HIPPOCRENE COMPACT DICTIONARY

BULGARIAN-ENGLISH
ENGLISH-BULGARIAN
DICTIONARY

IVAN TCHOMAKOV

HIPPOCRENE BOOKS
New York

Copyright© 1992 by Ivan Tchomakov.

Hippocrene Compact Dictionary edition, 1997.

For information, address:
HIPPOCRENE BOOKS, INC.
171 Madison Avenue
New York, NY 10016

ISBN 0-7818-0535-X

Printed in the United States of America.

FOREWORD

This Bulgarian-English English-Bulgarian Dictionary is addressed to business people, travelers and students. It contains over 8,000 entries in Bulgarian and English.

The use of this Dictionary is facilitated by the adoption of a simple transliteration scheme. Each word is supplied by a transliteration in the alphabet of the other language. This, naturally, entails a degree of imprecision, particularly in differentiating the pronunciation of sounds unique to the English language, such as open, short or long "o." Only one graphic symbol is employed. In the English-Bulgarian Dictionary, a hyphen following the letter "a" is used to denote the sound (a) in words such as "sad" and "cat." In the Bulgarian-English Dictionary, the hyphen is used to divide two letters indicating that they are to be pronounced separately, rather than as one sound. Such is the case with the combination of the letters "z" and "h," which, if divided by a hyphen, should be pronounced as in "zero" and "hotel." If used in combination without a dividing mark, they sould be pronounced as the sound "zh" in the English word "measure." Duplication of characters is used to denote long vowels in English or separate pronunciation of the two identical sounds in Bulgarian.

I.T.

THE KEY TO PRONUNCIATION

Bulgarian symbol	English pronunciation	Example
а	a	harbor
б	b	boy
в	v	victory
г	g	grammar
д	d	door
е	e	net
ж	zh	division
з	z	zebra
и	i	little
й	i	young
к	k	kettle
л	l	lonely
м	m	money
н	n	never
о	o	opera
п	p	open
р	r	rest
с	s	still
т	t	touch
у	ou	youth
ф	f	fig
х	h	hotel
ц	ts	shuts
ч	ch	choose
ш	sh	shoe
щ	sht	fishtail
ъ	u	gum
ь	denotes softening of vowel "o"	
ю	yu	you
я	ya	yard

BULGARIAN-ENGLISH
DICTIONARY

ABBREVIATIONS USED IN THIS DICTIONARY

adj	adjective
adv	adverb
conj	conjunction
f	feminine
interj	interjection
m	masculine
n	neuter (Bulgarian-English Section)
n	noun (English-Bulgarian Section)
num	numeral
part	particle
pl	plural
prep	preposition
pron	pronoun
v	verb

A

a [a] *conj* and, while, yet, but
абажу́р [abazhour] *m* lampshade
абонаме́нт [abonament] *m* subscription
абони́рам [aboniram] *v* subscribe to
абсолю́тен [absolyuten] *adj* absolute
абсу́рден [absourden] *adj* absurd
аванту́ра [avantyura] *f* adventure
ава́рия [avariya] *f* damage, break down
а́вгуст [avgoust] *m* August
авиа́ция [aviatsiya] *f* aviation, aircraft
автобу́с [aftobous] *m* bus, coach
автомати́чен [aftomatichen] *adj* automatic
автомоби́л [aftomobil] *m* motorcar
а́втор [aftor] *m* author
авторите́т [aftoritet] *m* authority, prestige
авторемо́нтна работи́лница [aftoremontna rabotilnitsa] *f* auto-repair shop
аге́нт [agent] *m* agent
аге́нция [agentsiya] *f* agency, bureau
а́гне [agne] *n* lamb
агре́сия [agresiya] *f* agression
агроно́м [agronom] *m* agronomist, agriculturalist
ад [ad] *m* inferno, hell
адвока́т [advokat] *m* lawyer, solicitor, barrister

администра́ция [administratsiya] *f* administration, management

адре́с [adres] *m* address

аерога́ра [aerogara] *f* airport

аз [as] *pron* I

а́збука [azbouka] *f* alphabet

азиа́тски [aziatski] *adj* Asiatic

азо́т [azot] *m* nitrogen

акаде́мия [akademiya] *f* academy

акваре́л [akvarel] *m* watercolor

аква́риум [akvarium] *m* aquarium

ако́ [ako] *conj* if

акроба́т [akrobat] *m* acrobat

акт [akt] *m* act, deed, certificate

акти́вен [aktiven] *adj* active

активизи́рам [aktiviziram] *v* activate, rouse, stir up

аку́ла [akoula] *f* shark

акумула́тор [akoumoulator] *m* battery

акура́тен [akouraten] *adj* accurate, precise

аку́стика [akoustika] *f* acoustics

акуше́рка [akousherka] *f* midwife

акце́нт [aktsent] *m* accent, stress

а́лен [alen] *adj* scarlet

але́я [aleya] *f* alley, lane, walk

алкохо́л [alkohol] *m* alcohol

а́ло [alo] *intej* hello

алпини́зъм [alpinizum] *m* mountaineering, mountain climbing

алуми́ний [aluminii] *m* aluminum

а́лчен [alchen] *adj* greedy, avid, covetous

аматьо́рски [amatyorski] *adj* amateur

амбала́ж [ambalazh] *m* packing

амбицио́зен [ambitsiozen] *adj* ambitious

амби́ция [ambitsiya] *f* ambition

америка́нски [amerikanski] *adj* American

ана́лиз [analis] *m* analysis

анато́мия [anatomiya] *f* anatomy

ангажиме́нт [angazhiment] *m* commitment, engagement

а́нгел [angel] *m* angel

англи́йски [angliiski] *adj* English

анекдо́т [anekdot] *m* anecdote

анке́та [anketa] *f* inquiry, investigation

анони́мен [anonimen] *adj* anonymous

анса́мбъл [ansambul] *m* ensemble, group, company

анте́на [antena] *f* aerial

антра́кт [antrakt] *m* interval, intermission

антре́ [antre] *n* entrance hall

апара́т [aparat] *m* apparatus, appliance

апартаме́нт [apartament] *m* flat, rooms, apartment

апели́рам [apeliram] *v* appeal to

аперити́в [aperitif] *m* appetizer

апети́т [apetit] *m* appetite

аплоди́рам [aplodiram] *v* applaud, acclaim

апри́л [april] *m* April

апте́ка [apteka] *f* pharmacy, drugstore

апте́кар [aptekar] *m* chemist, druggist

аргуме́нт [argument] *m* argument

аресту́вам [arestouvam] *v* arrest, take into custody

аристокра́ция [aristokratsiya] *f* aristocracy

аритме́тика [aritmetika] *f* arithmetic

а́рка [arka] *f* arch

а́рмия [armiya] *f* army

арога́нтност [arogantnost] *f* arrogance

арома́т [aromat] *m* aroma, fragrance, perfume

арома́тен [aromaten] *adj* aromatic, fragrant

арте́рия [arteriya] *f* artery

артиле́рия [artileriya] *f* artillery

арти́ст [artist] *m* actor

археоло́гия [arheologiya] *f* archaeology

архи́ва [arhiva] *f* records

архите́кт [arhitekt] *m* architect

архитекту́ра [arhitektoura] *f* architecture

асансьо́р [asansyor] *m* lift, elevator

асисте́нт [asistent] *m* assistant

асоциа́ция [asotsiatsiya] *f* association

аспири́рам [aspiriram] *v* aspire

астроно́мия [astronomiya] *f* astronomy

ата́ка [ataka] *f* attack, assault, onset

атаку́вам [atakouvam] *v* attack, assault

ателие́ [atelie] *n* shop, work room, studio

атента́т [atentat] *m* attempt, on smb's life, outrage

атле́т [atlet] *m* athlete

атлети́чески състеза́ния [atleticheski sustezaniya] *noun pl* track-and-field events

аудие́нция [audientsiya] *f* audience

аудито́рия [auditoriya] *f* auditorium, lecture hall

афекти́рам се [afektiram se] *v* become overexcited, exasperated

афи́ш [afish] *m* poster, bill, placard

африка́нски [afrikanski] *adj* African

а́хвам [ahvam] *v* exclaim, gasp

Б

ба́ба [baba] *f* grandmother, old woman

ба́вен [baven] *adj* slow, tardy, sluggish

ба́вене [bavene] *n* delay, protraction

бага́ж [bagazh] *m* luggage, baggage

ба́гер [bager] *m* excavator

ба́гра [bagra] *f* color, tint, hue, shade

баде́м [badem] *m* almond

баджана́к [badzhanak] *m* brother-in-law

ба́за [baza] *f* base, basis

баи́р [bair] *m* hill, elevation

бака́лница [bakalnitsa] *f* grocery

бакши́ш [bakshish] *m* tip

бал [bal] *m* ball

бала́нс [balans] *m* balance

балдъ́за [balduza] *f* sister-in-law

бале́т [balet] *m* ballet
балка́н [balkan] *m* mountain
балко́н [balkon] *m* balcony
бало́н [balon] *m* balloon
балто́н [balton] *m* overcoat, topcoat
бана́лен [banalen] *adj* commonplace, ordinary, banal
бана́н [banan] *m* banana
ба́нда [banda] *f* gang, band
ба́нка [banka] *f* bank
банкно́та [banknota] *f* banknote, bill
ба́нски [banski] *adj* bathing
ба́ня [banya] *f* bathroom, public baths
бар [bar] *m* bar, night club
бараба́н [baraban] *m* drum
бара́ка [baraka] *f* shed
баре́та [bareta] *f* cap, beret
барие́ра [bariera] *f* barrier, bar
бару́т [barout] *m* gunpowder
басе́йн [basein] *m* swimming pool
баскетбо́л [basketbol] *m* basketball
басносло́вен [basnosloven] *adj* fabulous
ба́сня [basnya] *f* fable
басту́н [bastoun] *m* cane, walking stick
батери́я [bateriya] *f* battery
баща́ [bashta] *m* father
бди́телен [bditelen] *adj* vigilant, watchful, alert
бе́бе [bebe] *n* baby
бега́ч [begach] *m* runner

беда́ [beda] *f* misfortune, disaster, trouble

бе́ден [beden] *adj* poor, needy

бе́дност [bednost] *f* poverty, poorness

бедро́ [bedro] *n* thigh

бе́дствие [bedstvie] *n* calamity, disaster

бежане́ц [bezhanets] *m* refugee

бе́жов [bezhof] *adj* beige

без [bes] *prep* without, to

безбро́ен [bezbroen] *adj* countless, innumerable

безво́ден [bezvoden] *adj* waterless, dry

безво́лев [bezvolev] *adj* weak-willed, irresolute

безвре́ден [bezvreden] *adj* harmless, innocuous

безвъзвра́тен [bezvuzvraten] *adj* irretrievable, irrevocable

безвъзме́зден [bezvuzmezden] *adj* free

безграни́чен [bezgranichen] *adj* boundless, infinite

безгри́жие [bezgrizhie] *n* unconcern, ease

безде́ен [bezdeen] *adj* inactive, passive, inert

бе́здна [bezdna] *f* chasm, abyss

бездо́мник [bezdomnik] *m* waif, homeless person

безжи́знен [bezzhiznen] *adj* lifeless, dull

беззаве́тен [bezzaveten] *adj* devoted, selfless

безизхо́ден [bezis-hoden] *adj* hopeless

безизхо́дица [bezis-hoditsa] *f* impasse, deadlock

безинтересен [bezinteresen] *adj* uninterested, dull

безир [bezir] *m* linseed oil

безкористен [beskoristen] *adj* unselfish

безкрайност [beskrainost] *f* infinity, boundlessness

безлихвен [bezlihven] *adj* free of interest

безлюден [bezlyuden] *adj* deserted, empty, uninhabited

безмилостен [bezmilosten] *adj* merciless, ruthless

безмитен [bezmiten] *adj* duty-free

безмълвен [bezmulven] *adj* silent, mute

безнравствен [beznravstven] *adj* immoral

безоблачен [bezoblachen] *adj* cloudless

безобразен [bezobrazen] *adj* repulsive, hideous

безобразие [bezobrazie] *n* outrage, scandal, disgrace

безопасен [bezopasen] *adj* secure, safe

безочлив [bezochlif] *adj* impudent

безплатен [besplaten] *adj* free

безплоден [besploden] *adj* fruitless, vain

безпокойствие [bespokoystvie] *n* uneasiness, anxiety

безпокоя [bespokoya] *v* trouble, disturb, worry

безполезен [bespolezen] *adj* useless, vain, futile

безпомощен [bespomoshten] *adj* helpless

безпоря́дък [besporyaduk] *m* disorder, confusion

безпоща́ден [besposhtaden] *adj* ruthless, merciless

безпристра́стен [bespristrasten] *adj* impartial, unbiased

безрабо́тен [bezraboten] *adj* unemployed, jobless

безразбо́рно [bezrazborno] *adv* at random, indiscriminately

безразли́чие [bezrazlichie] *n* indifference

безре́дие [bezredie] *n* disorder, disturbance

безрезулта́тен [bezrezoultaten] *adj* ineffective, futile

безси́лие [besilie] *n* impotence, weakness

безсми́слен [besmislen] *adj* meaningless, senseless

безсм́ртен [besmurten] *adj* immortal

безспи́рен [bespiren] *adj* incessant, continual

безспо́рно [besporno] *adv* indisputably, certainly

безсра́мен [besramen] *adj* shameless, impudent

безсро́чен [besrochen] *adj* termless, permanent

безстра́шен [bestrashen] *adj* fearless

безсъзна́ние [besuznanie] *n* unconsciousness

безс́ние [besunie] *n* sleeplessness, insomnia

безу́мен [bezoumen] *adj* mad, insane

безупречен [bezouprechen] *adj* flawless, impeccable

безуспешен [bezouspeshen] *adj* unsuccessful

безхарактерен [bes-harakteren] *adj* weak-willed

безцветен [bestsveten] *adj* colorless

безценен [bestsenen] *adj* priceless, precious

безчестя [beschestya] *v* disgrace, dishonor, defame

безчовечен [beschovechen] *adj* inhuman, cruel

безчувствен [beschouvstven] *adj* unconscious, indifferent, insensitive

безшумен [beshoumen] *adj* noiseless

белег [beleg] *m* scar, mark, sign

бележа [belezha] *v* mark, note, show, register

бележит [belezhit] *adj* notable, distinguished

бележник [belezhnik] *m* notebook

бельо [belyo] *n* underwear, linen

беля [belya] *f* nuisance, trouble

бензин [benzin] *m* petrol, gasoline

бензиностанция [benzinostantsiya] *f* gas station

бера [bera] *v* pick, gather

беседа [beseda] *f* talk, lecture, discourse

бетон [beton] *m* concrete

би, бих [bi, bih] *v* would

библиотека [biblioteka] *f* library, bookcase

библия [bibliya] *f* the Bible

бижу́ [bizhou] *n* jewel, gem

бик [bik] *m* bull

биле́т [bilet] *m* ticket

би́лка [bilka] *f* herb

бинт [bint] *m* bandage

биогра́фия [biografiya] *f* biography

биоло́гия [biologiya] *f* biology

би́ра [bira] *f* beer, ale

бис [bis] *m* encore

би́сер [biser] *m* pearl

би́стър [bistur] *adj* clear

битие́ [bitie] *n* being, existence

би́тка [bitka] *f* battle, fight

би́я [biya] *v* beat, lash, ring

благ [blag] *n* gentle, kind, sweet

благода́рен [blagodaren] *adj* thankful, grateful

благода́рност [blagodarnost] *f* gratitude

благодаря́ [blagodarya] *conj* thank

благода́тен [blagodaten] *adj* beneficial

благозву́чен [blagozvouchen] *adj* harmonious, melodious

благонаде́жен [blagonadezhen] *adj* reliable, dependable

благополу́чен [blagopolouchen] *adj* successful

благоприли́чие [blagoprilichie] *n* propriety, decency

благоприя́тен [blagopriyaten] *adj* favorable

благоразумие [blagorazoumie] *n* prudence, reasonableness, common sense

благороден [blagoroden] *adj* noble, generous

благородство [blagorodstvo] *n* nobility, generosity

благосклонен [blagosklonen] *adj* favorable, benevolent

благословия [blagosloviya] *f* blessing

благосъстояние [blagosustoyanie] *n* prosperity, well-being

благотворен [blagotvoren] *adj* beneficial

благотворителен [blagotvoritelen] *adj* charitable

благочестив [blagochestif] *adj* pious, devout

блажен [blazhen] *adj* blessed, happy

блато [blato] *n* marsh, swamp

бледен [bleden] *adj* pale

блестя [blestya] *v* sparkle, shine, glitter

блестящ [blestyasht] *adj* shining, brilliant

блещукам [bleshtoukam] *v* twinkle, glimmer

близжа [blizha] *v* lick

близнак [bliznak] *m* twin

близо [blizo] *adv* near

близък [blizuk] *adj* near, recent, future

блуждая [blouzhdaya] *v* roam, wander

блуза [blouza] *f* blouse

блъскам [bluskam] *v* push, shove

блюдо [blyudo] *n* dish

бог [bog] *m* God

богат [bogat] *adj* rich, wealthy

богатство [bogatstvo] *n* wealth, fortune

боготворя [bogotvorya] *v* worship, adore, deify

бодър [bodur] *adj* cheerful, lively

боен [boen] *adj* military, fighting

боеприпаси [boepripasi] *noun pl* ammunition

божествен [bozhestven] *adj* divine

бозайник [bozainik] *m* mammal

бозая [bozaya] *v* suck

бой [boi] *m* beating, battle, fight

бойлер [boiler] *m* boiler, water-heater

боклук [boklouk] *m* rubbish, garbage

боледувам [boledouvam] *v* be ill, suffer

болен [bolen] *adj* ill, sick

болест [bolest] *f* sickness, disease

болка [bolka] *f* pain, ache

болница [bolnitsa] *f* hospital

болшинство [bolshinstvo] *n* majority

бомба [bomba] *f* bomb

бонбон [bonbon] *m* candy

бор [bor] *m* pine

борба [borba] *f* fight, struggle, wrestling

борд [bord] *m* deck

борец [borets] *m* fighter, wrestler

борса [borsa] *f* exchange

боря се [borya se] *v* fight, wrestle

бос [bos] *adj* barefoot

ботаника [botanika] *f* botany

ботуш [botoush] *m* boot

боя [boya] *f* paint, dye

бояджия [boyadzhiya] *m* painter
боя се [boya se] *v* be afraid of, fear
боядисвам [boyadisvam] *v* paint, dye
брава [brava] *f* lock
брадва [bradva] *f* axe
брак [brak] *m* marriage, matrimony
браня [branya] *v* defend, protect
брат [brat] *m* brother
братовчед [bratovched] *m* cousin
брашно [brashno] *n* flour
бреза [breza] *f* birch
бреме [breme] *n* burden
бременна [bremenna] *adj* pregnant
бридж [bridzh] *m* bridge
брой [broy] *n* number, issue, copy
броня [bronya] *f* armor
броя [broya] *v* count, reckon
брутален [broutalen] *adj* brutal, cruel
бръмбар [brumbar] *m* beetle
бръсна [brusna] *v* shave
бръснач [brusnach] *m* razor
бряг [bryag] *m* coast, shore
буден [bouden] *adj* awake, intelligent
будилник [boudilnik] *m* alarm clock
будя [boudya] *v* wake, awaken
буен [bouen] *adj* hot-tempered, violent
буза [bouza] *f* cheek
буква [boukva] *f* letter
буквално [boukvalno] *adv* literally
булевард [boulevard] *m* avenue, boulevard

бу́лка [boulka] *f* bride, wife

бунт [bount] *m* revolt, riot, rebellion

бу́рен [bouren] *adj* stormy, violent, rapid

бурка́н [bourkan] *m* jar

бу́ря [bourya] *f* storm, tempest

бут [bout] *m* leg, round

бу́там [boutam] *v* push, shove

бути́лка [boutilka] *f* bottle

буто́н [bouton] *m* button

буча́ [boucha] *v* rumble, roar

бъ́брек [bubrek] *m* kidney

бъбри́в [bubriv] *adj* talkative

бъ́да [buda] *v* be

бъ́деш [budesht] *adj* future, coming

бъ́деще [budeshte] *n* future

бъ́лгарски [bulgarski] *adj* Bulgarian

бърз [burs] *adj* fast, quick, rapid

бъ́рзам [burzam] *v* hurry, be in a hurry

бъ́ркам [burkam] *v* stir, mix, make a mistake

бъркоти́я [burkotiya] *f* confusion, disorder

бъ́рша [bursha] *v* wipe

бю́ро [byuro] *n* desk, office

бя́гам [byagam] *v* run, fly

бя́гство [byagstvo] *n* flight, escape

бял [byal] *adj* white, fair

В

в [v] *prep* in, on, at, to

вагóн [vagon] *m* carriage, coach, car

вáдя [vadya] *v* pull out, take out

вáжен [vazhen] *adj* important, haughty

вáжност [vazhnost] *f* importance

вакáнция [vakantsiya] *f* holiday, vacation

ваксинúрам се [vaksiniram se] *v* be vaccinated

валú [vali] *v* it snows, it rains

валúден [validen] *adj* valid, good

валс [vals] *m* waltz

валýта [valouta] *f* currency

вáна [vana] *f* tub, bathtub

вар [var] *f* lime

варúрам [variram] *v* vary

варúола [variola] *f* smallpox

варя́ [varya] *v* boil, cook

вас [vas] *pron* you

ваш [vash] *pron* your

вбеся́вам се [vbesyavam se] *v* be furious, be enraged

вгле́ждам се [vglezhdam se] *v* stare, gaze

вдúгам [vdigam] *v* raise, lift

вдúшвам [vdishvam] *v* inhale, breathe in

вдлъбнат [vdlubnat] *adj* concave

вдове́ц [vdovets] *m* widower

вдовúца [vdovitsa] *f* widow

вдъхновѐние [vduhnovenie] *n* inspiration
вегетариа́нец [vegetarianets] *m* vegetarian
ведна́га [vednaga] *adv* immediately, at once, right away
веднъ̀ж [vednuzh] *adv* once
ве́жда [vezhda] *f* eyebrow
ве́жлив [vezhlif] *adj* polite, civil, courteous
везни́ [vezni] *noun pl* scales, balance
век [vek] *m* century
вели́к [velik] *adj* great
велика́н [velikan] *m* giant
Вели́кден [velikden] *m* Easter
великобрита́нски [velikobritanski] *adj* British
великоду́шен [velikodoushen] *adj* generous, noble
великоле́пен [velikolepen] *adj* magnificient
вели́чествен [velichestven] *adj* majestic
велисипе́д [velosiped] *m* bicycle
ве́на [vena] *f* vein
вентила́тор [ventilator] *m* fan
венча́вка [venchafka] *f* wedding
ве́рен [veren] *adj* correct, right, true, loyal
вери́га [veriga] *f* chain
вероизповеда́ние [veroizpovedanie] *n* faith, religion
вероло́мен [verolomen] *adj* treacherous, perfidious
вероя́тен [veroyaten] *adj* probable, likely
вероя́тно [veroyatno] *adv* probably, likely

вертика́лен [vertikalen] *adj* vertical
ве́сел [vesel] *adj* cheerful, jolly
веселя́ се [veselya se] *v* enjoy oneself, have fun
весло́ [veslo] *n* oar
ве́стник [vesnik] *m* newspaper, journal
ве́хна [vehna] *v* fade, wither, languish
ве́че [veche] *adv* already
ве́чен [vechen] *adj* eternal, everlasting
ве́чер [vecher] *f* evening
вече́ря [vecherya] *f* supper, dinner
вече́рям [vecheryam] *v* have supper, dine
ве́чност [vechnost] *f* eternity
вещ [vesht] *f* thing
вещ [vesht] *adj* experienced, clever
вещество́ [veshtestvo] *n* matter, substance
вещина́ [veshtina] *f* experience, skill
ве́щица [veshtitsa] *f* witch
взаи́мен [vzaimen] *adj* mutual, reciprocal
взе́мам [vzemam] *v* take, get, pick up
взиска́телен [vziskatelen] *adj* exacting
взрив [vzrif] *m* explosion
вид [vid] *m* appearance, air
вид [vid] *m* kind, sort
ви́ден [viden] *adj* eminent, outstanding, notable
ви́дим [vidim] *adj* visible
ви́е [vie] *pron* you
вие́лица [vielitsa] *f* blizzard
ви́ждам [vizhdam] *v* see, realize

ви́за [viza] *f* visa

вик [vik] *m* cry, shout

ви́кам [vikam] *v* cry, call out, shout

ви́лица [vilitsa] *f* fork

вина́ [vina] *f* guilt, fault

ви́наги [vinagi] *adv* always, ever

ви́но [vino] *n* wine

вино́вен [vinoven] *adj* guilty

винт [vint] *m* screw

виня́ [vinya] *v* blame, find fault

виоле́тов [violetof] *adj* violet, purple

виря́ [vireya] *v* grow, flourish

висо́к [visok] *adj* high, tall, loud

висо́ко [visoko] *adv* high

висо́коговори́тел [visokogovoritel] *m* loudspeaker

височина́ [visochina] *f* height, altitude, hill

вися́ [visya] *v* hang

витри́на [vitrina] *f* shop window

виц [vits] *m* anecdote, funny story

вклю́чвам [fklyuchvam] *v* include, switch on

включи́телно [fklyuchitelno] *adv* including, inclusive

вкус [fkous] *m* taste

вку́сен [fkousen] *adj* tasty, delicious

вла́га [vlaga] *f* moisture, humidity

владе́тел [vladetel] *m* ruler, monarch

владе́я [vladeya] *v* rule, govern, possess, master, speak

влади́ка [vladika] *m* bishop

влак [vlak] *m* train

власт [vlast] *f* power, rule

влача [vlacha] *v* drag, pull, tow

влечение [vlechenie] *n* inclination, bent

влечуго [vlechougo] *n* reptile

влизам [vlizam] *v* enter, go in

влияние [vliyanie] *n* influence

влиятелен [vliyatelen] *adj* influential

влог [vlog] *m* deposit

влошавам [vloshavam] *v* make worse, aggravate

влюбвам се [vlyubvam se] *v* fall in love

вместо [vmesto] *adv* instead of

внасям [vnasyam] *v* bring in, import

внезапен [vnezapen] *adj* sudden, unexpected

внимавам [vnimavam] *v* pay attention, be careful

внимание [vnimanie] *n* attention, care

внук [vnouk] *m* grandson

внучка [vnouchka] *f* granddaughter

внушавам [vnoushavam] *v* suggest

внушение [vnoushenie] *n* suggestion

вода [voda] *f* water

водач [vodach] *m* leader, guide

водовъртеж [vodovurtezh] *m* whirlpool

водолаз [vodolas] *m* diver

водопад [vodopad] *m* waterfall

водоравен [vodoraven] *adj* horizontal

водорасли [vodorasli] *noun pl* seaweed

водород [vodorod] *m* hydrogen

во́дя [vodya] *v* lead, conduct
вое́нен [voenen] *adj* military
во́зя [vozya] *v* ride
война́ [voina] *f* war, warfare
войни́к [voinik] *m* soldier
войска́ [voiska] *f* army
во́лейбол [voleibol] *m* volleyball
во́лен [volen] *adj* free, unrestricted
во́лност [volnost] *f* liberty
во́ля [volya] *f* will
впечатле́ние [fpechatlenie] *n* impression
впро́чем [fprochem] *adv* anyhow, besides, by the way
врабче́ [vrabche] *n* sparrow
враг [vrag] *m* enemy, foe
враждбе́н [vrazhdeben] *adj* hostile
вра́на [vrana] *f* crow
врат [vrat] *m* neck
врата́ [vrata] *f* door
врата́р [vratar] *m* goalkeeper
вратовръ́зка [vratovruska] *f* necktie
вреда́ [vreda] *f* damage, injury, harm
вре́ден [vreden] *adj* harmful
вре́ме [vreme] *n* time, tense
вре́ме [vreme] *n* weather
вре́менен [vremenen] *adj* temporary
връ́зка [vruska] *f* string, lace, relation, connection, link
връх [vruh] *m* top, peak, height
връ́щам [vrushtam] *v* send back, return

всеки [fseki] *pron* everyone, anyone, each

всекидневен [fsekidneven] *adj* daily, everyday

вселена [fselena] *f* universe, cosmos

всемогъщ [fsemogusht] *adj* almighty, omnipotent

всенароден [fsenaroden] *adj* national, nationwide

всеобщ [fseobsht] *adj* universal, common, general

всички [fsichki] *pron* all, everybody

всичко [fsichko] *pron* all, everything

вследствие [fsledstvie] *conj* as a result of, owing to

всред [fsred] *adv* amid, among

всякакъв [fsyakakuv] *adj* various, of all kinds

всякога [fsyakoga] *adv* always, ever

всякъде [fsyakude] *adv* everywhere

втори [ftori] *adj* second

вторник [ftornik] *m* Tuesday

вход [fhod] *m* entrance

вчера [fchera] *adv* yesterday

въведение [vuvedenie] *n* introduction

въглерод [vuglerod] *m* carbon

въглища [vuglishta] *noun pl* coal

въже [vuzhe] *n* rope, cord, line

възбуждам [vuzbouzhdam] *v* excite

възвание [vuzvanie] *n* appeal

възглавница [vuzglavnitsa] *f* pillow, cushion

въздействие [vuzdeistvie] *n* effect, influence, impact

въздух [vuzdouh] *m* air

въздържам се [vuzdurzham se] *v* refrain, abstain

въздъхвам [vuzduhvam] *v* sigh

възел [vuzel] *m* knot

възклицавам [vusklitsavam] *v* exclaim

възклицание [vusklitsanie] *n* exclamation

възкресение [vuskresenie] *n* resurrection, Easter

възможен [vuzmozhen] *adj* possible, likely

възможност [vuzmozhnost] *f* possibility

възмущение [vuzmoushtenie] *n* indignation

възнаграждение [vuznagrazhdenie] *n* reward, remuneration

възпрепятствувам [vusprepyatstvouvam] *v* impede, prevent

възраждане [vuzrazhdane] *n* revival, renaissance

възраст [vuzrast] *f* age

възрастен [vuzrasten] *adj* elderly, old

възстановявам [vuzstanovyavam] *v* restore, recover, reconstruct

възхищавам се [vus-hishtavam se] *v* admire

възхищение [vus-hishtenie] *n* admiration

възход [vus-hod] *m* progress, advance

вълк [vulk] *m* wolf

вълна [vulna] *f* wool

вълна [vulna] *f* wave

вълне́ние [vulnenie] *n* riot, emotion, excitement

вълше́бен [vulsheben] *adj* magic, enchanting

вън [vun] *prep* out of

вѣншност [vunshnost] *f* appearance

въображе́ние [vuobrazhenie] *n* imagination

въобразя́вам си [vuobrazyavam si] *v* imagine, fancy

въобще́ [vuobshte] *adv* in general, on the whole, at all

въоръжа́вам [vuoruzhavam] *v* arm

въоръже́ние [vuoruzhenie] *n* armament

въпреки́ [vupreki] *conj* in spite of, despite

въпро́с [vupros] *m* question

вървя́ [vurvya] *v* go, walk

въртя́ [vurtya] *v* turn, revolve

върху́ [vurhou] *prep* on, upon, over

въ́рша [vursha] *v* do

въста́ние [vustanie] *n* rebellion, uprising

въ́тре [vutre] *prep* in, inside, within

вя́рвам [vyarvam] *v* believe in, trust in

вя́рно [vyarno] *adv* truly, right

вя́тър [vyatur] *m* wind

Г

газ [gas] *m* gas

га́ля [galya] *v* caress, stroke

га́ра [gara] *f* railway station

гара́ж [garazh] *m* garage

гаранти́рам [garantiram] *v* guarantee, warrant

гара́нция [garantsiya] *m* warranty, guarantee

гардеро́б [garderob] *m* wardrobe

гари́рам [gariram] *v* park

га́ся [gasya] *v* put out, extinguish, turn off

га́танка [gatanka] *f* riddle

гаще́та [gashteta] *noun pl* trunks, pants

геогра́фия [geografiya] *f* geography

геоло́гия [geologiya] *f* geology

геоме́трия [geometriya] *f* geometry

герма́нски [germanski] *adj* German

геро́йзъм [geroizum] *m* heroism, gallantry

геро́йчен [geroichen] *adj* heroic

геро́й [geroi] *m* hero

ги [gi] *pron* them

гига́нт [gigant] *m* giant

гимна́зия [gimnaziya] *f* high-school

глава́ [glava] *f* head, chapter

гла́вен [glaven] *adj* chief, main, principal

главобо́лие [glavobolie] *n* headache

глаго́л [glagol] *m* verb

глад [glad] *m* hunger, famine

гла́ден [gladen] *adj* hungry

гладу́вам [gladouvam] *v* starve, be hungry

гла́дък [gladuk] *adj* smooth, even

гла́дя [gladya] *v* iron

глас [glas] *m* voice

гласу́вам [glasouvam] *v* vote, poll

гле́дам [gledam] *v* look at, watch, see, gaze

гле́зя [glezya] *v* spoil, behave badly

гло́ба [globa] *f* fine, penalty

глу́пав [gloupaf] *adj* foolish, silly, stupid

глух [glouh] *adj* deaf

гне́вен [gneven] *adj* angry, wrathful

гнездо́ [gnezdo] *n* nest

гни́я [gniya] *v* rot, decay

гняв [gnyav] *m* anger, wrath, rage

го [go] *pron* him

гове́ждо [govezhdo] *n* beef

го́вор [govor] *m* speech, dialect

говори́тел [govoritel] *m* speaker

гово́ря [govorya] *v* speak, talk

годени́к [godenik] *m* fiancé

годени́ца [godenitsa] *f* fiancée

годи́на [godina] *f* year

годи́шен [godishen] *adj* yearly, annual

годи́шно вре́ме [godishno vreme] *n* season

годи́шнина [godishnina] *f* anniversary

гол [gol] *adj* naked

голя́м [golyam] *adj* big, large, great

го́ня [gonya] *v* chase, pursue

гора́ [gora] *f* forest, wood

горд [gord] *adj* proud

го́рдост [gordost] *f* pride

го́ре [gore] *adv* above, up

го́рен [goren] *adj* upper, top

горе́щ [goresht] *adj* hot, fervent

горещина́ [goreshtina] *f* heat
гори́во [gorivo] *n* fuel
горчи́в [gorchif] *adj* bitter
горчи́ца [gorchitsa] *f* mustard
горя́ [gorya] *v* burn
господа́р [gospodar] *m* master
господи́н [gospodin] *m* Mr., Sir
госпожа́ [gospozha] *f* Mrs., Madam
госпо́жица [gospozhitsa] *f* Miss
гост [gost] *m* guest, visitor
гостоприе́мство [gostopriemstvo] *n* hospitality
госту́ване [gostouvane] *n* visit
готва́ч [gotvach] *m* cook
го́твя [gotvya] *v* cook, prepare
гото́в [gotof] *adj* ready, prepared
грабе́ж [grabezh] *m* robbery, plunder
град [grad] *m* town, city
град [grad] *m* hail
гради́на [gradina] *f* garden
гра́дус [gradous] *m* degree
гра́жданин [grazhdanin] *m* citizen
гра́ждански [grazhdanski] *adj* civil, civilian
грама́ден [gramaden] *adj* huge, enormous, tremendous
грамо́тен [gramoten] *adj* literate
грамофо́нна пло́ча [gramofonna plocha] *f* record, disc
гра́ница [granitsa] *f* frontier, border
грах [grah] *m* peas

грациозен [gratsiozen] *adj* graceful

грация [gratsiya] *f* grace

грешка [greshka] *f* mistake, error

гривна [grivna] *f* bracelet

грижа [grizha] *f* care

грижа се [grizha se] *v* take care of, worry, look after

грим [grim] *m* make-up

грип [grip] *m* influenza, flu

гроб [grob] *m* grave

гробище [grobishte] *n* cemetery

грозде [grozde] *n* grapes

грозен [grozen] *adj* ugly, plain

груб [groub] *adj* coarse, rude

група [groupa] *f* group, party

гръб [grub] *m* back

гръбнак [grubnak] *m* spine, backbone

гръд [grud] *f* breast, bosom

гръм [grum] *m* thunder

грях [gryah] *m* sin

губернатор [goubernator] *m* governor

губя [goubya] *v* lose

гума [gouma] *f* rubber, tire

гуменки [goumenki] *noun pl* tennis shoes

гуша [gousha] *f* throat

гущер [goushter] *m* lizard

гъба [guba] *f* mushroom

гъвкав [gufkav] *adj* flexible, pliable

гълтам [gultam] *v* swallow

гълъб [gulub] *m* pigeon, dove

гъ́лъб [gulub] *m* pigeon, dove
гъ́рло [gurlo] *n* throat
гъ́ска [guska] *f* goose
гъст [gust] *adj* thick, dense

Д

да [da] *prep* to
да [da] *part* yes
да́вам [davam] *v* give, pass, grant
да́вя [davya] *v* drown
дале́ч [dalech] *adv* far, far away
дали́ [dali] *conj* if, whether
да́ма [dama] *f* lady
да́нни [danni] *noun pl* data
да́нък [danuk] *m* tax, rate
да́рба [darba] *f* talent, gift
да́та [data] *f* date
два [dva] *num* two
два́десет [dvadeset] *num* twenty
двана́десет [dvanadeset] *num* twelve
двига́тел [dvigatel] *m* motor, engine
дви́жа се [dvizha se] *v* move, stir, work
дво́ен [dvoen] *adj* double
двоето́чие [dvoetochie] *n* colon
дворе́ц [dvorets] *m* palace
двоумя́ се [dvooumya se] *v* hesitate
дебе́л [debel] *adj* thick, fat

дебелогла́в [debeloglaf] *adj* stubborn, obstinate

де́вер [dever] *m* brother-in-law

де́вет [devet] *num* nine

деветна́десет [devetnadeset] *num* nineteen

де́йсност [deisnost] *f* activity, work

де́йствие [deistvie] *n* action, operation, act

действи́телен [deistvitelen] *adj* real, actual, valid

деке́мври [dekemvri] *m* December

деклари́рам [deklariram] *v* declare

деле́ние [delenie] *n* division, partition

де́ло [delo] *n* case, suit

делфи́н [delfin] *m* dolphin

деля́ [delya] *v* divide

демокра́ция [demokratsiya] *f* democracy

ден [den] *m* day

депози́рам [depoziram] *v* deposit

де́сен [desen] *adj* right

десетиле́тие [desetiletie] *n* decade

дете́ [dete] *n* child

дефе́кт [defect] *m* defect, fault, flaw

джоб [dzhob] *m* pocket

джу́нгла [dzhoungla] *f* jungle

диагно́за [diagnoza] *f* diagnosis

диама́нт [diamant] *m* diamond

див [dif] *adj* wild

дива́н [divan] *m* couch, sofa

ди́вен [diven] *adj* marvellous, wonderful

ди́веч [divech] *m* game

диета [dieta] *f* diet
диктатура [diktatoura] *f* dictatorship
дим [dim] *m* smoke
диня [dinya] *f* watermelon
директор [direktor] *m* director, manager, principal
диригент [dirigem] *m* conductor
дискриминация [diskriminatsiya] *f* discrimination
дискусия [diskousiya] *f* discussion, debate
дисциплина [distsiplina] *f* discipline, subject
дишам [disham] *v* breathe
длан [dlan] *f* palm
длъжност [dluzhnost] *f* office, position
дневник [dnevnik] *m* diary
днес [dnes] *adv* today, at present
до [do] *prep* at, by, beside, to, till
добив [dobif] *m* production, crop
добитък [dobituk] *m* cattle, livestock
добре [dobre] *adv* good, well, right
добрина [dobrina] *f* goodness, kindness
доброволец [dobrovolets] *m* volunteer
добродетел [dobrodetel] *f* virtue
добър [dobur] *adj* good
доверие [doverie] *n* confidence, faith, trust
довечера [dovechera] *adv* tonight, this evening
довод [dovod] *m* argument
договор [dogovor] *m* contract, agreement, treaty

догоди́на [dogodina] *adv* next year
дого́нвам [dogonvam] *v* catch up
доказа́телство [dokazatelstvo] *n* proof, evidence
дока́звам [dokazvam] *v* prove
докла́д [doklad] *m* report, lecture, talk
докога́ [dokoga] *adv* how long, till when
доко́лкото [dokolkoto] *adv* as far as
доко́свам [dokosvam] *v* touch lightly
до́ктор [doktor] *m* doctor
докуме́нт [dokoument] *m* document
долина́ [dolina] *f* valley
до́лу [dolou] *adv* down, below
дом [dom] *m* home
домаки́н [domakin] *m* host
домаки́ня [domakinya] *f* housewife
дома́т [domat] *m* tomato
дона́сям [donasyam] *v* bring, fetch
допу́скам [dopouskam] *v* admit
допълне́ние [dopulnenie] *n* addition, supplement
дори́ [dori] *adv* even
доса́да [dosada] *f* boredom, tediousness
доса́ждам [dosazhdam] *v* bore, tire, bother
досе́щам се [doseshtam se] *v* guess, remember
доспи́ва ми се [dospiva mi se] *v* be sleepy
досрамя́ва ме [dosramyava me] *v* feel ashamed

до́ста [dosta] *adv* fairly, somewhat, very, quite

доста́вка [dostafka] *f* shipment, delivery

доста́вям [dostavyam] *v* supply, furnish, provide

доста́тъчен [dostatuchen] *adj* sufficient, enough

достове́рен [dostoveren] *adj* reliable, authentic

досто́йнство [dostoinstvo] *n* dignity

до́ход [dohod] *m* income, revenue

до́ходен [dohoden] *adj* profitable

дра́зня [draznya] *v* irritate, tease

дра́ма [drama] *f* drama

драмату́рг [dramatourg] *m* dramatist, playwright

дре́бен [dreben] *adj* small, fine

дре́вен [dreven] *adj* ancient, antique

дре́ха [dreha] *f* garment, clothes

дроб [drob] *m* lung, liver

друг [droug] *adj* other, different

дру́жество [drouzhestvo] *n* association, society

дръ́жка [druzhka] *f* handle

дузи́на [douzina] *f* dozen

ду́ма [douma] *f* word

ду́пка [doupka] *f* hole, cavity

ду́хам [douham] *v* blow

духо́вен [douhoven] *adj* spiritual, of the mind

духо́венство [douhovenstvo] *n* clergy, priesthood

душ [doush] *m* shower

душа́ [dousha] *f* soul, heart

душе́вен [dousheven] *adj* spiritual, mental

дъб [dub] *m* oak tree

дъ́вка [dufka] *f* chewing gum

дъ́вча [dufcha] *v* chew

дъга́ [duga] *f* rainbow

дъжд [duzhd] *m* rain

дълбо́к [dulbok] *adj* deep

дълбочина́ [dulbochina] *f* depth

дъ́лго [dulgo] *adv* for a long time

дължа́ [dulzha] *v* owe, be indebted

дължина́ [dulzhina] *m* length, longitude

дъ́лъг [dulug] *adj* long

дъ́нки [dunki] *noun pl* blue jeans

дъ́но [duno] *n* bottom

дървеси́на [durvesina] *f* wood

дърво́ [durvo] *n* tree

държа́ [durzha] *v* hold, support, keep

държа́ва [durzhava] *f* state, country

държа́ние [durzhanie] *n* behavior, manners

дъска́ [duska] *f* board, plank

дъщеря́ [dushterya] *f* daughter

дюше́к [dyushek] *m* mattress

дя́вол [dyavol] *m* devil

дя́до [dyado] *m* grandfather

дял [dyal] *m* share, part, branch

дя́сно [dyasno] *adv* right

Е

Ева́нгелие [evangelie] *n* gospel

евре́ин [evrein] *m* Jew

европе́йски [evropeiski] *adj* European

е́втин [eftin] *adj* cheap, inexpensive

егои́зъм [egoizum] *m* selfishness, egoism

еди́н [edin] *num* one

едина́десет [edinadeset] *num* eleven

едини́ца [edinitsa] *f* unit

едини́чен [edinichen] *adj* single

еди́нство [edinstvo] *n* unity

еднообра́зие [ednoobrazie] *n* uniformity

еднопосо́чна у́лица [ednoposochna oulitsa] *f* one-way street

езда́ [ezda] *f* riding

е́зеро [ezero] *n* lake, pond

ези́к [ezik] *m* tongue, language, speech

екра́н [ekran] *m* screen

екску́рзия [ekskourziya] *f* excursion, hike, trip

екскурзово́д [ekskourzovod] *m* guide

експериме́нт [eksperiment] *m* experiment, test

експе́рт [ekspert] *m* expert, specialist

експло́зия [eksploziya] *f* explosion

експона́т [eksponat] *m* exhibit

ела́ [ela] *v* come

елега́нтен [eleganten] *adj* elegant, smart

електри́чески [elektricheski] *adj* electric
елемента́рен [elementaren] *adj* elementary
елха́ [elha] *f* Christmas tree
емигра́нт [emigrant] *m* emigrant
емигри́рам [emigriram] *v* emigrate
емо́ция [emotsiya] *f* emotion
енерги́чен [energichen] *adj* energetic
ене́ргия [energiya] *f* energy
енциклопе́дия [entsiklopediya] *f*
encyclopedia
епиде́мия [epidemiya] *f* epidemic
епи́скоп [episkop] *m* bishop
ерге́н [ergen] *m* bachelor
е́сен [esen] *f* autumn, fall
есте́ствен [estestven] *adj* natural
есте́ствено [estestveno] *adv* certainly, of
course
ета́ж [etazh] *m* floor, storey
ета́п [etap] *m* stage
е́тика [etika] *f* ethics
ефе́кт [efect] *m* effect, result
ефекти́вен [efektiven] *adj* effective,
efficient
е́хо [eho] *n* echo

Ж

жа́ба [zhaba] *f* frog, toad
жа́ден [zhaden] *adj* thirsty

жа́жда [zhazhda] *f* thirst, lust
жела́ние [zhelanie] *n* wish, desire
жела́я [zhelaya] *v* wish, desire
железари́я [zhelezariya] *f* hardware
желе́зен [zhelezen] *adj* iron
желе́зница [zheleznitsa] *f* railway
желя́зо [zhelyazo] *n* iron
жена́ [zhena] *f* woman, wife
жесто́к [zhestok] *adj* cruel, fierce
живе́я [zhiveya] *v* live
живопи́с [zhivopis] *f* painting
живо́т [zhivot] *m* life
живо́тно [zhivotno] *n* animal
жиле́тка [zhiletka] *f* vest
жи́лище [zhilishte] *n* home, house
жи́то [zhito] *n* wheat
жи́ца [zhitsa] *f* wire
журна́л [zhournal] *m* magazine
журнали́ст [zhournalist] *m* journalist,
pressman
жълт [zhult] *adj* yellow
жълтъ́к [zhultuk] *m* yolk
жъ́тва [zhutva] *f* harvest

З

за [za] *prep* to, for, till
забавле́ние [zabavlenie] *n* entertainment
заба́вям [zabavyam] *v* delay, retard

забележи́телен [zabelezhitelen] *adj*
remarkable, notable
заблужда́вам [zablouzhdavam] *v* mislead
забогатя́вам [zabogatyavam] *v* grow rich
забра́вям [zabravyam] *v* forget
забра́на [zabrana] *f* prohibition, ban
забраня́вам [zabranyavam] *v* forbid, prohibit
зава́рвам [zavarvam] *v* find
заве́са [zavesa] *f* curtain
завеща́ние [zaveshtanie] *n* will, testament
завзе́мам [zavzemam] *v* seize, capture,
occupy
зави́сим [zavisim] *adj* dependent
зави́симост [zavisimost] *f* dependence
за́вист [zavist] *f* envy
зави́ся [zavisya] *v* depend on
заво́д [zavod] *m* plant, mill
заво́й [zavoi] *m* turn, curve
завою́вам [zavoyuvam] *v* conquer, win
завръ́щане [zavrushtane] *v* return
загла́вие [zaglavie] *n* title, heading
за́говор [zagovor] *m* plot, conspiracy
загри́жен [zagrizhen] *adj* worried, anxious
загри́женост [zagrizhenost] *f* anxiety,
concern, care
за́губа [zagouba] *f* loss, damage
зада́вам [zadavam] *v* assign, ask
зада́ча [zadacha] *f* task, problem
задоволи́телен [zadovolitelen] *adj*
satisfactory, satisfying

задълбоче́н [zadulbochen] *adj* profound, thorough

задълже́ние [zadulzhenie] *n* duty, obligation, engagement

задължи́телен [zadulzhitelen] *adj* obligatory, compulsory

за́едно [zaedno] *adv* together, along with

за́ек [zaek] *m* rabbit, hare

за́ем [zaem] *m* loan

зае́т [zaet] *adj* busy, taken, occupied

заинтересо́ван [zainteresovan] *adj* interested, concerned, partial

зака́нвам се [zakanvam se] *v* threaten

зака́чалка [zakachalka] *f* hat rack, hanger

зака́чам [zakacham] *v* hang up

заклю́чвам [zaklyuchvam] *v* lock

заключе́ние [zaklyuchenie] *n* conclusion

зако́н [zakon] *m* law, act

зако́нен [zakonen] *adj* lawful, legitimate, legal

законода́телство [zakonodatelstvo] *n* legislation

законопрое́кт [zakonoproekt] *m* bill

закопча́вам [zakopchavam] *v* button

заку́свам [zakousvam] *v* have breakfast

заку́ска [zakouska] *f* breakfast, snack

закъсне́ние [zakusnenie] *n* delay

закъсня́вам [zakusnyavam] *v* be late

зала́вям [zalavyam] *v* catch

за́лез [zales] *n* sunset

зале́пвам [zalepvam] *v* stick
зали́в [zalif] *m* bay, gulf
заме́свам [zamesvam] *v* involve
заме́ствам [zamestvam] *v* replace, substitute
заможен [zamozhen] *adj* well-to-do, well off
замразе́н [zamrazen] *adj* frozen
замразя́вам [zamrazyavam] *v* freeze, ice
замя́на [zamyana] *f* exchange
заня́тие [zanyatie] *n* occupation
за́пад [zapad] *m* west
запа́лвам [zapalvam] *v* light, kindle
запа́лка [zapalka] *f* lighter
запаля́нко [zapalyanko] *m* fan
запла́та [zaplata] *f* salary, pay, wages
запла́ха [zaplaha] *f* threat, menace
запла́швам [zaplashvam] *v* threaten, menace
за́повед [zapoved] *f* command, order
запозна́вам [zapoznavam] *v* acquaint, introduce
запо́чвам [zapochvam] *v* begin, start
запу́швам [zapoushvam] *v* plug, cork
зар [zar] *m* die
зара́вям [zaravyam] *v* bury
зара́за [zaraza] *f* infection, contagion
заро́диш [zarodish] *m* embryo, foetus
заса́да [zasada] *f* ambush
заса́ждам [zasazhdam] *v* plant
заседа́ние [zasedanie] *n* conference, session
заспи́вам [zaspivam] *v* go to sleep
заста́вям [zastavyam] *v* force, compel

застрахо́вка [zastrahofka] *f* insurance
затва́рям [zatvaryam] *v* shut, close
затво́р [zatvor] *m* prison, jail
затво́рен [zatvoren] *adj* closed, shut
затво́рник [zatvornik] *m* prisoner
затова́ [zatova] *adv* therefore, that is why
зато́плям [zatoplyam] *v* warm up
затъмне́ние [zatumnenie] *n* black out, eclipse
затя́гам [zatyagam] *v* tighten, make fast
зауча́вам [zaouchavam] *v* learn
за́ушки [zaoushki] *noun pl* mumps
за́хар [zahar] *m* sugar
за́харна бо́лест [zaharna bolest] *f* diabetes
захарни́ца [zaharnitsa] *f* sugar bowl
защи́та [zashtita] *f* defence, protection
защища́вам [zashtishtavam] *v* defend, protect
защо́ [zashto] *conj* why, what for
защо́то [zashtoto] *conj* because, for, as
звезда́ [zvezda] *f* star
звук [zvouk] *m* sound
звуча́ [zvoucha] *v* ring, sound
звъне́ц [zvunets] *m* bell
звъня́ [zvunya] *v* ring
звяр [zvyar] *m* beast, wild animal
зда́ние [zdanie] *n* building
здрав [zdraf] *adj* healthy, strong, solid
здра́ве [zdrave] *n* health
зе́ле [zele] *n* cabbage
зеле́н [zelen] *adj* green, unripe
зеленчу́к [zelenchouk] *m* vegetables

земевладе́лец [zemevladelets] *m* landowner
земеде́лец [zemedelets] *m* farmer
земеде́лие [zemedelie] *n* agriculture, farming
земетресе́ние [zemetresenie] *n* earthquake
земя́ [zemya] *f* soil, earth, ground
зет [zet] *m* son-in-law, brother-in-law
зехти́н [zehtin] *m* olive oil
зид [zid] *m* wall
зи́ма [zima] *f* winter
зла́то [zlato] *n* gold
зло́ба [zloba] *f* spite, malice
злове́щ [zlovesht] *adj* sinister, ominous
злополу́ка [zlopolouka] *f* accident
злоупотре́ба [zlooupotreba] *f* abuse, misuse
змия́ [zmiya] *f* snake
знак [znak] *m* sign, mark, symbol
зна́ме [zname] *n* flag, banner
знамени́т [znamenit] *adj* famous, eminent
зна́ча [znacha] *v* mean
значе́ние [znachenie] *n* meaning,
importance, significance
значи́телен [znachitelen] *adj* considerable,
important
значка́ [znachka] *f* badge
зна́я [znaya] *v* know, be aware of
зоологи́ческа гради́на [zoologicheska
gradina] *f* zoo
зооло́гия [zoologiya] *f* zoology
зре́ние [zrenie] *n* eyesight, vision
зре́я [zreya] *v* ripen, mature

зри́тел [zritel] *m* spectator, viewer
зрял [zryal] *adj* ripe, mature
зъб [zub] *m* tooth
зъбобо́л [zubobol] *m* toothache
зъболе́кар [zubolekar] *m* dentist
зърно́ [zurno] *n* grain

И

и [i] *conj* and, even, also, too
игла́ [igla] *f* needle
игра́ [igra] *f* game, play
игра́чка [igrachka] *f* toy
игра́я [igraya] *v* play
игри́ще [igrishte] *n* playground
и́двам [idvam] *v* come
идеа́лен [idealen] *adj* ideal, perfect
иде́я [ideya] *f* idea, notion, concept
идио́т [idiot] *m* idiot, fool
избира́тел [izbiratel] *m* voter
и́збори [izbori] *noun pl* elections
избя́гвам [izbyagvam] *v* run away, escape, avoid
изва́ждане [izvazhdane] *n* removal, subtraction
изве́стен [izvesten] *adj* famous, certain
извине́ние [izvinenie] *n* excuse, apology, forgiveness
и́звод [izvod] *m* deduction, conclusion

и́звор [izvor] *m* spring

извою́вам [izvoyuvam] *v* win, gain

извъ́н [izvun] *adv* outside, out of

и́зглед [izgled] *m* view

изгна́ние [izgnanie] *n* exile

и́зговор [izgovor] *m* pronunciation, articulation

изго́да [izgoda] *f* advantage, interest, profit

изго́ден [izgoden] *adj* advantageous, profitable

изго́нвам [izgonvam] *v* drive away, expel

изгот́вям [izgotvyam] *v* prepare, make

и́згрев [izgrev] *m* sunrise

изгря́вам [izgryavam] *v* rise

изгу́бен [izgouben] *adj* lost, hopeless

изда́вам [izdavam] *v* betray, give away

изда́вам [izdavam] *v* publish, issue

изда́ние [izdanie] *n* publication, edition

изда́тел [izdatel] *m* publisher

изда́телство [izdatelstvo] *n* publishing house

изди́швам [izdishvam] *v* exhale, expire, breathe out

издръжли́вост [izdruzhlivost] *f* tenacity, resistance

изи́сканост [iziskanost] *f* refinement, fineness, good taste

изи́сквам [iziskvam] *v* demand, require

изи́скване [iziskvane] *n* requirement

изка́зване [iskazvane] *n* statement, speech, contribution

изключвам [isklyuchvam] *v* exclude, rule out, bar

изключение [isklyuchenie] *n* exception

изкуствен [iskoustven] *adj* artificial

изкуство [iskoustvo] *n* art, skill

изкушавам [iskoushavam] *v* tempt, allure

изкушение [iskoushenie] *n* temptation, allurement

изливам [izlivam] *v* pour out, empty

излизам [izlizam] *v* come out

излитам [izlitam] *v* fly out, take off

излишен [izlishen] *adj* superfluous, redundant

излишък [izlishuk] *m* surplus, excess

изложба [izlozhba] *f* exhibition, show, display

измама [izmama] *f* deceit, fraud, delusion

измамвам [izmamvam] *v* deceive, cheat, fool

измервам [izmervam] *v* measure, weigh

измерение [izmerenie] *n* dimension

измествам [izmestvam] *v* displace

измивам [izmivam] *v* wash

измислям [izmislyam] *v* invent, contrive, fabricate

изморен [izmoren] *adj* tired, weary

изморителен [izmoritelen] *adj* tiresome

измръзнал [izmruznal] *adj* frozen, chilled

измъчвам [izmuchvam] *v* torture, torment

изнасилвам [iznasilvam] *v* rape

изневяра [iznevyara] *f* unfaithfulness

изненада [iznenada] *f* surprise

износ [iznos] *m* export, exportation

изобилие [izobilie] *n* abundance, profusion, plenty

изобразително искуство [izobrazitelno iskoustvo] *n* painting

изобретателен [izobretatelen] *adj* inventive, resourceful

изобретение [izobretenie] *n* invention, device

изолация [izolatsiya] *f* insulation, isolation

изолирам [izoliram] *v* insulate, isolate

изоставам [izostavam] *v* fall behind, lose

изоставям [izostavyam] *v* desert, abandon

изпарение [isparenie] *n* evaporation, fumes

изпарявам [isparyavam] *v* evaporate

изпит [ispit] *m* examination

изплащам [isplashtam] *v* pay off

изповед [ispoved] *f* confession

изпотявам се [ispotyavam se] *v* sweat, perspire

изправен [ispraven] *adj* upright

изпразвам [isprazvam] *v* empty, discharge

изпробвам [isprobvam] *v* test, try, fit

изпускам [ispouskam] *v* drop

изпълнение [ispulnenie] *n* execution, fulfilment, performance

изравям [izravyam] *v* dig out, excavate

изражение [izrazhenie] *n* expression, air

изразходвам [izraz-hodvam] *v* spend, use up

изразя́вам [izrazyavam] *v* express, voice

изрече́ние [izrechenie] *n* sentence

изря́звам [izryazvam] *v* cut, clip

изска́чам [iskacham] *v* jump out, pop up

изсле́дване [isledvane] *n* study, investigation, research

изследова́тел [isledovatel] *m* researcher, explorer

и́зстрел [istrel] *m* shot, report

изтеза́вам [istezavam] *v* torture, torment

изтеза́ние [istezanie] *n* torture, torment

изти́чам [isticham] *v* run out, expire

и́зток [istok] *m* east

и́зточен [istochen] *adj* eastern, oriental

и́зточник [istochnik] *m* source

изтоща́вам [istoshtavam] *v* exhaust, drain

изтоще́ние [istoshtenie] *n* exhaustion

изтреби́тел [istrebitel] *m* fighter

изтри́вам [istrivam] *v* wipe, rub, erase

изтъ́кнат [istuknat] *adj* outstanding, distinguished, eminent

изтърва́вам [isturvavam] *v* drop, let fall

изуча́вам [izouchavam] *v* study, learn

изхвъ́рлям [is-hvurlyam] *v* throw out, eject

и́зход [is-hod] *m* exit, way out, outcome, issue

изче́звам [ischezvam] *v* disappear, vanish

изче́рпан [ischerpan] *adj* exhausted, out of print

изчерпа́телен [ischerpatelen] *adj* thorough, comprehensive

изчисле́ние [ischislenie] *n* calculation

изчисля́вам [ischislyavam] *v* calculate, estimate

изчи́ствам [ischistvam] *v* clean out, clear

изя́щен [izyashten] *adj* graceful, refined, exquisite

изя́щество [izyashtestvo] *n* grace, refinement

ико́на [ikona] *f* icon

иконо́мика [ikonomika] *f* economy

икономи́свам [ikonomisvam] *v* save, economize, put aside

икономи́чен [ikonomichen] *adj* economical, thrifty

илю́зия [ilyuziya] *f* illusion

илюстра́ция [ilyustratsiya] *f* illustration

и́ма [ima] *v* there is, there are

и́мам [imam] *v* have, own, possess

и́ме [ime] *n* name

имо́т [imot] *m* property, belongings

имуните́т [imounitet] *m* immunity

иму́щество [imoushtestvo] *n* property

инвали́д [invalid] *m* invalid, disabled person

индиви́д [individ] *m* individual, specimen

индивидуа́лен [individoualen] *adj* individual, personal

инди́йски [indiiski] *adj* Indian

индустриа́лен [indoustrialen] *adj* industrial

инду́стрия [indoustriya] *f* industry

инже́кция [inzhektsiya] *f* injection
инжене́р [inzhener] *m* engineer
инсти́нкт [instinkt] *m* instinct
институ́т [institout] *m* institute
инстру́кция [instrouktsiya] *f* instructions
инструме́нт [instrument] *m* instrument, tool
интеле́кт [intelekt] *m* intellect, brains
интелектуа́лен [intelektoualen] *adj* intellectual
интелиге́нтен [inteligenten] *adj* intelligent, clever, bright
интензи́вен [intenziven] *adj* intensive
интерва́л [interval] *m* interval, space, gap
интервю́ [intervyu] *n* interview
интере́с [interes] *m* interest
интере́сен [interesen] *adj* interesting
инти́мен [intimen] *adj* intimate, close
инти́мност [intimnost] *f* intimacy
инфе́кция [infektsiya] *f* infection
инфла́ция [inflatsiya] *f* inflation
информа́ция [informatsiya] *f* information, news
информи́рам [informiram] *v* inform, notify, advise
брони́чен [ironichen] *adj* ironical, derisive
иск [isk] *m* claim
и́скам [iskam] *v* want, require, demand
и́скрен [iskren] *adj* sincere, frank
и́скреност [iskrenost] *f* sincerity, frankness
и́стина [istina] *f* truth

и́стински [istinski] *adj* true, real, genuine
истори́чески [istoricheski] *adj* historical
исто́рия [istoriya] *f* history, tale, affair

К

ка́бел [kabel] *m* cable
каби́на [kabina] *f* cabin, booth
кабине́т [kabinet] *m* study
кави́чки [kavichki] *noun pl* quotation marks
кадифе́н [kadifen] *adj* velvet
каза́рма [kazarma] *f* barracks
ка́звам [kazvam] *v* say, tell
как [kak] *adv* how
кака́о [kakao] *n* cocoa
какво́ [kakvo] *adv* what
ка́кто [kakto] *adv* as
какъ́в [kakuf] *adv* what, what kind of
кал [kal] *f* mud, dirt
календа́р [kalendar] *m* calendar
камба́на [kambana] *f* bell
ками́ла [kamila] *f* camel
камио́н [kamion] *m* truck
камши́к [kamshik] *m* whip, lash
кана́л [kanal] *m* canal, channel
канапе́ [kanape] *n* sofa, couch
кандида́т [kandidat] *m* candidate
канцела́рия [kantselariya] *f* office
ка́ня [kanya] *v* invite, ask

капа́к [kapak] *m* lid, cover

капа́н [kapan] *m* trap

капиталовложе́ние [kapitalovlozhenie] *n* investment

ка́пка [kapka] *f* drop

ка́рам [karam] *v* drive

ка́рам се [karam se] *v* scold, quarrel

карамфи́л [karamfil] *m* carnation

карие́ра [kariera] *f* career

карикату́ра [karikatoura] *f* caricature, cartoon

ка́рта [karta] *f* card

карте́чница [kartechnitsa] *f* machine-gun

карти́на [kartina] *f* picture, painting

ка́ртичка [kartichka] *f* postcard

картон [karton] *m* cardboard, pasteboard

карто́ф [kartof] *m* potato

ка́са [kasa] *f* safe, cash-drawer

катало́г [katalog] *m* catalog

катастро́фа [katastrofa] *f* accident, crash, disaster

катастрофи́рам [katastrofiram] *v* crash, have an accident

катедра́ла [katedrala] *f* cathedral

ка́терица [kateritsa] *f* squirrel

кате́ря се [katerya se] *v* climb

като́ [kato] *v* like

като́лик [katolik] *m* catholic

ка́уза [kauza] *f* cause, idea

кафе́ [kafe] *n* coffee

кафене́ [kafene] *n* cafe
кафя́в [kafyav] *adj* brown
ка́цане [katsane] *n* landing
ка́цам [katsam] *v* land
ка́чество [kachestvo] *n* quality
ка́шлям [kashlyam] *v* cough, have a cough
квадра́т [kvadrat] *m* square
квадра́тен [kvadraten] *adj* square
квалифика́ция [kvalifikatsiya] *f* qualification
кварти́ра [kvartira] *f* lodging(s)
кварти́ра́нт [kvartirant] *m* lodger, tenant
кей [keil] *m* quay
кера́мика [keramika] *f* ceramics, pottery
керами́да [keramida] *f* tile
ке́стен [kesten] *m* chestnut
ке́цове [ketsove] *noun pl* sneakers
кибри́т [kibrit] *m* match, box of matches
крили́м [kilim] *m* carpet, rug
ки́но [kino] *n* cinema, movie
кинорежисьо́р [kinorezhisyor] *m* film
director
кипя́ [kipya] *v* boil, seethe
ки́сел [kisel] *adj* sour, acid
киселина́ [kiselina] *f* acid
кислоро́д [kislorod] *m* oxygen
кит [kit] *m* whale
кита́йски [kitaiski] *adj* Chinese
кита́ра [kitara] *f* guitar
ки́фла [kifla] *f* roll, bun
ки́хам [kiham] *v* sneeze

клави́ш [klavish] *m* key, note
кла́денец [kladenets] *m* well
кла́мер [klamer] *m* paper–clip
клас [klas] *m* class, grade
класи́чески [klasicheski] *adj* classic
кла́тя [klatya] *v* shake, rock, dangle
клепа́ч [klepach] *m* eyelid
кле́пка [klepka] *f* eyelash
кле́тва [kletva] *f* oath, curse
кле́тка [kletka] *f* cage, cell
клие́нт [klient] *m* customer, patron
кли́мат [klimat] *m* climate
климати́чна инстала́ция [klimatichna instalatsiya] *f* air–conditioning
клон [klon] *m* branch, bough
кло́ун [kloun] *m* clown, joker
клуб [kloub] *m* club
клю́ка [klyuka] *f* gossip, scandal
ключ [klyuch] *m* key
ключа́лка [klyuchalka] *f* lock
кмет [kmet] *m* mayor
кни́га [kniga] *f* book
книжа́ [knizha] *noun pl* papers, documents
книжа́рница [knizharnitsa] *f* bookstore
коали́ция [koalitsiya] *f* coalition
кова́рство [kovarstvo] *n* treachery, perfidy
ковче́г [kofcheg] *m* coffin
кога́ [koga] *adv* when
ко́жа [kozha] *f* skin, fur, leather
ко́жен [kozhen] *adj* leather, fur

козá [koza] *f* goat

кой [koi] *pron* who, which

кóкал [kokal] *m* bone

кокóшка [kokoshka] *f* hen

колáн [kolan] *m* bell

колебáние [kolebanie] *n* hesitation, wavering

колебáя се [kolebaya sе] *v* hesitate, waver

колéга [kolega] *m* colleague, mate

кóледа [koleda] *f* Christmas

колéкция [kolektsiya] *f* collection

колелó [kolelo] *n* wheel, bicycle

колúчество [kolichestvo] *n* quantity, amount, number

кóлко [kolko] *adv* how much, how many

кóлкото [kolkoto] *adv* as, as much as, as many as

колóна [kolona] *f* column, pillar, post

колóния [koloniya] *f* colony

кóля [kolya] *v* slaughter, kill, butcher

командúр [komandir] *m* commander

комáр [komar] *m* mosquito, gnat

комáр [komar] *f* gambling

комéдия [komediya] *f* comedy

коментáр [komentar] *m* commentary, comment

коментúрам [komentiram] *v* comment

комúн [komin] *m* chimney

комúсия [komisiya] *f* commission, committee, board

комитéт [komitet] *m* committee

компа́с [kompas] *m* compass

компенса́ция [kompensatsiya] *f* compensation, recompense

компенси́рам [kompensiram] *v* compensate, make amends

компете́нтен [kompetenten] *adj* competent

компете́нтност [kompetentnost] *f* competence

компози́тор [kompozitor] *m* composer

комуни́зъм [komounizum] *m* communism

комфо́рт [komfort] *m* comfort, luxury

комюнике́ [komyunike] *n* communique, official statement

кон [kon] *m* horse, steed, knight

конгре́с [kongres] *m* congress

ко́нец [konets] *m* thread

конкуре́нт [konkourent] *m* competitor

конкуре́нция [konkourentsiya] *f* competition

конку́рс [konkours] *m* competition (in arts, sport)

ко́нница [konnitsa] *f* cavalry

консервати́вен [konservativen] *adj* conservative

консе́рвена кути́я [konservena koutiya] *f* tin, can

конспе́кт [konspekt] *m* syllabus

ко́нсулство [konsoulstvo] *n* consulate

консулти́рам [konsoultiram] *v* consult, see

контине́нт [kontinent] *m* continent

контраба́нда [kontrabanda] *f* smuggling, contraband

контра́ст [kontrast] *m* contrast
контро́л [kontrol] *m* control, checking
ко́нус [konous] *m* cone
конфитю́р [konfityur] *m* jam, preserve
конфли́кт [konflict] *m* conflict
конце́рт [kontsert] *m* concert
коня́к [konyak] *m* cognac, brandy
копа́я [kopaya] *v* dig
ко́пие [kopie] *n* spear, pike
ко́пие [kopie] *n* copy, duplicate
копри́на [koprina] *f* silk
ко́пче [kopche] *n* button
кора́ [kora] *f* bark, peal, crust
ко́раб [korab] *m* ship, boat
коре́ктор [korektor] *m* proof-reader
коре́кция [korektsiya] *f* correction, amendment
коре́м [korem] *m* stomach, belly
ко́рен [koren] *m* root
кореспонде́нт [korespondent] *m* correspondent
коридо́р [koridor] *m* corridor
кори́ца [koritsa] *f* cover
коро́на [korona] *f* crown
коса́ [kosa] *f* hair
космона́вт [kosmonaft] *m* astronaut
кост [kost] *f* bone
костену́рка [kostenourka] *f* turtle, tortoise
костю́м [kostyum] *m* suit, costume
ко́съм [kosum] *m* hair

ко́тва [kotva] *f* anchor
ко́тка [kotka] *f* cat
ко́шница [koshnitsa] *f* basket
кра́ва [krava] *f* cow
крада́ [krada] *v* steal, lift
краде́ц [kradets] *m* thief
кра́жба [krazhba] *f* theft, burglary
кра́йник [krainik] *m* limb
кра́йност [krainost] *f* extreme, excess
крак [krak] *m* leg, foot
крал [kral] *m* king
крали́ца [kralitsa] *f* queen
кра́лство [kralstvo] *n* kingdom
краса́вица [krasavitsa] *f* beauty
краси́в [krasif] *adj* beautiful, lovely, handsome
красота́ [krasota] *f* beauty
кра́ставица [krastavitsa] *f* cucumber
кра́тък [kratuk] *adj* short, brief, concise
кра́чка [krachka] *f* step, pace
крева́т [krevat] *m* bed, bedstead
креди́т [kredit] *m* credit
крем [krem] *m* cream
кре́нвирш [krenvirsh] *m* Frankfurter
кресло́ [kreslo] *n* armchair, easychair
креща́ [kreshtya] *v* scream, yell, shout
кривогле́д [krivogled] *adj* cross-eyed
кри́за [kriza] *f* crisis
крило́ [krilo] *n* wing
кримина́лен [kriminalen] *adj* criminal

криста́л [kristal] *m* crystal
кри́тик [kritik] *m* critic
кри́я [kriya] *v* hide, conceal
крокоди́л [krokodil] *m* crocodile
кру́ша [krousha] *f* pear
кру́шка [kroushka] *f* light bulb
кръ́вно наля́гане [kruvno nalyagane] *n*
blood pressure
кръг [krug] *m* circle
кръст [krust] *m* cross
кръст [krust] *m* waist
кръстосло́вица [krustoslovitsa] *f* crossword
puzzle
кръ́чма [kruchma] *f* pub, tavern
кръще́лно свиде́телство [krushtelno
svidetelstvo] *n* birth certificate
куб [koub] *m* cube
ку́ка [kouka] *f* hook, knitting needle
ку́кла [koukla] *f* doll
ку́ла [koula] *f* tower
култ [koult] *m* cult
култу́ра [koultoura] *f* culture, civilization
куп [koup] *m* heap, pile, stack
ку́па [koupa] *f* bowl, cup
купле́т [kouplet] *m* verse, couplet
купу́вам [koupouvam] *v* buy, get, purchase
купува́ч [koupouvach] *m* buyer, purchaser
курс [kours] *m* course
куршу́м [kourshoum] *m* bullet, lead
кути́я [koutiya] *f* box

ку́хня [kouhnya] *f* kitchen
ку́че [kouche] *n* dog
къде́ [kude] *adv* where
кълбо́ [kulbo] *n* ball, globe, sphere
към [kum] *adv* toward, to
къ́пя [kupya] *v* bathe
кѝрпа [kurpa] *f* cloth, handkerchief, towel
къс [kus] *adj* short, brief
кѝсен [kusen] *adj* late
кѝсме́т [kusmet] *m* luck, fortune
късогле́д [kusogled] *adj* short-sighted
къ́ща [kushta] *f* home, house
кюфте́ [kyufte] *n* meatball

Л

лаборато́рия [laboratoriya] *f* laboratory
лави́на [lavina] *f* avalanche
ла́вка [lafka] *f* canteen
ла́гер [lager] *m* camp
ла́зя [lazya] *v* creep, crawl
лак [lak] *m* varnish, polish
ла́кът [lakut] *m* elbow
ла́мпа [lampa] *f* lamp
ла́па [lapa] *f* paw
ла́стик [lastik] *m* elastic, rubber band
лати́нски [latinski] *adj* Latin
ла́я [laya] *v* bark
ле́бед [lebed] *m* swan

леге́нда [legenda] *f* legend
легло́ [leglo] *n* bed
лед [led] *m* ice
лежа́ [lezha] *v* lie, recline, be situated
ле́кар [lekar] *m* physician, doctor
лека́рство [lekarstvo] *n* medicine, drug
леке́ [leke] *n* stain, spot
лекоми́слие [lekomislie] *n* frivolity
ле́ксика [leksika] *f* vocabulary
леку́вам [lekouvam] *v* cure, treat
ле́кция [lektsiya] *f* lecture
леля́ [lelya] *f* aunt
лепи́ло [lepilo] *n* gum, glue, paste
ле́пкав [lepkaf] *adj* sticky
ле́сен [lesen] *adj* easy, light
ле́сно [lesno] *adv* easily
лети́ще [letishte] *n* airport, airfield
летя́ [letya] *v* fly, soar
ли́жа [lizha] *v* lick
лила́в [lilav] *adj* purple, violet
лимо́н [limon] *m* lemon
лимона́да [limonada] *f* lemonade
лине́йка [lineika] *f* ambulance
ли́ния [liniya] *f* line, ruler, straightedge
ли́пса [lipsa] *f* lack, want, shortage
ли́псвам [lipsvam] *v* be wanting, be absent
ли́ра [lira] *f* pound
лиси́ца [lisitsa] *f* fox
лист [list] *m* leaf, petal, sheet
литерату́ра [literatoura] *f* literature

ли́хва [lihva] *f* interest
лицеме́рие [litsemerie] *n* hypocrisy
ли́чен [lichen] *adj* personal, private, eminent
ли́чност [lichnost] *f* personality
лов [lof] *m* hunting, shooting
лове́ц [lovets] *m* hunter
ловя́ [lovya] *v* catch, seize
ло́дка [lodka] *f* boat
ло́жа [lozha] *f* box
локомоти́в [lokomotif] *m* engine
лопа́та [lopata] *f* spade, shovel
лост [lost] *m* lever
лота́рия [lotariya] *f* lottery, raffle
лош [losh] *adj* bad, wicked, poor
луд [loud] *adj* mad, crazy, insane
лу́дост [loudost] *f* madness, insanity
лук [louk] *m* onion
лукс [louks] *m* luxury
лула́ [loula] *f* pipe
луна́ [louna] *f* moon
лу́па [loupa] *f* magnifying glass
лъв [luv] *m* lion
лъжа́ [luzha] *v* lie
лъжа́ [luzha] *f* lie, falsehood
лъжи́ца [luzhitsa] *f* spoon
лъч [luch] *m* ray, beam
любе́зен [lyubezen] *adj* polite, kind
любе́зност [lyubeznost] *f* kindness, courtesy
люби́мец [lyubimets] *m* favorite

люби́тел [lyubitel] *m* lover, amateur
любо́в [lyubov] *f* love, affection, romance
любо́вник [lyubovnik] *m* lover, sweetheart
любо́вница [lyubovnitsa] *f* mistress, sweetheart
любопи́тен [lyubopiten] *adj* curious, inquisitive
любопи́тство [lyubopitstvo] *n* curiosity
любя́ [lyubya] *v* make love to, be in love with
лю́лка [lyulka] *f* swing, cradle
лю́ляк [lyulyak] *m* lilac
лют [lyut] *adj* hot, pungent
ляв [lyaf] *adj* left
ля́гам [lyagam] *v* lie down
ля́то [lyato] *n* summer

M

магази́н [magazin] *m* shop, store
мага́ре [magare] *n* donkey, ass
магнетофо́нен за́пис [magnetofonen zapis] *m* recording, tape
маза́ [maza] *f* cellar, basement
мазнина́ [maznina] *f* fat, grease
май [mai] *m* May
ма́йка [maika] *f* mother
маймуна [maimouna] *f* monkey, ape
майо́р [mayor] *m* major

ме́стен [mesten] *adj* local, native
ме́стност [mestnost] *f* locality, place, country
местожи́телство [mestozhitelstvo] *n* residence
местоиме́ние [mestoimenie] *n* pronoun
местонахожде́ние [mestonahozhdenie] *n* location, whereabouts
месторожде́ние [mestorozhdenie] *n* birthplace
ме́стя [mestya] *v* move, transfer
мета́ [meta] *v* sweep
мета́лен [metalen] *adj* metal
метеороло́гия [meteorologiya] *f* meteorology
метла́ [metla] *f* broom
ме́тод [metod] *m* method
метро́ [metro] *n* subway
меха́ник [mehanik] *m* mechanic
мехле́м [mehlem] *m* ointment, cream
меч [mech] *m* sword
ме́чка [mechka] *f* bear
мечта́ [mechta] *f* day-dream
мечта́я [mechtaya] *v* dream of, long for
ми́вка [mifka] *f* wash-basin, sink
ми́да [mida] *f* mussel, clam
мизе́рия [mizeriya] *f* misery, poverty
микро́б [mikrob] *m* microbe, germ
микроско́п [mikroskop] *m* microscope
микрофо́н [mikrofon] *m* microphone
мил [mil] *adj* dear, nice, kind
милиа́рд [miliard] *m* billion
милио́н [milion] *m* million
милионе́р [milioner] *m* millionaire

ми́лост [milost] *f* mercy, pity, compassion

ми́ля [milya] *f* mile

ми́на [mina] *f* mine

мина́вам [minavam] *v* pass, go by, be over

ми́нало [minalo] *n* past

минера́л [mineral] *m* mineral

минима́лен [minimalen] *adj* minimum

министе́рство [ministerstvo] *n* ministry, department

мини́стър [ministur] *m* minister, secretary of state

мину́та [minouta] *f* minute, moment, instant

миньо́р [minyor] *m* miner

мир [mir] *m* peace

мири́зма [mirizma] *f* smell, odor, scent

мири́ша [mirisha] *v* smell

ми́сия [misiya] *f* mission

ми́сля [mislya] *v* think, reason, intend

ми́съл [misul] *f* thought, reflection, idea

ми́тинг [miting] *m* rally

ми́тница [mitnitsa] *f* custom house

ми́то [mito] *n* duty

ми́шка [mishka] *f* mouse

ми́я [miya] *v* wash, clean

млад [mlad] *adj* young

мла́дост [mladost] *f* youth

мле́чен [mlechen] *adj* milky, of milk

мля́ко [mlyako] *n* milk

мне́ние [mnenie] *n* opinion

мно́го [mnogo] *adv* much, many, plenty

многолю́ден [mnogolyuden] *adj* crowded, populous

мно́жество [mnozhestvo] *n* multitude, great number

мо́га [moga] *v* can, be able to, may

могъ́щ [mogusht] *adj* powerful, mighty

мо́да [moda] *f* fashion, vogue

моде́л [model] *m* model, pattern, design

моде́рен [moderen] *adj* modern, contemporary, fashionable

мо́же [mozhe] *v* may

мо́зък [mozuk] *m* brain

мой [moi] *pron* my, mine

мо́кър [mokur] *adj* wet, damp

молба́ [molba] *f* request, application

мо́лив [molif] *m* pencil

моли́тва [molitva] *f* prayer

мо́ля [molya] *v* beg, ask, request

моме́нт [moment] *m* moment, instant

моми́че [momiche] *n* girl, lass

момче́ [momche] *n* boy, lad, youngster

моне́та [moneta] *f* coin

моноло́г [monolog] *m* monologue

мора́л [moral] *m* morality, morals

море́ [more] *n* sea

морепла́ване [moreplavane] *n* navigation

мо́рков [morkof] *m* carrot

моря́к [moryak] *m* sailor, seaman

мост [most] *m* bridge

мо́стра [mostra] *f* sample, specimen

мотел [motel] *m* motel
мотоциклет [mototsiklet] *m* motocycle, bike
мошеник [moshenik] *m* swindler, rascal
мощ [mosht] *f* might, power
мощен [moshten] *adj* powerful
мравка [mrafka] *f* ant
мраз [mras] *m* frost, chill
мразя [mrazya] *v* hate, detest, dislike
мрамор [mramor] *m* marble
мрежа [mrezha] *f* net, network
мръсен [mrusen] *adj* dirty, soiled
мръсотия [mrusotiya] *f* dirt, squalor
му [mou] *pron* him
музей [mouzei] *m* museum
музика [mouzika] *f* music
музикален [mouzikalen] *adj* musical
мускул [mouskoul] *m* muscle
мустаци [moustatsi] *noun pl* moustaches, whiskers
муха [mouha] *f* fly
мъгла [mugla] *f* mist, fog
мъдрост [mudrost] *f* wisdom, prudence
мъдър [mudur] *adj* wise, judicious
мъж [muzh] *m* man
мъжки [muzhki] *adj* male, masculine
мъка [muka] *f* pain, torment
мълча [mulcha] *v* keep silence
мързел [murzel] *m* laziness, indolence
мързелив [murzelif] *adj* lazy, idle
мърморя [murmorya] *v* mumble, grumble

мъ́ртъв [murtuf] *adj* dead
мъх [muh] *m* moss, lichen
мъ́ча [mucha] *v* torture, torment
мъчени́к [muchenik] *m* martyr
мя́рка [myarka] *f* measure, measurement
мя́сто [myasto] *n* place, room

Н

на [na] *prep* on, upon, to, at, of, by
наблюда́вам [nablyudavam] *v* observe, watch
наблюда́тел [nablyudatel] *m* observer
наблюде́ние [nablyudenie] *n* observation, control
набля́гам [nablyagam] *v* stress, emphasize
набо́жен [nabozhen] *adj* religious, devout
наве́ждам [navezhdam] *v* bend down
на́вик [navik] *m* habit, custom
наводне́ние [navodnenie] *n* flood
навъ́н [navun] *adv* out, outside
навя́рно [navyarno] *adv* probably, most likely
навя́хвам [navyahvam] *v* sprain
наго́ре [nagore] *adv* upwards, uphill
награ́да [nagrada] *f* prize, award
награжда́вам [nagrazhdavam] *v* award, decorate
нагрева́тел [nagrevatel] *m* heater
нагрубя́вам [nagroubyavam] *v* insult, be rude

нагря́вам [nagryavam] *v* heat, warm

над [nad] *prep* over, above

надале́ч [nadalech] *adv* far away, a long way off

надбя́гване [nadbyagvane] *n* race

наде́жда [nadezhda] *f* hope

на́дница [nadnitsa] *f* wage

надни́чам [nadnicham] *v* peep

на́дпис [nadpis] *m* inscription

надя́вам се [nadyavam se] *v* hope

надя́сно [nadyasno] *adv* on, to the right

на́ем [naem] *m* rent

нае́мам [naemam] *v* rent, hire

наема́тел [naematel] *m* tenant, lodger

напа́дам [napadam] *v* attack, assail

напада́тел [napadatel] *m* assailant, aggressor

нападе́ние [napadenie] *n* attack, assault

напеча́твам [napechatvam] *v* print

напи́вам се [napivam se] *v* get drunk

напосо́ки [naposoki] *adv* at random

напоя́вам [napoyavam] *v* irrigate, water, soak

напоя́ване [napoyavane] *n* irrigation

напра́во [napravo] *adv* straight, straight ahead

напра́зен [naprazen] *adj* vain, futile

напре́д [napred] *adv* forward, ahead

напре́дък [napreduk] *m* progress, advance

напреже́ние [naprezhenie] *n* tension, strain, effort

напри́мер [naprimer] *adv* for instance, for example

напу́квам [napoukvam] *v* crack

напъ́лно [napulno] *adv* completely, fully, quite

нараня́вам [naranyavam] *v* wound, injure, hurt

наре́дба [naredba] *f* regulation, instruction, order

нари́чам [naricham] *v* call, name

наро́д [narod] *m* people, nation

наро́чно [narochno] *adv* on purpose, deliberately

наруша́вам [naroushavam] *v* violate, break, transgress

наруше́ние [naroushenie] *n* breach, violation, offense

наруши́тел [naroushitel] *m* offender

наръ́чник [naruchnik] *m* handbook, manual, guide

нас [nas] *pron* us

наса́м [nasam] *adv* this way, here

насеко́мо [nasekomo] *n* insect

населе́ние [naselenie] *n* population, inhabitants

наси́лие [nasilie] *n* force, violation

наси́лствен [nasilstven] *adj* forcible

насле́дник [naslednik] *m* heir

насле́дствен [nasledstven] *adj* hereditary, inherited

насле́дственост [nasledstvenost] *f* heredity

насле́дство [nasledstvo] *n* inheritance, legacy

насле́дявам [nasledyavam] *v* inherit, succeed to

насме́шка [nasmeshka] *f* mockery, ridicule

насти́вам [nastivam] *v* catch cold

насти́гам [nastigam] *v* catch up with, overtake, reach

насто́йник [nastoinik] *m* guardian

насто́йчивост [nastoichivost] *f* insistence, perseverance

настоя́вам [nastoyavam] *v* insist, persist

настоя́ще [nastoyashte] *n* present

настрое́ние [nastroenie] *n* mood, temper, spirits

насърча́вам [nasurchavam] *v* encourage, reassure

на́тиск [natisk] *m* pressure

нати́скам [natiskam] *v* press

натова́рвам [natovarvam] *v* load, charge, entrust with

нау́ка [naouka] *f* science

науча́вам [naouchavam] *v* learn

нау́чен [naouchen] *adj* scientific, scholarly

наха́лен [nahalen] *adj* impertinent, saucy

наха́лство [nahalstvo] *n* impertinence, cheek

нахо́дка [nahodka] *f* find

нахо́дчив [nahodchif] *adj* resourceful, inventive, ingenious

находчивост [nahodchivost] *f*
resourcefulness, ingenuity
националност [natsionalnost] *f* nationality
нация [natsiya] *f* nation
началник [nachalnik] *m* head, chief, boss
начало [nachalo] *n* beginning, start
наш [nash] *pron* our
нашествeник [nashestvenik] *m* invader
нашествие [nashestvie] *n* invasion
не [ne] *part* no, not
небе [nebe] *n* sky, heaven
небрежност [nebrezhnost] *f* carelessness,
negligence
невежество [nevezhestvo] *n* ignorance
невероятен [neveroyaten] *adj* improbable,
unbelievable
невидим [nevidim] *adj* invisible
невинен [nevinen] *adj* innocent
невинност [nevinnost] *f* innocence,
harmlessness
невнимание [nevnimanie] *n* carelessness
невнимателен [nevnimatelen] *adj* careless,
thoughtless
невралгия [nevralgiya] *f* neuralgia
невроза [nevroza] *f* neurosis
невролог [nevrolog] *m* neurologist
невъзможен [nevuzmozhen] *adj* impossible
невъзпитан [nevuspitan] *adj* ill-bred,
bad-mannered

невъзпита́ние [nevuspitanie] *n* ill-breeding, bad manners

не́го [nego] *pron* him, it

не́гов [negof] *pron* his, its

негодува́ние [negodouvanie] *n* indignation, remonstrance

неграмо́тност [negramotnost] *f* illiteracy

не́гър [negur] *m* black person

неде́ля [nedelya] *f* Sunday

недове́рие [nedoverie] *n* mistrust, suspicion

недово́лен [nedovolen] *adj* dissatisfied, displeased

недово́лство [nedovolstvo] *n* discontent, dissatisfaction

недовъ́ршен [nedovurshen] *adj* unfinished, incomplete

недопусти́м [nedopoustim] *adj* inadmissible, unthinkable

недоразуме́ние [nedorazoumenie] *n* misunderstanding

недоста́тък [nedostatuk] *m* defect, fault, shortcoming

недоста́тъчен [nedostatuchen] *adj* insufficient, inadequate

недо́стиг [nedostik] *m* shortage, lack

недостъ́пен [nedostupen] *adj* inaccessible, out of reach

нежела́ние [nezhelanie] *n* reluctance, unwillingness

нежелателен [nezhelatelen] *adj* undesirable, objectionable

нежен [nezhen] *adj* tender, delicate, fine

неженен [nezhenen] *adj* unmarried, single

нежност [nezhnost] *f* tenderness, delicacy

незабавно [nezabavno] *adv* immediately, at once

независим [nezavisim] *adj* independent

независимост [nezavisimost] *f* independence

незаконен [nezakonen] *adj* illegal, unlawful

незначителен [neznachitelen] *adj* insignificant, negligible

неизбежен [neizbezhen] *adj* inevitable

неизвестен [neizvesten] *adj* unknown

неизлечим [neizlechim] *adj* incurable

неизменен [neizmenen] *adj* invariable, unchanging

неизправен [neispraven] *adj* out of order

неин [nein] *pron* her

неквалифициран [nekvalifitsiran] *adj* unskilled

некомпетентен [nekompetenten] *adj* incompetent

нелогичен [nelogichen] *adj* illogical

немец [nemets] *m* German

неминуем [neminouem] *adj* inevitable

неморален [nemoralen] *adj* immoral

немски [nemski] *adj* German

ненавиждам [nenavizhdam] *v* hate, detest

ненавист [nenavist] *f* hatred, abhorrence, dislike

необмислен [neobmislen] *adj* hasty, rash

необходим [neobhodim] *adj* necessary, indispensable

необходимост [neobhodimost] *f* necessity

необясним [neobyasnim] *adj* inexplicable, unaccountable

неограничен [neogranichen] *adj* unlimited, boundless

неодобрение [neodobrenie] *n* disapproval

неомъжена [neomuzhena] *adj* unmarried, single

неопитен [neopiten] *adj* inexperienced, unpractised

неопитност [neopitnost] *f* inexperience

неоснователен [neosnovatelen] *adj* groundless, unfounded

неоспорим [neosporim] *adj* indisputable, irrefutable

неосъществим [neosushtestvim] *adj* infeasible, impracticable

неотдавна [neotdavna] *adv* recently, not long ago

неотдавнашен [neotdavnashen] *adj* recent

неофициален [neofitsialen] *adj* informal, unofficial

неочакван [neochakvan] *adj* unexpected, sudden

непобедим [nepobedim] *adj* invincible

неподви́жен [nepodvizhen] *adj* immovable, motionless

неподходя́щ [nepodhodyasht] *adj* unsuitable, inappropriate

непозна́т [nepoznat] *adj* unknown, unfamiliar

непоноси́м [neponosim] *adj* intolerable, unbearable

непослу́шен [neposloushen] *adj* disobedient, naughty

непотре́бен [nepotreben] *adj* useless

непра́вда [nepravda] *f* injustice

непра́вилен [nepravilen] *adj* incorrect, wrong

непредвидли́в [nepredvidlif] *adj* improvident

непредвидли́вост [nepredvidlivost] *f* improvidence

непредпазли́в [nepredpazlif] *adj* imprudent, careless

непредпазли́вост [nepredpazlivost] *f* imprudence, carelessness

непредубеде́н [nepredoubeden] *adj* unprejudiced, unbiased

непреќъ́снато [neprekusnato] *adv* ceaselessly, incessantly

непривлека́телен [neprivlekatelen] *adj* unattractive

неприе́млив [nepriemlif] *adj* unacceptable, inadmissible

неприли́чен [neprilichen] *adj* indecent, improper

неприя́зън [nepriyazun] *f* hostility, ill-will

неприя́тел [nepriyatel] *m* enemy, foe

неприя́тен [nepriyaten] *adj* unpleasant, disagreeable

неприя́тност [nepriyatnost] *f* trouble, nuisance

непълноле́тен [nepulnoleten] *adj* under age, minor

нера́венство [neravenstvo] *n* inequality

неравноме́рен [neravnomeren] *adj* uneven, irregular

неразби́раем [nerazbiraem] *adj* unintelligible

неразположе́ние [neraspolozhenie] *n* indisposition

неразу́мен [nerazoumen] *adj* unwise, unreasonable

нерв [nerf] *m* nerve

не́рвен [nerven] *adj* nervous

нерви́рам [nerviram] *v* get on someone's nerves

не́рвност [nervnost] *f* nervousness

нередо́вен [neredoven] *adj* irregular

нереши́телен [nereshitelen] *adj* irresolute, hesitating

нереши́телност [nereshitelnost] *f* indecision, irresolution

неръжда́ем [neruzhdaem] *adj* stainless

ни́кой [nikoi] *pron* nobody, no one
ни́къде [nikude] *adv* nowhere
нима́ [nima] *adv* really, indeed
ни́ско [nisko] *adv* low
ни́сък [nisuk] *adj* low, short, undersized
нит [nit] *m* rivet
ни́шка [nishka] *f* thread
ни́що [nishto] *pron* nothing
но [no] *conj* but
нов [nof] *adj* new
нова́тор [novator] *m* innovator
новина́ [novina] *f* news
новодошъ́л [novodoshul] *m* newcomer
ное́мври [noemvri] *m* November
нож [nozh] *m* knife
но́жица [nozhitsa] *f* scissors
но́кът [nokut] *m* nail
но́мер [nomer] *m* number, size
норма́лен [normalen] *adj* normal
нос [nos] *m* nose
носи́лка [nosilka] *f* stretcher
но́ся [nosya] *v* carry, bring, wear
нощ [nosht] *f* night
но́щница [noshtnitsa] *f* nightgown
нрав [nraf] *m* temper, disposition
нужда́ [nouzhda] *f* need, necessity
нужда́я се [nouzhdaya se] *v* need, require
ну́жен [nouzhen] *adj* necessary, requisite
ну́ла [noula] *f* zero
няка́къв [nyakakuf] *adj* some, some kind

някога [nyakoga] *adv* once, formerly
някой [nyakoi] *pron* somebody
някъде [nyakude] *adv* somewhere
ням [nyam] *adj* dumb, mute
няма [nyama] *v* there is not, there are not

О

оазис [oazis] *m* oasis
обаждам [obazhdam] *v* tell, inform, report
обаче [obache] *conj* but, however
обаяние [obayanie] *n* fascination, charm
обвинение [obvinenie] *n* accusation, charge
обвинявам [obvinyavam] *v* accuse, charge, blame
обвиняем [obvinyaem] *m* defender
обграждам [obgrazhdam] *v* surround, encircle
обяд [obyad] *m* lunch, dinner
обединение [obedinenie] *n* union, society
обеднявам [obednyavam] *v* unite, combine
обезоръжавам [obezoruzhavam] *v* disarm
обезпокоявам [obespokoyavam] *v* disturb, trouble
обезщетение [obeshtetenie] *n* compensation, amends, damages
обезщетявам [obeshtetyavam] *v* compensate, indemnify
обект [obekt] *m* object

обекти́вен [obektiven] *adj* objective, unbiased

обекти́вност [obektivnost] *f* objectivity

обём [obem] *m* volume

обёсвам [obesvam] *v* hang

обеца́ [obetsa] *f* earring

обеща́вам [obeshtavam] *v* promise

обеща́ние [obeshtanie] *n* promise

обжа́лвам [obzhalvam] *v* appeal

обзавёждам [obzavezhdam] *v* furnish

обзала́гам се [obzalagam se] *v* bet, wager

обзо́р [obzor] *m* survey

оби́да [obida] *f* insult, affront

оби́ден [obiden] *adj* insulting, offensive

оби́ждам [obizhdam] *v* offend, insult

обика́лям [obikalyam] *v* go round, tour, travel over

обикновён [obiknoven] *adj* ordinary, usual

обикновёно [obiknoveno] *adv* usually, as a rule

обико́лка [obikolka] *f* tour

оби́лен [obilen] *adj* abundant, plentiful

о́бир [obir] *m* robbery

обита́вам [obitavam] *v* inhabit, dwell in

обита́тел [obitatel] *m* inhabitant, dweller

обича́й [obichai] *m* habit, custom

оби́чам [obicham] *v* love, like

о́блак [oblak] *m* cloud

о́бласт [oblast] *f* district, region, sphere

о́блачен [oblachen] *adj* cloudy, overcast

облега́ло [oblegalo] *n* back

облекло́ [obleklo] *n* clothes, dress

облекче́ние [oblekchenie] *n* relief

облига́ция [obligatsiya] *f* share, bond, stock

обли́чам [oblicham] *v* dress, clothe

обло́г [oblok] *m* bet, wager

обля́гам [oblyagam] *v* lean, rest

обме́ням [obmenyam] *v* exchange

обобща́вам [obobshtavam] *v* generalize, summarize

обобще́ние [obobshtenie] *n* generalization, summary

обожа́вам [obozhavam] *v* adore, worship

обожа́тел [obozhatel] *m* admirer

обоня́ние [obonyanie] *n* smell

обрабо́твам [obrabotvam] *v* cultivate, process

обрабо́тка [obrabotka] *f* treatment, processing

о́браз [obras] *m* shape, form, appearance, image

образо́ван [obrazovan] *adj* educated, well-read

образова́ние [obrazovanie] *n* education

образова́телен [obrazovatelen] *adj* educational

образу́вам [obrazouvam] *v* form, make

обра́т [obrat] *m* turn, change

обра́тно [obratno] *adv* back

обре́д [obred] *m* ritual, rite

о́брив [obrif] *m* rash

обръще́ние [obrushtenie] *n* address, appeal, circulation

обса́да [obsada] *f* siege

о́бсег [obseg] *m* sphere, range

обсервато́рия [observatoriya] *f* observatory

обстано́вка [obstanofka] *f* condition, situation

обстоя́телство [obstoyatelstvo] *n* circumstance

обсъ́ждам [obsuzhdam] *v* discuss, consider

обува́лка [obouvalka] *f* shoehorn

обу́вам се [obouvam se] *v* put on shoes

обу́вка [oboufka] *f* shoe

обуча́вам [obouchavam] *v* teach, instruct, train

общ [obsht] *adj* common, general

обще́ствен [obshtestven] *adj* social, public

обще́ственост [obshtestvenost] *f* public, society

общество́ [obshtestvo] *n* society

общи́на [obshtina] *f* community

о́бщност [obshtnost] *f* community, commonwealth

о́бщо [obshto] *adv* generally, altogether

общоприе́т [obshtopriet] *adj* generally accepted

общопризна́т [obshtopriznat] *adj* universally acknowledged

объ́рквам [oburkvam] *v* mix, confuse

обя́ва [obyava] *f* announcement, notice

обявя́вам [obyavyavam] *v* announce, declare, proclaim

обя́двам [obyadvam] *v* have lunch, dine

обясне́ние [obyasnenie] *n* explanation

обясня́вам [obyasnyavam] *v* explain

ова́ции [ovatsii] *noun pl* ovation, cheers, applause

ове́н [oven] *m* ram

ове́с [oves] *m* oats

о́внешко [ovneshko] *n* mutton

овца́ [ovtsa] *f* sheep

овча́р [ovchar] *m* shepherd

огладня́вам [ogladnyavam] *v* grow hungry

огледа́ло [ogledalo] *n* mirror, looking-glass

огнестре́лно оръ́жие [ognestrelno oruzhie] *n* firearm

огни́ще [ognishte] *n* hearth, fireplace

огра́бвам [ograbvam] *v* rob, plunder

огра́да [ograda] *f* fence, enclosure

огра́ждам [ograzhdam] *v* fence in, enclose

ограни́чавам [ogranichavam] *v* limit, confine

огро́мен [ogromen] *adj* huge, enormous, immense

о́гън [ogun] *f* fire

огъ́рлица [ogurlitsa] *f* necklace

одеколо́н [odekolon] *m* eau-de-cologne

одеа́ло [odealo] *n* blanket

одобре́ние [odobrenie] *n* approval, sanction

одобря́вам [odobryavam] *v* approve of, ratify

ожадня́вам [ozhadnyavam] *v* become thirsty

озаглавя́вам [ozaglavyavam] *v* entitle

оздравя́вам [ozdravyavam] *v* recover, become well

океа́н [okean] *m* ocean

о́кис [okis] *m* oxide

окисля́вам [okislyavam] *v* oxidize

око́ [oko] *n* eye

око́лност [okolnost] *f* vicinity, surroundings

о́коло [okolo] *adv* around, about

окончáние [okonchanie] *n* ending

окончáтелен [okonchatelen] *adj* final, conclusive

о́кръг [okrug] *m* district, county, region

окръ́жност [okruzhnost] *f* circle

октóмври [oktomvri] *m* October

окупáция [okoupatsiya] *f* occupation

окупи́рам [okoupiram] *v* occupy

олимпиáда [olimpiada] *f* Olympiad

о́лио [olio] *n* oil

оло́во [olovo] *n* lead

олтáр [oltar] *m* altar

омагьо́свам [omagyosvam] *v* cast a spell on, bewitch

омéквам [omekvam] *v* grow softer, get warmer

омлéт [omlet] *m* omelette

омрáза [omraza] *f* hate, hatred

омрáзен [omrazen] *adj* hateful, odious

омъ́жвам [omuzhvam] *v* marry

опáзвам [opazvam] *v* preserve

опа́зване [opazvane] *n* preservation
опако́вам [opakovam] *v* pack up, wrap up
опако́вка [opakofka] *f* packing
опа́сен [opasen] *adj* dangerous, perilous
опасе́ние [opasenie] *n* fear, apprehension
опа́сност [opasnost] *f* danger, peril
опа́шка [opashka] *f* tail, queue
о́пера [opera] *f* opera
опера́тор [operator] *m* cameraman
опера́ция [operatsiya] *f* operation
опере́та [opereta] *f* musical
опери́рам [operiram] *v* operate
о́пис [opis] *m* list, inventory
описа́ние [opisanie] *n* description
опи́свам [opisvam] *v* describe, portray
о́пит [opit] *m* attempt, test
опи́твам [opitvam] *v* try, make an attempt
о́питен [opiten] *adj* experienced, skilled,
experimental
о́питност [opitnost] *f* experience, proficiency
опла́квам се [oplakvam se] *v* complain
опла́кване [oplakvane] *n* complaint
оповестя́вам [opovestyavam] *v* announce
опози́ция [opozitsiya] *f* opposition
опозна́вам [opoznavam] *v* get to know
опо́ра [opora] *f* support, bulwark
оправда́вам [opravdavam] *v* excuse, vindicate
оправда́ние [opravdanie] *n* justification,
vindication

опроверга́вам [oprovergavam] *v* refute, disprove

опроверже́ние [oproverzhenie] *n* refutation, denial

опроща́вам [oproshtavam] *v* pardon, remit

опъ́вам [opuvam] *v* stretch, pull, strain

ора́ [ora] *v* plough

ора́нжев [oranzhef] *adj* orange

о́рбита [orbita] *f* orbit

организа́ция [organizatsiya] *f* organization

организи́рам [organiziram] *v* organize

органи́зъм [organizum] *m* organism

органи́чен [organichen] *adj* organic

оре́л [orel] *m* eagle

о́рех [oreh] *m* walnut

оригина́лен [originalen] *adj* original

ори́з [oris] *m* rice

орке́стър [orkestur] *m* orchestra

оръ́дие [orudie] *n* instrument, tool

оръ́жие [oruzhie] *n* arms, weapons

ос [os] *f* axis

оса́ [osa] *f* wasp

осведомя́вам [osvedomyavam] *v* inform, notify, ask

освежа́вам [osvezhavam] *v* refresh

осве́н [osven] *prep* except for, but

осветле́ние [osvetlenie] *n* light

осветля́вам [osvetlyavam] *v* light up, illuminate

освободи́тел [osvoboditel] *m* liberator

освобожда́вам [osvobozhdavam] *v* liberate, free

освобожде́ние [osvobozhdenie] *n* liberation

осеза́ем [osezaem] *v* tangible

о́сем [osem] *num* eight

осемдесе́т [osemdeset] *num* eighty

осигуро́вка [osigourofka] *f* insurance, assurance

осиновя́вам [osinovyavam] *v* adopt

оскърбле́ние [oskurblenie] *n* insult

оскърбя́вам [oskurbyavam] *v* insult, offend, hurt

осно́ва [osnova] *f* foundation, base

основа́вам [osnovavam] *v* found

основа́ние [osnovanie] *n* grounds, reason

основа́тел [osnovatel] *m* founder

осно́вен [osnoven] *adj* basic, fundamental, thorough

осо́бен [osoben] *adj* special, peculiar, strange

осребря́вам [osrebryavam] *v* cash

оста́вам [ostavam] *v* remain

оста́вка [ostafka] *f* resignation

остаря́вам [ostaryavam] *v* grow old

остаря́л [ostaryal] *v* old

оста́тък [ostatuk] *m* remainder, rest

остри́е [ostrie] *n* edge, point

остри́лка [ostrilka] *f* pencil-sharpener

о́стров [ostrof] *m* island

о́стря [ostrya] *v* sharpen

о́стър [ostur] *adj* sharp, keen

осъждам [osuzhdam] *v* blame, sentence
осъществявам [osushtestvyavam] *v* realize, carry out
от [ot] *prep* out, of, from, off, than
отбор [otbor] *m* team
отбрана [otbrana] *f* defense
отбранителен [otbranitelen] *adj* defensive
отварям [otvaryam] *v* open, turn on
отверка [otverka] *f* screwdriver
отвесен [otvesen] *adj* vertical
отвор [otvor] *m* opening, hole
отворен [otvoren] *adj* open
отвратителен [otvratitelen] *adj* disgusting, repugnant
отвращение [otvrashtenie] *n* disgust, loathing
отвързвам [otvurzvam] *v* untie, undo
отговарям [otgovaryam] *v* answer, reply
отговор [otgovor] *m* answer, reply
отговорност [otgovornost] *f* responsibility
отгоре [otgore] *adv* upon, above
отдавна [otdavna] *adv* long ago
отдалечавам се [otdalechavam se] *v* move away
отдалечен [otdalechen] *adj* distant, remote
отдел [otdel] *m* department
отделен [otdelen] *adj* separate, individual
отделям [otdelyam] *v* separate, detach
отдясно [otdyasno] *adv* to the right
отегчавам [otegchavam] *v* bore
отегчение [otegchenie] *n* boredom

отзад [otzat] *adv* behind
отивам [otivam] *v* go
отказ [otkas] *m* refusal
отказвам [otkazvam] *v* refuse, decline
откак [otkak] *conj* since
отклонявам [otklonyavam] *v* divert, branch off
отключвам [otklyuchvam] *v* unlock
отколкото [otkolkoto] *pron* than
откривам [otkrivam] *v* open, discover, find out
откривател [otkrivatel] *m* discoverer, inventor
открит [otkrit] *adj* open
откритие [otkritie] *n* discovery, invention
откровен [otkroven] *adj* frank, sincere
откровеност [otkrovenost] *f* frankness, sincerity
откуп [otkoup] *m* ransom
отлагам [otlagam] *v* put off, postpone
отлитам [otlitam] *v* fly away
отличен [otlichen] *adj* excellent
отличие [otlichie] *n* distinction
отляво [otlyavo] *adv* to the left
отменям [otmenyam] *v* abolish, cancel, repeal
отмъщавам [otmushtavam] *v* revenge
отмъщение [otmushtenie] *n* revenge, vengeance
отначало [otnachalo] *adv* from the beginning
отново [otnovo] *adv* again

отноше́ние [otnoshenie] *n* relation, bearing
отопле́ние [otoplenie] *n* heating
отопля́вам [otoplyavam] *v* heat
отпо́р [otpor] *m* resistance
отпре́д [otpred] *adv* in front of
о́тпуск [otpousk] *m* holiday, leave
отпу́швам [otpoushvam] *v* open, unclog
отрица́телен [otritsatelen] *adj* negative, unfavorable
отри́чам [otricham] *v* deny
отро́ва [otrova] *f* poison
отро́вен [otroven] *adj* poisonous
отря́звам [otryazvam] *v* cut
отсла́бвам [otslabvam] *v* grow weak, lose weight
отстраня́вам [otstranyavam] *v* remove
отстъпле́ние [otstuplenie] *n* retreat
оттегля́м [otteglyam] *v* withdraw, retire
оттегля́не [otteglyane] *n* withdrawal, retirement
отте́нък [ottenuk] *m* shade, tint, hue
оттога́ва [ottogava] *conj* since
отту́к [ottouk] *adv* from here, this way
отча́ян [otchayan] *adj* desperate, downcast
отча́яние [otchayanie] *n* despair, despondency
отче́т [otchet] *m* account, report
офе́рта [oferta] *f* offer
офице́р [ofitser] *m* officer
охла́ждам [ohlazhdam] *v* cool, chill

о́хлюв [ohlyuf] *m* snail

охо́лен [oholen] *adj* rich, opulent

охра́на [ohrana] *f* guard, protection

оце́нка [otsenka] *f* valuation, estimation, mark

оценя́вам [otsenyavam] *v* evaluate, estimate, value

оце́т [otset] *m* vinegar

оча́квам [ochakvam] *v* expect, look forward to

оча́кване [ochakvane] *n* expectation

очаро́вам [ocharovam] *v* charm, enchant

очарова́телен [ocharovatelen] *adj* charming, fascinating

очеви́ден [ocheviden] *adj* obvious, evident, clear, conspicuous

очерта́вам [ochertavam] *v* outline, describe

очерта́ние [ochertanie] *n* outline, delineation

очила́ [ochila] *noun pl* eye-glasses, spectacles

о́ще [oshte] *adv* more, still, yet

П

пава́ж [pavazh] *n* pavement

па́дам [padam] *v* fall

па́дане [padane] *m* fall

паза́р [pazar] *m* market

пазару́вам [pazarouvam] *v* buy, go shopping

пазаря́ се [pazarya se] *v* bargain
па́зя [pazya] *v* guard, protect, keep
пак [pak] *adv* again
паке́т [paket] *m* package, parcel
пала́тка [palatka] *f* tent
палачи́нка [palachinka] *f* pancake
па́лец [palets] *m* thumb
па́лма [palma] *f* palm
палто́ [palto] *n* coat, overcoat
па́луба [palouba] *f* deck
па́ля [palya] *v* light
паля́чо [palyacho] *m* clown, fool
па́мет [pamet] *f* memory
па́метник [pametnik] *m* monument, memorial
паму́к [pamouk] *m* cotton
пана́ир [panair] *m* fair
па́нделка [pandelka] *f* ribbon
па́ника [panika] *f* panic
пани́ца [panitsa] *f* bowl
панора́ма [panorama] *f* panorama, view
пансио́н [pansion] *m* boarding-house
панталóни [pantaloni] *noun pl* trousers, pants
панто́фи [pantofi] *noun pl* slippers
па́па [papa] *m* pope
папага́л [papagal] *m* parrot
па́пка [papka] *f* portfolio
па́ра [para] *f* steam, vapor
пара́д [parad] *m* parade

парали́за [paraliza] *f* paralysis
парахо́д [parahod] *m* steamer
парашу́т [parashout] *m* parachute
пари́ [pari] *noun pl* money
парк [park] *m* park
парламе́нт [parlament] *m* parliament
па́ртер [parter] *m* ground floor
па́ртия [partiya] *f* party
парфю́м [parfyum] *m* perfume, scent
парца́л [partsal] *m* rag
парче́ [parche] *n* piece, fragment, slice
па́спорт [pasport] *m* passport
па́ста [pasta] *f* paste
пате́нт [patent] *m* patent
патрио́т [patriot] *m* patriot
патриоти́зъм [patriotizum] *m* patriotism
па́уза [paouza] *f* interval, pause
пацие́нт [patsient] *m* patient
па́як [payak] *m* spider
певе́ц [pevets] *m* singer
пе́ене [peene] *n* singing
пе́йка [peika] *f* bench
пека́ [peka] *v* bake, roast
пелена́ [pelena] *f* diaper
пенсионе́р [pensioner] *m* pensioner
пенсиони́рам се [pensioniram se] *v* retire
пе́пел [pepel] *m* ash
пе́пелник [pepelnik] *m* ash-tray
пеперу́да [peperouda] *f* butterfly
пера́ [pera] *v* wash

пера́лня [peralnya] *f* washing machine, laundry

перде́ [perde] *n* curtain

перио́д [period] *m* period

пе́рка [perka] *f* propeller, fin

пе́рла [perla] *f* pearl

перо́ [pero] *n* feather

перо́н [peron] *m* platform

перпендикуля́рен [perpendikoulyaren] *adj* perpendicular

перси́йски [persiiski] *adj* Persian

персона́л [personal] *m* personnel, staff

пе́сен [pesen] *f* song

песимисти́чен [pesimistichen] *adj* pessimistic

пестели́в [pestelif] *adj* thrifty, sparing

пестя́ [pestya] *v* save

пет [pet] *num* five

петдесе́т [petdeset] *num* fifty

пете́л [petel] *m* rooster

петна́десет [petnadeset] *num* fifteen

петно́ [petno] *n* spot, stain

пе́тък [petuk] *m* Friday

пехо́та [pehota] *f* infantry

печа́лба [pechalba] *f* gain, profit, prize

печа́там [pechatam] *v* print, publish

печата́р [pechatar] *m* printer

печа́тница [pechatnitsa] *f* printing house

печеля [pechelya] *v* earn, gain, win

пе́чка [pechka] *f* stove

пешехо́дец [peshehodets] *m* pedestrian

пещ [pesht] *f* oven, furnace
пещера́ [peshtera] *f* cave
пе́я [peya] *v* sing
пиа́но [piano] *n* piano
пие́са [piesa] *f* play
пижа́ма [pizhama] *f* pyjamas
пила́ [pila] *f* file
пи́ле [pile] *n* chicken
пило́т [pilot] *m* pilot
пи́пам [pipam] *v* touch
пипе́р [piper] *m* pepper
пирами́да [piramida] *f* pyramid
писа́лка [pisalka] *f* pen
писмо́ [pismo] *n* letter
пи́ста [pista] *f* racetrack
пистоле́т [pistolet] *m* pistol
пи́там [pitam] *v* ask, question, inquire
пи́ша [pisha] *v* write
пи́я [piya] *v* drink, sip
пия́н [piyan] *v* drunk
плаж [plazh] *m* beach
плака́т [plakat] *m* poster
пла́мък [plamuk] *m* flame, blaze
план [plan] *m* plan, scheme, design
плане́та [planeta] *f* planet
планина́ [planina] *f* mountain
плани́рам [planiram] *v* plan, lay out
пла́стмаса [plastmasa] *f* plastics
пла́стмасов [plastmasof] *adj* plastic
плат [plat] *m* cloth, material

платёж [platezh] *m* payment
плача [placha] *v* cry, weep
племе [pleme] *n* tribe
племенник [plemennik] *m* nephew
племенница [plemennitsa] *f* niece
пленник [plennik] *m* captive, prisoner
пленявам [plenyavam] *v* capture, take prisoner
плета [pleta] *v* knit
плетиво [pletivo] *n* knitwear
плешив [pleshif] *adj* bald
плик [plik] *m* envelope
плитка [plitka] *f* plait, tress, braid
плитък [plituk] *adj* shallow
плод [plod] *m* fruit
плодороден [plodoroden] *adj* fertile
плодородие [plodorodie] *n* fertility
плодотворен [plodotvoren] *adj* fruitful
пломба [plomba] *f* filling
плосък [plosuk] *adj* flat
плоча [plocha] *f* slab, record
площ [plosht] *f* area
площад [ploshtad] *m* square
плувам [plouvam] *v* swim, sail
плътен [pluten] *adj* thick, dense
плътност [plutnost] *f* thickness, density
плъх [pluh] *m* rat
плюя [plyuya] *v* spit
пневмония [pnevmoniya] *f* pneumonia
по [po] *prep* along, on, over, by

побе́да [pobeda] *f* victory
победи́тел [pobeditel] *m* victor, winner
побежда́вам [pobezhdavam] *v* defeat, win
поби́рам [pobiram] *v* hold, contain
повди́гам [povdigam] *v* lift, raise
поведе́ние [povedenie] *n* conduct, behavior
повери́телен [poveritelen] *adj* confidential
по́вече [poveche] *adv* more
по́вечето [povecheto] *adv* most
пови́квам [povikvam] *v* call, summon, send for
по́вод [povod] *m* occasion, cause, ground
повръ́щам [povrushtam] *v* vomit, be sick
повръ́хност [povurhnost] *f* surface
повръ́хностен [povurhnosten] *adj* superficial
по́глед [pogled] *m* look, gaze, stare
погле́ждам [poglezhdam] *v* look at, glance
поглъ́щам [poglushtam] *v* swallow, absorb
погово́рка [pogovorka] *f* proverb, saying
погре́бвам [pogrebvam] *v* bury
погребе́ние [pogrebenie] *n* funeral, burial
под [pod] *m* floor
под [pod] *prep* under, below
по́даник [podanik] *m* subject
по́данство [podanstvo] *n* citizenship, nationality
пода́рък [podaruk] *m* present, gift
подаря́вам [podaryavam] *v* make a present
пода́тел [podatel] *m* sender
подво́дница [podvodnitsa] *f* submarine

подвързвам [podvurzvam] *v* bind
подготвям [podgotvyam] *v* prepare, train
подготовка [podgotofka] *f* preparation
поддържам [poddurzham] *v* support, maintain
подземен [podzemen] *adj* underground
подигравка [podigrafka] *f* mockery
подиум [podioum] *m* platform
подкрепа [podkrepa] *f* support, backing
подкрепям [podkrepyam] *v* support, back
подметка [podmetka] *f* sole
поднасям [podnasyam] *v* serve, present, offer
поднос [podnos] *m* tray
подобрение [podobrenie] *n* improvement
подобрявам [podobryavam] *v* improve
подозирам [podoziram] *v* suspect
подозрение [podozrenie] *n* suspicion
подпис [podpis] *m* signature
подписвам [podpisvam] *v* sign
подправка [podprafka] *f* condiment, spice, seasoning
подробен [podroben] *adj* detailed
подробност [podrobnost] *f* detail
подслаждам [podslazhdam] *v* sweeten
подслон [podslon] *m* shelter
подувам се [podouvam se] *v* swell
подут [podout] *adj* swollen
подушвам [podoushvam] *v* scent, sniff
подход [podhod] *m* approach
подходящ [podhodyasht] *adj* suitable, appropriate

подхо́ждам [podhozhdam] *v* suit, fit

подценя́вам [podtsenyavam] *v* underestimate, underrate

подчерта́вам [podchertavam] *v* underline, emphasize, stress

по́дъл [podul] *adj* mean, base

поéзия [poeziya] *f* poetry

поéт [poet] *m* poet

пожа́р [pozhar] *m* fire

пожа́рен кран [pozharen kran] *m* fire hydrant

пожарника́р [pozharnikar] *m* fireman

пожела́вам [pozhelavam] *v* wish

пожела́ние [pozhelanie] *n* wish

по́за [poza] *f* pose, attitude

позволéние [pozvolenie] *n* permission, permit

позволя́вам [pozvolyavam] *v* allow, permit, let

по́здрав [pozdraf] *m* greeting, regards

поздравлéние [pozdravlenie] *n* greeting, congratulation

поздравя́вам [pozdravyavam] *v* greet, congratulate

пози́ция [pozitsiya] *f* position, stand

позна́вам [poznavam] *v* guess, know

позна́ние [poznanie] *n* knowledge, learning

позна́т [poznat] *m* acquaintance

позна́т [poznat] *adj* well-known, familiar

позо́р [pozor] *m* disgrace, shame

показа́лец [pokazalets] *m* forefinger
показа́ние [pokazanie] *n* evidence, testimony
показа́тел [pokazatel] *m* index, indicator
пока́звам [pokazvam] *v* show, point, exhibit
пока́на [pokana] *f* invitation
пока́нвам [pokanvam] *v* invite, ask
покло́н [poklon] *m* bow
поколе́ние [pokolenie] *n* generation
по́крив [pokrif] *m* roof
покри́вам [pokrivam] *v* cover
поку́пка [pokoupka] *f* purchase
пол [pol] *m* sex
пола́ [pola] *f* skirt
поле́ [pole] *n* field
поле́зен [polezen] *adj* useful, beneficial
по́лет [polet] *m* flight
по́лза [polza] *f* advantage, benefit, use
полиле́й [polilei] *m* chandelier
полити́к [politik] *m* politician
полити́ка [politika] *f* politics
полица́й [politsai] *m* policeman
поли́ция [politsiya] *f* police
по́лов [polof] *adj* sexual
полови́на [polovina] *f* half
положе́ние [polozhenie] *n* position, situation
по́лски [polski] *adj* Polish
полукълбо́ [poloukulbo] *n* hemisphere
полуме́сец [poloumesets] *m* crescent
полуно́щ [polounosht] *m* midnight
полуо́стров [polouostrov] *m* peninsula

получа́вам [polouchavam] *v* get, receive, obtain

получа́тел [polouchatel] *m* recipient, addressee

поля́к [polyak] *m* Pole

пома́гам [pomagam] *v* help, assist, aid

помире́ние [pomirenie] *n* reconciliation

по́мощ [pomosht] *f* help, assistance, aid

помо́щник [pomoshtnik] *m* assistant, helper, deputy

по́мпа [pompa] *f* pump

поне́ [pone] *adv* at least

понеде́лник [ponedelnik] *m* Monday

поне́же [ponezhe] *conj* because, since

поня́кога [ponyakoga] *adv* sometimes, occasionally

поня́тие [ponyatie] *n* concept, notion

попра́вка [poprafka] *f* correction, repairs

попра́вям [popravyam] *v* correct, repair, mend

популя́рен [popoulyaren] *adj* popular

поро́да [poroda] *f* breed, race

портати́вен [portativen] *adj* portable

портока́л [portokal] *m* orange

портре́т [portret] *m* portrait, picture

портфе́йл [portfeil] *m* wallet, pocketbook

порцела́н [portselan] *m* china

поръ́чвам [poruchvam] *v* tell, ask, commission

посети́тел [posetitel] *m* visitor

посеща́вам [poseshtavam] *v* visit, call on, attend

посеще́ние [poseshtenie] *n* visit, attendance

посла́ние [poslanie] *n* message

посла́ник [poslanik] *m* ambassador

после́ден [posleden] *adj* last, final

после́дица [posleditsa] *f* consequence, result

посло́вица [poslovitsa] *f* proverb, saying

посо́ка [posoka] *f* direction

посо́лство [posolstvo] *n* embassy

посре́щам [posreshtam] *v* meet, welcome

пост [post] *m* post

поста́вям [postavyam] *v* put, place, set, stage

постепе́нен [postepenen] *adj* gradual

постепе́нно [postepenno] *adv* gradually

пости́гам [postigam] *v* achieve, attain

постиже́ние [postizhenie] *n* achievement, attainment

постоя́нен [postoyanen] *adj* constant, permanent, steady

постоя́нно [postoyanno] *adv* always, constantly

постро́явам [postroyavam] *v* build, construct

пот [pot] *f* sweat, perspiration

потвържда́вам [potvurzhdavam] *v* confirm

потвържде́ние [potvurzhdenie] *n* confirmation

пото́к [potok] *m* stream, brook

потъ́вам [potuvam] *v* sink, be lost in

потя́ се [potya se] *v* sweat, prespire

похвала [pohvala] *f* praise
по́чва [pochva] *f* soil, ground
по́чвам [pochvam] *v* begin, start
по́черк [pocherk] *m* handwriting
по́чест [pochest] *f* honor
по́четен [pocheten] *adj* honorary
почи́вам [pochivam] *v* rest, die
почи́вен ден [pochiven den] *m* day off
почти́ [pochti] *adv* almost, nearly,
practically
по́ща [poshta] *f* mail
появя́вам се [poyavyavam se] *v* appear,
come into view
пра́вен [praven] *adj* legal
пра́вилен [pravilen] *adj* regular, correct
пра́вило [pravilo] *n* rule
прави́телство [pravitelstvo] *n* government
пра́во [pravo] *n* right, law
правопи́с [pravopis] *m* spelling
правосла́вен [pravoslaven] *adj* orthodox
правоъ́гълен [pravougulen] *adj* rectangular
пра́вя [pravya] *v* do, make
праг [prag] *m* threshold, doorstep
пра́зник [praznik] *m* holiday
пра́ктика [praktika] *f* practice
практику́вам [praktikouvam] *v* practise
практи́чен [praktichen] *adj* practical
прасе́ [prase] *n* pig
пра́сковa [praskova] *f* peach
прах [prah] *m* dust, powder

прахосмука́чка [prahosmoukachka] *f*
vacuum cleaner

пра́шен [prashen] *adj* dusty

пребива́вам [prebivavam] *v* stay, sojourn

пребива́ване [prebivavane] *n* stay

преброя́ване [prebroyavane] *n* census

преве́ждам [prevezhdam] *v* translate,
interpret

превра́т [prevrat] *m* coup d'etat

пре́вод [prevod] *m* translation

прево́да́ч [prevodach] *m* translator,
interpreter

пре́воз [prevos] *m* transport, shipping

прево́звам [prevozvam] *v* transport, carry,
ship

прево́зно сре́дство [prevozno sredstvo] *n*
vehicle

превръ́зка [prevruska] *f* bandage, dressing

превръ́щам [prevrushtam] *v* turn, change

превъзхо́дство [prevus-hodstvo] *n*
superiority, excellence

превъзхо́ждам [prevus-hozhdam] *v* surpass,
exceed

превъ́рзвам [prevurzvam] *v* dress, bandage

пре́глед [pregled] *m* survey, inspection,
examination

прегле́ждам [preglezhdam] *v* examine

прегръ́дка [pregrudka] *f* embrace

прегръ́щам [pregrushtam] *v* embrace

пред [pred] *prep* before, in front of

предáвам [predavam] *v* hand in, deliver, teach

предáвам се [predavam se] *v* surrender

предавáтел [predavatel] *m* transmitter

прéданост [predanost] *f* devotion, attachment

предáтел [predatel] *m* traitor, betrayer

предáтелство [predatelstvo] *n* treachery, betrayal

предварúтелен [predvaritelen] *adj* preliminary, beforehand

прéдговор [predgovor] *m* preface, foreword

предгрáдие [predgradie] *n* suburb

прéден [preden] *adj* front

предú [predi] *adv* before

предúмство [predimstvo] *n* advantage, priority

предúшен [predishen] *adj* previous, former

предлáгам [predlagam] *v* offer, suggest, propose

предлóг [predlog] *m* pretext, preposition

предложéние [predlozhenie] *n* offer, proposal, suggestion

предмéт [predmet] *m* object, topic

предпáзвам [predpazvam] *v* protect, preserve

предпáзен [predpazen] *adj* preventive

предпазлúв [predpazlif] *adj* cautious, wary

предпазлúвост [predpazlivost] *f* caution, wariness

предпúсвам [predpisvam] *v* prescribe

предпола́гам [predpolagam] v suppose, guess
предположе́ние [predpolozhenie] n
supposition, conjecture
предпочи́там [predpochitam] v prefer
предпочита́ние [predpochitanie] n preference
предприя́тие [predpriyatie] n enterprise
предразсъ́дък [predrasuduk] m prejudice,
bias
председа́тел [predsedatel] m president,
chairman
предста́ва [predstava] f idea, notion
предста́вител [predstavitel] m
representative, agent
предста́вка [predstavka] f prefix
представле́ние [predstavlenie] n performance
предста́вям [predstavyam] v represent,
introduce
предубежде́ние [predoubezhdenie] n
prejudice, bias
предупрежда́вам [predouprezhdavam] v
warn, notify
предупрежде́ние [predouprezhdenie] n
warning, notice
предше́ственик [predshestvenik] m
predecessor, forerunner
пре́жда [prezhda] f yarn
през [prez] conj through, via
президе́нт [prezident] m president
прези́ме [prezime] n surname
прези́рам [preziram] v despise, scorn

презре́ние [prezrenie] *n* contempt, scorn

презри́телен [prezritelen] *adj*
contemptuous, scornful

прекале́н [prekalen] *adj* excessive, too great

прекра́сен [prekrasen] *adj* beautiful,
wonderful, splendid

прекъ́свам [prekusvam] *v* interrupt, break off

прекъ́сване [prekusvane] *n* interruption,
break

премие́ра [premiera] *f* first night
performance

пренебре́гвам [prenebregvam] *v* neglect,
disregard, ignore

пренощу́вам [prenoshtouvam] *v* spend the
night

преодоля́вам [preodolyavam] *v* overcome,
surmount

пре́пис [prepis] *m* copy

препи́свам [prepisvam] *v* copy

препода́вам [prepodavam] *v* teach

препода́ване [prepodavane] *n* teaching

преподава́тел [prepodavatel] *m* teacher

препоръ́ка [preporuka] *f* recommendation

препоръ́чвам [preporuchvam] *v* recommend

пре́сен [presen] *adj* fresh, new

пресе́чка [presechka] *f* crossing

пресле́дване [presledvane] *n* persecution,
pursuit

пресмя́там [presmyatam] *v* calculate

прести́лка [prestilka] *f* apron

престру́вам се [prestrouvam se] *v* pretend, make believe

престъ́пен [prestupen] *adj* criminal

престъ́пник [prestupnik] *m* criminal

престъпле́ние [prestuplenie] *n* crime

прете́нция [pretentsiya] *f* claim

преустановя́вам [preoustanovyavam] *v* stop, suspend

пре́ход [prehod] *m* transition

пре́ходен [prehoden] *adj* transitional

пре́чка [prechka] *f* obstacle, hindrance

при [pri] *prep* at, near, to

приби́рам [pribiram] *v* put away, gather

приближа́вам [priblizhavam] *v* bring near, approach

приблизи́телно [priblizitelno] *adv* approximately

привиле́гия [privilegiya] *f* privilege

привлека́телен [privlekatelen] *adj* attractive, appealing

привлека́телност [privlekatelnost] *f* attractiveness, charm

приго́твям [prigotvyam] *v* prepare, make ready

приготовле́ние [prigotovlenie] *n* preparation, arrangement

придружа́вам [pridrouzhavam] *v* accompany, escort

прие́м [priem] *m* reception

прие́млив [priemlif] *adj* acceptable, plausible

при́зив [prizif] *m* call, appeal

призна́вам [priznavam] *v* acknowledge, admit

призо́вка [prizofka] *f* summons

при́казка [prikaska] *f* tale, story

приключе́ние [priklyuchenie] *n* adventure

прила́гам [prilagam] *v* apply to, enclose

прилага́телно и́ме [prilagatelno ime] *n* adjective

приме́р [primer] *m* example

прими́рие [primirie] *n* armistice

примити́вен [primitiven] *adj* primitive

принадлежа́ [prinadlezha] *v* belong to

принадле́жност [prinadlezhnost] *f* belonging

при́нос [prinos] *m* contribution

принужда́вам [prinouzhdavam] *v* compel, force

принужде́ние [prinouzhdenie] *n* compulsion

принц [prints] *m* prince

принце́са [printsesa] *f* princess

при́нцип [printsip] *m* principle

припа́дам [pripadam] *v* faint

припо́мням [pripomnyam] *v* recall, bring to mind

приспособя́вам се [prisposobyavam se] *v* adapt, accommodate

приста́нище [pristanishte] *n* port, harbor

присти́гам [pristigam] *v* arrive

пристигане [pristigane] *n* arrival

пристъп [pristup] *m* fit, attack

присъда [prisuda] *f* sentence

присъединявам се [prisuedinyavam se] *v* join, attach

присъствие [prisustvie] *n* presence, attendance

притежание [pritezhanie] *n* possession

притежател [pritezhatel] *m* owner, possessor

притискам [pritiskam] *v* press

приход [prihod] *m* income, revenue

причина [prichina] *f* cause, reason

причинявам [prichinyavam] *v* cause, bring about

приятел [priyatel] *m* friend

приятелски [priyatelski] *adj* friendly

приятелство [priyatelstvo] *n* friendship

приятен [priyaten] *adj* pleasant, agreeable, nice

проба [proba] *f* trial, test, experiment

пробвам [probvam] *v* test

пробивам [probivam] *v* pierce, bore

проблем [problem] *m* problem

провалям [provalyam] *v* frustrate

проверка [proverka] *f* examination, check up

проверявам [proveryavam] *v* verify, check, examine

провинция [provintsiya] *f* province

проводник [provodnik] *m* conductor, wire

провокѝрам [provokiram] *v* provoke, instigate

прогно́за [prognoza] *f* weather forecast

програ́ма [programa] *f* program

прогре́с [progres] *m* progress

прода́вам [prodavam] *v* sell

продава́ч [prodavach] *m* salesman

прода́жба [prodazhba] *f* sale, retail

проду́кт [prodoukt] *m* product

проду́кция [prodouktsiya] *f* production, output

продължа́вам [produlzhavam] *v* continue, go on

продълже́ние [produlzhenie] *n* continuation, extension

прое́кт [proekt] *m* project, design

про́за [proza] *f* prose

прозо́рец [prozorets] *m* window

прозра́чен [prozrachen] *adj* transparent

прозя́вам се [prozyavam se] *v* yawn

произве́ждам [proizvezhdam] *v* produce, turn out

производѝтел [proizvoditel] *m* producer

производѝтелност [proizvoditelnost] *f* productivity

произво́дство [proizvodstvo] *n* production, output

произноше́ние [proiznoshenie] *n* pronunciation

про́изход [prois-hod] *m* origin, descent

произше́ствие [proizshestvie] *n* accident
прокуро́р [prokouror] *m* public prosecutor
про́лет [prolet] *f* spring
проме́нлив [promenliv] *adj* changeable, variable
проме́ням [promenyam] *v* change, alter
проми́шлен [promishlen] *adj* industrial
проми́шленост [promishlenost] *f* industry
промя́на [promyana] *f* change
прони́квам [pronikvam] *v* penetrate, permeate
про́паст [propast] *f* precipice
про́повед [propoved] *f* sermon
про́пуск [propousk] *m* pass
прост [prost] *adj* simple, ordinary
про́сто [prosto] *adv* simply, merely, just
простота́ [prostota] *f* simplicity, plainness
простра́нство [prostranstvo] *n* space, area
просту́да [prostouda] *f* cold, chill
про́ся [prosya] *v* beg
про́сяк [prosyak] *m* beggar
проте́ст [protest] *m* protest, remonstrance
протести́рам [protestiram] *v* protest
про́тив [protif] *prep* against
проти́вник [protivnik] *m* opponent, enemy
противореча́ [protivorecha] *v* contradict
противоре́чие [protivorechie] *n* contradiction
протоко́л [protokol] *m* protocol, report
профе́сия [profesiya] *f* profession, trade
профе́сор [profesor] *m* professor

процедура [protsedoura] *f* procedure
процент [protsent] *m* percentage
процес [protses] *m* process, course, trial
прошка [proshka] *f* forgiveness, pardon
прощавам [proshtavam] *v* forgive, pardon
пружина [prouzhina] *f* spring
пръст [prust] *f* earth, soil
пръст [prust] *m* finger, toe
пръстен [prusten] *m* ring
пръчка [pruchka] *f* stick
пряк [pryak] *m* nickname
психиатър [psihiatur] *m* psychiatrist
психология [psihologiya] *f* psychology
псувам [psouvam] *v* swear
птица [ptitsa] *f* bird
публика [poublika] *f* public, audience
публикувам [poublikouvam] *v* publish
пудра [poudra] *f* face powder
пуйка [pouika] *f* turkey
пуловер [poulover] *m* sweater
пулс [pouls] *m* pulse
пура [poura] *f* cigar
пустиня [poustinya] *f* desert
пуша [pousha] *v* smoke
пушач [poushach] *m* smoker
пушек [poushek] *m* smoke
пушка [poushka] *f* gun, rifle
пчела [pchela] *f* bee
пшеница [pshenitsa] *f* wheat
пълен [pulen] *adj* full, complete

пълномо́щно [pulnomoshtno] *n* power of attorney
пъ́лня [pulnya] *v* fill, stuff
пъ́пеш [pupesh] *m* melon
пъ́рви [purvi] *adj* first
пъ́ржа [purzha] *v* fry
пържо́ла [purzhola] *f* chop, cutlet
пъстъ́рва [pusturva] *f* trout
път [put] *m* road, path, track
пъ́тник [putnik] *m* traveller, passenger
пъ́тнически [putnicheski] *adj* passenger
пъту́вам [putouvam] *v* travel, voyage
пъту́ване [putouvane] *n* trip, journey, voyage
пя́на [pyana] *f* foam
пя́сък [pyasuk] *m* sand

Р

ра́бота [rabota] *f* work, job, labor
работи́лница [rabotilnitsa] *f* workshop
рабо́тник [rabotnik] *m* worker, workman
работода́тел [rabotodatel] *m* employer
рабо́тя [rabotya] *v* work
ра́вен [raven] *adj* even, level, equal
ра́венство [ravenstvo] *n* equality
равнина́ [ravnina] *f* plain
равни́ще [ravnishte] *n* level
равнове́сие [ravnovesie] *n* balance, equilibrium

ра́дио [radio] *n* radio

радиопреда́ване [radiopredavane] *n* broadcast

ра́дост [radost] *f* joy, gladness

ра́достен [radosten] *adj* joyful

ра́ждам [razhdam] *v* bear, give birth to, yield

разби́ра се [razbira se] *adv* of course

разби́рам [razbiram] *v* understand, realize, find out

разби́ране [razbirane] *n* understanding, comprehension, opinion

разва́лям [razvalyam] *v* spoil, damage, break

разве́ден [razveden] *adj* divorced

разве́ждам се [razvezhdam se] *v* divorce

разви́вам [razvivam] *v* develop

разви́тие [razvitie] *n* development, growth

развлече́ние [razvlechenie] *n* entertainment, amusement

разво́д [razvod] *m* divorce

развъ́рзвам [razvurzvam] *v* untie, undo

разгле́ждам [razglezhdam] *v* examine, look at, see

разгова́рям [razgovaryam] *v* talk, converse

ра́зговор [razgovor] *m* conversation, talk, chat

разгово́рен [razgovoren] *adj* colloquial

раздава́ч [razdavach] *m* postman

разде́лям [razdelyam] *v* divide, part

раздя́ла [razdyala] *f* parting

ра́зказ [raskas] *m* story, tale

разка́звам [raskasvam] *v* tell, relate

разкри́вам [raskrivam] *v* reveal, disclose

разли́вам [razlivam] *v* spill

ра́злика [razlika] *f* difference

различа́вам [razlichavam] *v* distingiush, discern

разли́чен [razlichen] *adj* different, various, diverse

разме́р [razmer] *m* size, degree, extent

размя́на [razmyana] *f* exchange, barter

разнообра́зен [raznoobrazen] *adj* varied

разнообра́зие [raznoobrazie] *n* variety, diversity

разно́ски [raznoski] *noun pl* expenses

разоблича́вам [razoblichavam] *v* expose, unmask, lay bare

разоръжа́вам [razoruzhavam] *v* disarm

разоръжа́ване [razoruzhavane] *n* disarmament

разоря́вам [razoryavam] *v* ruin

разочаро́вам [razocharovam] *v* disappoint

разочарова́ние [razocharovanie] *n* disappointment

ра́списка [raspiska] *f* receipt

ра́зпит [raspit] *m* interrogation

разпи́твам [raspitvam] *v* interrogate, question

разпределя́м [raspredelyam] *v* distribute

разпрода́жба [rasprodazhba] *f* sale

разреша́вам [razreshavam] *v* allow, permit

разреше́ние [razreshenie] *n* permission, solution

разреши́телно [razreshitelno] *n* licence,
permit

разруша́вам [razroushavam] *v* destroy,
demolish

разруше́ние [razroushenie] *n* destruction,
ruin

рассе́ян [raseyan] *adj* absent-minded

разстоя́ние [rastoyanie] *n* distance

рассъ́дък [rasuduk] *m* reason, sense

рассъжда́вам [rasuzhdavam] *v* reason

рассъ́мване [rasumvane] *n* dawn, daybreak

разтво́р [rastvor] *m* solution

разтопя́вам [rastopyavam] *v* melt

разтя́гам [rastyagam] *v* stretch

ра́зум [razoum] *m* sense, reason, mind

разу́мен [razoumen] *adj* sensible, reasonable

разхлади́телен [ras-hladitelen] *adj* cooling,
refreshing

ра́зход [ras-hod] *m* expense, cost

разхо́дка [ras-hodka] *f* walk

разхо́ждам се [ras-hozhdam se] *v* take a walk

рай [rai] *m* paradise

райе́ [raie] *n* stripe

райо́н [raion] *m* district

рак [rak] *m* crab, cancer

раке́та [raketa] *f* rocket

ра́мка [ramka] *f* frame

ра́мо [ramo] *n* shoulder

ра́на [rana] *f* wound

ра́но [rano] *adv* early

раня́вам [ranyavam] *v* wound
ра́са [rasa] *f* race
раси́зъм [rasizum] *m* racialism
расти́телност [rastitelnost] *f* vegetation
реакти́вен [reaktiven] *adj* jet
реализи́рам [realiziram] *v* make, realize
реалисти́чен [realistichen] *adj* realistic
ребро́ [rebro] *m* rib
реве́р [rever] *m* lapel
ревмати́зъм [revmatizum] *m* rheumatism
ревни́в [revnif] *adj* jealous
ре́вност [revnost] *f* jealousy
револю́ция [revolyutsiya] *f* revolution
регистри́рам [registriram] *v* register
ред [red] *m* order, line, row
реда́ктор [redaktor] *m* editor
реди́ца [reditsa] *f* row, series, number
редо́вен [redoven] *adj* regular
ре́жа [rezha] *v* cut
режиси́рам [rezhisiram] *v* direct, produce
режисьо́р [rezhisyor] *m* director, producer
резе́рвни ча́сти [rezervni chasti] *noun pl*
spare parts
резулта́т [rezoultat] *m* result, outcome, score
рейс [reis] *m* bus
река́ [reka] *f* river, stream
рекла́ма [reklama] *f* advertisement
реклама́ция [reklamatsiya] *f* claim
реко́лта [rekolta] *f* crop
реко́рд [rekord] *m* record

рели́гия [religiya] *f* religion

ре́лса [relsa] *f* rail

ремо́нт [remont] *m* repairs

ремонти́рам [remontiram] *v* repair

рентге́нов [rentgenof] *adj* X-ray

репети́ция [repetitsiya] *f* rehearsal

репорта́ж [reportazh] *m* report

репортьо́р [reportyor] *m* reporter

репу́блика [repoublika] *f* republic

рестора́нт [restorant] *m* restaurant

реце́пта [retsepta] *f* recipe, prescription

реч [rech] *f* speech, address

ре́чник [rechnik] *m* dictionary, vocabulary

ре́ша [resha] *v* comb

реша́вам [reshavam] *v* decide

реше́ние [reshenie] *n* decision, determination

ри́ба [riba] *f* fish

риба́р [ribar] *m* fisherman

риболо́в [ribolof] *m* fishing

ри́за [riza] *f* shirt

риску́вам [riskouvam] *v* risk

рису́вам [risouvam] *v* draw, paint

рису́нка [risounka] *f* drawing

ри́там [ritam] *v* kick

роб [rob] *m* slave

рог [rog] *m* horn

ро́ден [roden] *adj* native, home

роде́н [roden] *adj* born

роди́тел [roditel] *m* parent

родни́на [rodnina] *m* relation, relative

рожде́н ден [rozhden den] *m* birthday
ро́за [roza] *f* rose
ро́зов [rozof] *adj* pink, rosy
ро́кля [roklya] *f* dress, gown, frock
ро́ля [rolya] *f* part, role
рома́н [roman] *m* novel
роса́ [rosa] *f* dew
ру́да [rouda] *f* ore
рус [rous] *adj* blond
ру́син [rousin] *m* Russian
ру́ски [rouski] *adj* Russian
ръж [ruzh] *f* rye
ръка́ [ruka] *f* arm, hand
ръка́в [rukaf] *m* sleeve
ръкави́ца [rukavitsa] *f* glove
ръкопи́с [rukopis] *m* manuscript
ръку́вам се [rukouvam se] *v* shake hands with
ръст [rust] *m* stature, height, size
ря́дък [ryaduk] *adj* thin, rare

С

с [s] *prep* with, and, by, in, of
са́бя [sabya] *f* sword, sabre
садя́ [sadya] *v* plant
сако́ [sako] *n* coat, jacket
сакси́я [saksiya] *f* flower-pot
сала́м [salam] *f* sausage, salami

сала́та [salata] *f* salad

сам [sam] *adj* alone

са́мо [samo] *adv* only, solely, merely

самобръсна́чка [samobrusnachka] *f* safety-razor

самоле́т [samolet] *m* airplane

самолетоноса́ч [samoletonosach] *m* aircraftcarrier

самоли́чност [samolichnost] *f* identity

самооблада́ние [samoobladanie] *n* self-control

самоотбра́на [samootbrana] *f* self-defense

самота́ [samota] *f* loneliness, solitude

само́тен [samoten] *adj* lonely, lonesome, solitary

самоуби́йство [samooubiistvo] *n* suicide

самоуве́рен [samoouveren] *adj* self-confident

самоуве́реност [samoouverenost] *f* self-confidence

самоуправле́ние [samooupravlenie] *n* self-government

санда́л [sandal] *m* sandal

са́ндвич [sandvich] *m* sandwich

сантимента́лен [santimentalen] *adj* sentimental

сапу́н [sapoun] *m* soap

сблъ́сквам се [sbluskvam se] *v* collide, clash

сблъ́скване [sbluskvane] *n* collision, conflict

сбо́гом [sbogom] *greet* good-bye, farewell

сбор [sbor] *m* sum

сборник [sbornik] *m* collection

свалям [svalyam] *v* take down, remove, take off

сватба [svatba] *f* wedding

сватбен [svatben] *adj* wedding, nuptial

свеж [svezh] *adj* fresh

свежест [svezhest] *f* freshness

свекър [svekur] *m* father-in-law

свекърва [svekurva] *f* mother-in-law

свет [svet] *adj* holy, sacred

светец [svetets] *m* saint

светкавица [svetkavitsa] *f* lightning

светлина [svetlina] *f* light

светло [svetlo] *adv* light, brightly

светя [svetya] *v* shine, beam

свещ [svesht] *f* candle

свещен [sveshten] *adj* holy, sacred

свещеник [sveshtenik] *m* priest, clergyman

свидетел [svidetel] *m* witness

свидетелство [svidetelstvo] *n* certificate

свинско месо [svinsko meso] *n* pork

свиня [svinya] *f* pig, swine

свирка [svirka] *f* whistle, pipe

свиря [svirya] *v* play, whistle

свобода [svoboda] *f* freedom, liberty

свободен [svoboden] *adj* free, vacant, unoccupied

свод [svod] *m* arch, vault

свой [svoi] *pron* one's own

свойство [svoistvo] *n* property, quality

свързвам [svurzvam] *v* connect, link, put in touch

свят [svyat] *m* world

сглобявам [sglobyavam] *v* assemble

сграда [sgrada] *f* building, house

сделка [sdelka] *f* transaction, bargain, deal

сдружение [sdrouzhenie] *n* corporation, society

се [se] *pron* oneself

север [sever] *m* north

северен [severen] *adj* northern

северозапад [severozapad] *m* northwest

северойзток [severoistok] *m* northeast

сега [sega] *adv* now, at present

сегашен [segashen] *adj* present, current

седалка [sedalka] *f* seat, bench

седем [sedem] *num* seven

седемдесет [sedemdeset] *num* seventy

седемнадесет [sedemnadeset] *num* seventeen

седло [sedlo] *n* saddle

седмица [sedmitsa] *f* week

седмичен [sedmichen] *adj* weekly

седя [sedya] *v* sit, be seated

сезон [sezon] *m* season

сека [seka] *v* cut, chop, fell

секретар [sekretar] *m* secretary

секретен [sekreten] *adj* secret, confidential

сексуален [seksoualen] *adj* sexual, sex

секунда [sekounda] *f* second

селище [selishte] *n* settlement

село [selo] *n* village

селскостопански [selskostopanski] *adj* agricultural

селянин [selyanin] *m* peasant, countryman

семе [seme] *n* seed gram

семейство [semeistvo] *n* family

семинар [seminar] *m* seminar

сензация [senzatsiya] *f* sensation

сено [seno] *n* hay

септември [septemvri] *m* September

сервиз [servis] *m* set, service

сервирам [serviram] *v* serve, help

сервитьор [servityor] *m* waiter

сериозен [seriozen] *adj* serious, earnest, grave

серия [seriya] *f* series, set

сестра [sestra] *f* sister

сечиво [sechivo] *n* tool, instrument

сив [siv] *adj* gray

сигнал [signal] *m* signal

сигурност [sigournost] *f* certainty, security, safety

сила [sila] *f* strength, force, power

силен [silen] *adj* strong, powerful

символ [simvol] *m* symbol

симетрия [simetriya] *f* symmetry

симфония [simfoniya] *f* symphony

син [sin] *m* son

син [sin] *adj* blue

сипвам [sipvam] *v* pour

си́рене [sirene] *n* cheese
систе́ма [sistema] *f* system
скала́ [skala] *f* rock, cliff
сканда́л [skandal] *m* scandal
ска́ра [skara] *f* grill
скеле́т [skelet] *m* skeleton
скепти́чен [skeptichen] *adj* sceptical
ски [ski] *noun pl* ski
скио́р [skior] *m* skier
склад [sklad] *m* storehouse, warehouse
склон [sklon] *m* slope
склоне́ние [sklonenie] *n* declension
скло́нност [sklonnost] *f* inclination,
propensity
склю́чвам [sklyuchvam] *v* conclude, contract
ско́ба [skoba] *f* clip, bracket
скок [skok] *m* jump, leap, spring
ско́ро [skoro] *adv* soon, presently, recently
ско́рост [skorost] *f* speed, rate, pace
скрива́лище [skrivalishte] *n* hiding place
скри́вам [skrivam] *v* hide, conceal
скрит [skrit] *adj* hidden, secret
скро́мен [skromen] *adj* modest, humble
скро́мност [skromnost] *f* modesty,
humbleness
скръб [skrub] *f* sorrow, grief
ску́ка [skouka] *f* boredom, tedium
ску́лптор [skoulptor] *m* sculptor
ску́лптура [skoulptoura] *f* sculpture
скъп [skup] *adj* dear, expensive

скъпе́рник [skupernik] *m* miner, skinflint

скъпо [skupo] *adv* costly, dearly

скъпоце́нност [skupotsennost] *f* jewel, gem

скърбя́ [skurbya] *v* grieve, mourn

скъсвам [skusvam] *v* tear, wear out, break

слаб [slab] *adj* weak, slender, lean

сла́ва [slava] *f* glory, fame

славя́нин [slavyanin] *m* Slav

славя́нски [slavyanski] *adj* Slavonic

сладка́рница [sladkarnitsa] *f* pastry shop

сла́дки [sladki] *noun pl* pastry

сладоле́д [sladoled] *m* ice-cream

сла́дък [sladuk] *adj* sweet

сла́ма [slama] *f* straw

следа́ [sleda] *f* track, trace, trail

сле́двам [sledvam] *v* follow, study, come after

сле́дващ [sledvasht] *adj* next, following

следо́бед [sledobed] *m* afternoon

сле́дствие [sledstvie] *n* investigation, inquiry

сли́ва [sliva] *f* plum, prune

сли́вица [slivitsa] *f* tonsil

сло́во [slovo] *n* word, speech, address

словоре́д [slovored] *m* word order

сло́жен [slozhen] *adj* complex, complicated

сло́жност [slozhnost] *f* complexity

слой [sloi] *m* layer, stratum

слон [slon] *m* elephant

сло́нова кост [slonova kost] *f* ivory

слуга́ [slouga] *m* servant

слу́жба [slouzhba] *f* work, employment
служе́бен [slouzheben] *adj* official, business
слух [slouh] *m* hearing, ear, rumor
слу́чай [slouchai] *m* case, occasion, opportunity
случа́йно [slouchaino] *adv* accidentally
случа́йност [slouchainost] *f* chance, accident
слуша́лка [sloushalka] *f* receiver, stethoscope
слуша́тел [sloushatel] *m* listener
слъ́нчев [slunchev] *adj* sunny
сляп [slyap] *adj* blind
смел [smel] *adj* courageous, daring
сме́лост [smelost] *f* courage, boldness
смес [smes] *f* mixture, blend
сме́свам [smesvam] *v* mix, blend
смета́на [smetana] *f* cream
сме́тка [smetka] *f* account, profit
сме́шен [smeshen] *adj* funny, ridiculous, absurd
сме́я се [smeya se] *v* laugh
смисъл [smisul] *m* sense, meaning
смоки́ня [smokinya] *f* fig
сму́ча [smoucha] *v* suck
смърт [smurt] *f* death, decease
смъ́ртен [smurten] *adj* mortal, deadly
смъ́ртност [smurtnost] *f* mortality, death rate
смъртоно́сен [smurtonosen] *adj* deadly
смя́на [smyana] *f* change, shift
смях [smyah] *m* laugh, laughter
снабдя́вам [snabdyavam] *v* provide, supply

снабдя́ване [snabdyavane] *n* supply, provisioning

снаря́д [snaryad] *m* shell, projectile

сна́сям [snasyam] *v* lay

снаха́ [snaha] *f* daughter-in-law, sister-in-law

сни́мка [snimka] *f* photograph, picture

сняг [snyag] *m* snow

со́бственик [sobstvenik] *m* owner, proprietor

со́бственост [sobstvenost] *f* property, possession

сода́ [soda] *f* soda

сок [sok] *m* juice

сол [sol] *f* salt

соле́н [solen] *adj* salty, saline

соля́ [solya] *v* salt

сос [sos] *m* sauce, gravy

социа́лен [sotsialen] *adj* social

социали́зъм [sotsializum] *m* socialism

спа́лня [spalnya] *f* bedroom

спана́к [spanak] *m* spinach

спасе́ние [spasenie] *n* rescue, salvation

спаси́тел [spasitel] *m* savior, rescuer

спестя́вам [spestyavam] *v* save, economize

спестя́вания [spestyavaniya] *noun pl* savings

специа́лен [spetsialen] *adj* special, particular

специали́ст [spetsialist] *m* specialist, expert

специалите́т [spetsialitet] *m* specialty

специа́лно [spetsialno] *adv* especially, in particular

специа́лност [spetsialnost] *f* specialty, subject

спе́шно [speshno] *adv* urgently, hastily

спе́шност [speshnost] *f* urgency

спира́чка [spirachka] *f* brake, curb

спи́рка [spirka] *f* stop, halt

спирт [spirt] *m* alcohol, spirit

списа́ние [spisanie] *n* magazine, journal

спи́сък [spisuk] *m* list

сплав [splaf] *f* alloy

спого́дба [spogodba] *f* agreement, accord

споко́ен [spokoen] *adj* calm, peaceful

споко́йствие [spokoistvie] *n* calmness, tranquility

спо́мен [spomen] *m* remembrance, recollection

спо́мням [spomnyam] *v* recall, call to mind

спор [spor] *m* dispute, argument

споразуме́ние [sporazoumenie] *n* agreement, understanding

спорт [sport] *m* sport

спорти́ст [sportist] *m* athlete

спо́ря [sporya] *v* dispute, argue

справедли́в [spravedlif] *adj* just, fair, equitable

справедли́вост [spravedlivost] *f* justice, equity

справо́чник [spravochnik] *m* handbook, manual

спреже́ние [sprezhenie] *n* conjugation

спринцо́вка [sprintsofka] *f* syringe
спу́скам [spouskam] *v* lower, drop, descend
спя [spya] *v* sleep, slumber
сравня́вам [sravnyavam] *v* compare, check
сраже́ние [srazhenie] *n* fight, battle, action
срам [sram] *m* shame, disgrace
срамежли́в [sramezhliuf] *adj* shy, bashful
сраму́вам се [sramouvam se] *v* be shy, be ashamed of
сребро́ [srebro] *n* silver
сред [sred] *prep* among, amidst
среда́ [sreda] *f* middle, environment
сре́дно [sredno] *adv* on the average
средновеко́вие [srednovekovie] *n* the Middle Ages
сре́дство [sredstvo] *n* means, device
сре́ща [sreshta] *f* meeting, appointment, date
сре́щам [sreshtam] *v* meet, see, encounter
срещу́ [sreshtou] *adv* against, opposite
сри́чка [srichka] *f* syllable
срок [srok] *m* term
сръ́чен [sruchen] *adj* dexterous, skilful
сръ́чност [sruchnost] *f* dexterity, skill
сря́да [sryada] *f* Wednesday
стаби́лен [stabilen] *adj* stable
стаби́лност [stabilnost] *f* stability
ста́ва [stava] *f* joint
ста́вам [stavam] *v* stand up, rise, happen, occur
ста́дий [stadii] *m* stage, phase

стадио́н [stadion] *m* stadium

ста́до [stado] *n* herd, flock

станда́ртен [standarten] *adj* standard

стар [star] *adj* old, ancient

ста́рец [starets] *m* old man

старе́я [stareya] *v* grow old

ста́рост [starost] *f* old age

ста́тия [statiya] *f* article

ста́туя [statouya] *f* statue

стафи́да [stafida] *f* raisin

ста́чка [stachka] *f* strike

ста́я [staya] *f* room

стена́ [stena] *f* wall

стеногра́фия [stenografiya] *f* shorthand

сти́гам [stigam] *v* reach, be sufficient, last out

стил [stil] *m* style

стипе́ндия [stipendiya] *f* scholarship

стих [stih] *m* verse, line

сто [sto] *num* one hundred

сто́йност [stoinost] *f* value, worth, cost

сто́ка [stoka] *f* commodity, wares

стол [stol] *m* chair

столе́тие [stoletie] *n* century

сто́лица [stolitsa] *f* capital, metropolis

столова́ [stolova] *f* diningroom

стома́на [stomana] *f* steel

стома́х [stomah] *m* stomach

стома́шен [stomashen] *adj* gastric

стопа́нски [stopanski] *adj* economic

стопа́нство [stopanstvo] *n* economy
стра́дам [stradam] *v* suffer
страда́ние [stradanie] *n* suffering
страна́ [strana] *f* side, aspect, country
стра́нен [stranen] *adj* strange, odd, queer
страни́ца [stranitsa] *f* page
страст [strast] *f* passion, ardor
страте́гия [strategiya] *f* strategy
страх [strah] *m* fear, dread, apprehension
страхли́в [strahlif] *adj* cowardly, timid
стра́шен [strashen] *adj* dreadful, terrible, awful
стрела́ [strela] *f* arrow, shaft
стрелка́ [strelka] *f* needle, hand
стре́лям [strelyam] *v* shoot, fire
строг [strog] *adj* strict, severe
стро́го [strogo] *adv* strictly, severely
строи́тел [stroitel] *m* builder
строи́телство [stroitelstvo] *n* building, construction
строя́ [stroya] *v* build, construct, put up
стру́ктура [strouktoura] *f* structure, texture
стру́на [strouna] *f* string, chord
струя́ [strouya] *f* stream, flush
стръ́мен [strumen] *adj* steep, precipitous
студ [stoud] *m* cold, chill
студе́н [stouden] *adj* cold, chilly
студе́нт [stoudent] *m* undergraduate, student
студио [stoudio] *n* studio
стъкло́ [stuklo] *n* glass

стълб [stulb] *m* post, pole, column
стълба [stulba] *f* stairs, ladder
стълбище [stulbishte] *n* staircase
стъпало [stupalo] *n* step, stair, foot
стъпвам [stupvam] *v* tread, step
стъпка [stupka] *f* step, pace, footprint
сувенир [souvenir] *m* souvenir, keepsake
суверенитет [souverenitet] *m* sovereignty
суеверен [soueveren] *adj* superstitious
суеверие [soueverie] *n* superstition
суетност [souetnost] *f* vanity, foppery
сума [souma] *f* sum, amount
супа [soupa] *f* soup
суров [sourof] *adj* raw, severe
суровина [sourovina] *f* raw material
сутиен [soutien] *adj* brassiere, bra
сутрин [soutrin] *f* morning
сух [souh] *adj* dry, arid
суча [soucha] *v* suck
суша [sousha] *f* dry land, mainland
суша [sousha] *f* drought
сушен [soushen] *adj* dry, dried
схема [s-hema] *f* diagram
сходен [s-hoden] *adj* similar, analogous
сцена [stsena] *f* stage, scene
сценарий [stsenarii] *m* scenario, script
счетоводител [schetovoditel] *m* accountant
счетоводство [schetovodstvo] *n* book-keeping
счупвам [schoupvam] *v* break
събирам [subiram] *v* gather, collect, contain

събитие [subitie] *n* event

събличам [sublicham] *v* take off, undress, strip

съболезнование [soboleznovanie] *n* condolence

събота [subota] *f* Saturday

събрание [subranie] *n* meeting, assembly

събувам [subouvam] *v* take off

събуждам [subouzhdam] *v* wake, awake

съвест [suvest] *f* conscience

съвестен [suvesten] *adj* conscientious, scrupulous

съвет [suvet] *m* advice, counsel

съветвам [suvetvam] *v* advise, admonish

съветник [suvetnik] *m* adviser, counselor

съвместен [suvmesten] *adj* joint, combined

съвпадам [sufpadam] *v* coincide, concur

съвпадение [sufpadenie] *n* coincidence, concurrence

съвременен [suvremenen] *adj* contemporary, modern, current

съвсем [sufsem] *adv* quite, entirely, altogether

съвършен [suvurshen] *adj* perfect, thorough

съгласие [suglasie] *n* consent, agreement

съгласно [suglasno] *adv* according to

съгражданин [sugrazhdanin] *m* fellow-citizen

съд [sud] *m* vessel, container, utensil

съд [sud] *m* court

съдба [sudba] *f* fate, fortune, destiny

съдбоно́сен [sudbonosen] *adj* fatal, fateful

съде́бен [sudeben] *adj* legal, judicial

съдия́ [sudiya] *m* judge, referee

съдру́жник [sudrouzhnik] *m* partner

съдържа́м [sudurzham] *v* contain, hold, comprise

съдържа́ние [sudurzhanie] *n* content

съдя́ [sudya] *v* judge, try, sue

съединя́вам [suedinyavam] *v* join, unite, connect

съжале́ние [suzhalenie] *n* regret, pity

съжаля́вам [suzhalyavam] *v* be sorry, regret, pity

създа́вам [suzdavam] *v* create, make, form

създа́ние [suzdanie] *n* creature, creation

създа́тел [suzdatel] *m* creator, founder

съзна́вам [suznavam] *v* realize, be aware of

съзна́ние [suznanie] *n* consciousness, awareness

съзна́телен [suznatelen] *adj* conscious, conscientious

съкраще́ние [sukrashtenie] *n* abbreviation

съкро́вище [sukrovishte] *n* treasury

сълза́ [sulza] *f* tear

съм [sum] *v* be, exist

съмне́ние [sumnenie] *n* doubt

съмни́телен [sumnitelen] *adj* doubtful, questionable

съмня́вам се [sumnyavam se] *v* doubt

сън [sun] *m* sleep, dream

сънаро́дник [sunarodnik] *m* compatriot, fellow-countryman

съну́вам [sunouvam] *v* dream, have a dream

съобща́вам [suobshtavam] *v* announce, tell

съобще́ние [suobshtenie] *n* announcement

съотве́тен [suotveten] *adj* corresponding, respective

съотве́тствувам [suotvetstvouvam] *v* correspond, fit

съотноше́ние [suotnoshenie] *n* correlation, ratio

съпе́рник [supernik] *m* rival

съпе́рничество [supernichestvo] *n* rivalry, competition

съproти́ва [suprotiva] *f* resistance, opposition

съпротивле́ние [suprotivlenie] *n* resistance

съпру́г [suproug] *m* husband

съпру́га [suprouga] *f* wife

сърбе́ж [surbezh] *m* itch

сърбя́ [surbya] *v* itch

сърди́т [surdit] *adj* angry, cross

сърдя [surdya] *v* make angry

сърна́ [surna] *f* deer, doe

сърце́ [surtse] *n* heart

сърцевина́ [surtsevina] *f* core, heart

съсе́д [sused] *m* neighbor

съсе́ден [suseden] *adj* neighboring, next

съсе́дски [susedski] *adv* neighborly

съста́в [sustaf] *m* composition, cast

състеза́вам се [sustezavam se] *v* compete, contend

състеза́ние [sustezanie] *n* contest, events, competition

състеза́тел [sustezatell] *m* competitor

състоя́ се [sustoya se] *v* consist of, take place

състоя́ние [sustoyanie] *n* condition, state

състоя́ние [sustoyanie] *n* wealth, fortune

състрада́ние [sustradanie] *n* compassion, sympathy

състрада́телен [sustradatelen] *adj* compassionate

съучени́к [suouchenik] *m* schoolmate

съ́хна [suhna] *v* dry, wither, fade

съчине́ние [suchinenie] *n* composition, work

съчиня́вам [suchinyavam] *v* compose, invent, make up

съчу́вствие [suchoufstvie] *n* sympathy

съчу́вствувам [suchoufstvouvam] *v* sympathize

съществи́телно [sushtestvitelno] *n* noun

същество́ [sushtestvo] *n* being, creature, thing

съществу́ване [sushtestvouvane] *n* existence

съществу́вам [soushtestvouvam] *v* exist, be

съ́що [sushto] *adv* also, too, as well

съю́з [suyus] *m* union, alliance

ся́нка [syanka] *f* shadow, shade

ся́ра [syara] *f* sulphur

Т

табе́ла [tabela] *f* sign-board
табле́тка [tabletka] *f* tablet
та́блица [tablitsa] *f* table
табло́ [tablo] *n* board
тава́н [tavan] *m* ceiling, attic
та́ен [taen] *adj* secret, covert
та́зи [tazi] *pron* this, that
та́йна [taina] *f* secret, secrecy
та́кса [taksa] *f* fee
тала́нт [talant] *m* talent, gift
талантли́в [talantlif] *adj* talented, gifted
та́лия [taliya] *f* waist
там [tam] *adv* there
танк [tank] *m* tank
танте́ла [tantela] *f* lace
танц [tants] *m* dance
танцу́вам [tantsouvam] *v* dance
твой [tvoi] *pron* your
твърд [tvurd] *adj* hard, stiff, solid, firm
твърде́ние [tvurdenie] *n* assertion, allegation
твъ́рдост [tvurdost] *f* firmness, hardness
те [te] *pron* they
театра́лен [teatralen] *adj* theatrical, theater
теа́тър [teatur] *m* theater
теб [teb] *pron* to you
тебеши́р [tebeshir] *m* chalk
тегло́ [teglo] *n* weight

тéгля [teglya] *v* weigh

тежá [tezha] *v* weigh, carry weight

тéжък [tezhuk] *adj* heavy, weighty, hard, difficulty

тéзи [tezi] *pron* these, those

тек [tek] *adj* odd

текá [teka] *v* flow, run, leak

текст [tekst] *m* text, words

текстúл [tekstil] *m* textile

тел [tel] *m* wire

телé [tele] *n* calf

телевúзия [televiziya] *f* television

телевúзор [televizor] *m* television set

телегрáма [telegrama] *f* telegram

телефóн [telefon] *m* telephone

телефóнен указáтел [telefonen oukazatel] *m* telephone directory

телефóнна слушалка [telefonna sloushalka] *f* receiver

тéлешко [teleshko] *n* veal

тéма [tema] *f* subject, theme, topic

теменýжка [temenouzhka] *f* violet

температýра [temperatoura] *f* temperature, fever

тéнджера [tendzhera] *f* pot, saucepan

тéнис [tenis] *m* tennis

теорéма [teorema] *f* theorem

теóрия [teoriya] *f* theory

територúя [teritoriya] *f* territory, area

тéрмин [termin] *m* term

термоме́тър [termometur] *m* thermometer
те́рмос [termos] *m* vacuum flask, thermos
теро́р [teror] *m* terror, terrorism
те́сен [tesen] *adj* narrow, tight
тесто́ [testo] *n* dough, paste
тетра́дка [tetradka] *f* notebook
те́хен [tehen] *pron* their
техни́к [tehnik] *m* mechanic, technician
те́хника [tehnika] *f* technics, technique
техни́чески [tehnicheski] *adj* technical
те́чен [techen] *adj* liquid, fluid
те́чност [technost] *f* liquid, fluid
ти [ti] *pron* you, your
тига́н [tigan] *m* frying pan
ти́гър [tigur] *m* tiger
ти́ква [tikva] *f* pumpkin, squash
тип [tip] *m* type, pattern
тих [tih] *adj* quiet, still, calm
ти́чам [ticham] *v* run
тишина́ [tishina] *f* silence, stillness
тла́сък [tlasuk] *m* push, stimulus
то [to] *pron* it, that
тоале́тна [toaletna] *f* lavatory
това́ [tova] *pron* this, that
това́р [tovar] *m* load, burden, cargo
товари́телница [tovaritelnitsa] *f* bill of lading
това́ря [tovarya] *v* load, charge
тога́ва [togava] *adv* then, at that time
той [toi] *pron* he

ток [tok] *m* current, electricity

ток [tok] *m* heel

том [tom] *m* volume

тон [ton] *m* tone, shade

тон [ton] *m* ton

то́пка [topka] *f* ball

топло́та [toplota] *f* warmth, cordiality

топля́ [toplya] *v* warm, heat

топо́ла [topola] *f* poplar

то́пъл [topul] *adj* warm, mild, cordial

топя́ [topya] *v* melt, thaw

топя́ [topya] *v* dip, soak

тор [tor] *m* fertilizer

то́рта [torta] *f* cake

тост [tost] *m* toast

то́чен [tochen] *adj* exact, precise, punctual

то́чка [tochka] *f* point, period

то́чно [tochno] *adv* exactly, just, precisely

то́чност [tochnost] *f* precision, punctuality

траге́дия [tragediya] *f* tragedy

траги́чен [tragichen] *adj* tragic

тради́ция [traditsiya] *f* tradition

тра́ктор [traktor] *m* tractor

транзи́стор [tranzistor] *m* transistor

тра́нспо́рт [transport] *m* transport, transportation

тра́ур [traour] *m* mourning

тра́я [traya] *v* last, endure

трева́ [treva] *f* grass

трево́жа [trevozha] *v* worry, be anxious

трѐзвен [trezven] *adj* sober
тренирòвка [trenirofka] *f* training, practice
треньòр [trenyor] *m* trainer, coach
трепèря [treperya] *v* tremble, shake, shudder
трèти [treti] *adj* third
три [tri] *num* three
трѝдесет [trideset] *num* thirty
тримèсечие [trimesechie] *n* quartet
тринàдесет [trinadeset] *num* thirteen
триòн [trion] *m* saw
триỳмф [trioumf] *m* triumph
триъ̀гълник [triugulnik] *m* triangle
трѝя [triya] *v* rub, scrub
трòвя [trovya] *v* poison
тропѝчески [tropicheski] *adj* tropical
тротоàр [trotouar] *m* pavement, sidewalk
труд [troud] *m* labor, work
трỳден [trouden] *adj* difficult, hard
трỳдност [troudnost] *f* difficulty, hardship
трỳдя се [troudya se] *v* labor, work
тръбà [truba] *f* pipe, tube
тръ̀гвам [trugvam] *v* start, set out, leave, depart
тръ̀н [trun] *m* thorn
трѝбва [tryabva] *v* must, have to, should
тук [touk] *adv* here
тунèл [tounel] *m* tunnel
турѝзъм [tourizum] *m* tourism, hiking
турѝст [tourist] *m* tourist, hiker
турнè [tourne] *n* tour

турни́р [toutnir] *m* tournament
ту́хла [touhla] *f* brick
тъга́ [tuga] *f* sorrow, grief, sadness
тъгу́вам [tugouvam] *v* grieve, sorrow
тълку́вам [tulkouvam] *v* interpret
тълпа́ [tulpa] *f* crowd, throng
тъ́мен [tumen] *adj* dark
тъ́нък [tunuk] *adj* thin, slender, subtle
търг [turg] *m* auction, tender
търго́вец [turgovets] *m* merchant, dealer
търгови́я [turgoviya] *f* trade, commerce, business
търка́лям [turkalyam] *v* roll
тъ́ркам [turkam] *v* rub, polish
търпя́ [turpya] *v* bear, suffer, tolerate
тъ́рсене [tursene] *n* search, quest, demand
тъ́рся [tursya] *v* look for, search, seek
тъст [tust] *m* father-in-law
тъ́ща [tushta] *f* mother-in-law
тютю́н [tyutyun] *m* tobacco
тя [tya] *pron* she
тя́ло [tyalo] *n* body
тя́сно [tyasno] *adv* tight, closely
тях [tyah] *pron* them

У

у [ou] *prep* at, to, with, on, about
убежда́вам [oubezhdavam] *v* convince, persuade

убеждéние [oubezhdenie] *n* conviction, belief

убéжище [oubezhishte] *n* refuge, shelter, asylum

убѝвам [oubivam] *v* kill, murder, assassinate

убѝец [oubiets] *m* killer, murderer

убѝйство [oubiistvo] *n* murder, assassination

уважáвам [ouvazhavam] *v* respect, esteem, honor

уважéние [ouvazhenie] *n* respect, regard, esteem

уведомя́вам [ouvedomyavam] *v* inform, notify

увеличáвам [ouvelichavam] *v* increase, enlarge

увеличéние [ouvelichenie] *n* increase

увéрен [ouveren] *adj* sure, certain, assured

уверéние [ouverenie] *n* assurance, certificate

увéреност [ouverenost] *f* confidence, assurance, conviction

увѝ [ouvi] *interj* alas

увѝвам [ouvivam] *v* wrap, wind

у́вод [ouvod] *m* introduction, preface

у́воден [ouvoden] *adj* introductory

уволнéние [ouvolnenie] *n* dismissal, discharge

уволня́вам [ouvolnyavam] *v* dismiss, fire

у́дар [oudar] *m* hit, blow, stroke, shock

ударéние [oudarenie] *n* accent, stress, emphasis

удóбен [oudoben] *adj* comfortable, convenient, handy

удо́бство [oudobstvo] *n* comfort, facilities

удовлетворя́вам [oudovletvoryavam] *v* satisfy, grant

удово́лствие [oudovolstvie] *n* pleasure

у́дрям [oudryam] *v* hit, strike, beat

удуша́вам [oudoushavam] *v* strangle, suffocate

удължа́вам [oudulzhavam] *v* prolong, extend

у́жас [ouzhas] *m* terror, horror, dread

ужа́сен [ouzhasen] *adj* awful, terrible, dreadful

узря́вам [ouzryavam] *v* ripen, mature

указа́тел [oukazatel] *m* index, directory

укра́са [oukrasa] *f* decoration

украше́ние [oukrashenie] *n* decoration, ornament

ула́вям [oulavyam] *v* catch, take hold of, seize

у́лица [oulitsa] *f* street

у́мен [oumen] *adj* clever, intelligent, bright

уме́ние [oumenie] *n* ability, skill

уме́рен [oumeren] *adj* moderate, temperate

уми́рам [oumiram] *v* die, pass away, depart

уми́съл [oumisul] *f* intention, design

уми́шлен [oumishlen] *adj* deliberate, intentional

умноже́ние [oumnozhenie] *n* multiplication

умо́ра [oumora] *f* weariness, fatigue

уморе́н [oumoren] *adj* tired, weary, worn out

умря́л [oumryal] *adj* dead, deceased

у́мствен [oumstven] *adj* mental, intellectual

универса́лен [ouniversalen] *adj* universal

университе́т [ouniversitet] *m* university

униже́ние [ounizhenie] *n* humiliation

унифо́рма [ouniforma] *f* uniform

унищожа́вам [ounishtozhavam] *v* destroy, annihilate

упла́ха [ouplaha] *f* fright, scare

упла́швам [ouplashvam] *v* frighten, scare

употре́ба [oupotreba] *f* use, usage

употребя́вам [oupotrebyavam] *v* use, make use of

упра́ва [ouprava] *f* management

управле́ние [oupravlenie] *n* management, administration, government

управля́вам [oupravlyavam] *v* govern, rule, run

упражне́ние [ouprazhnenie] *n* exercise, drill, practice

упражня́вам [ouprazhnyavam] *v* exercise, practise

упъ́тване [ouputvane] *n* direction

урага́н [ouragan] *m* hurricane, tornado

уро́к [ourok] *m* lesson

уси́лие [ousilie] *n* effort, exertion

ускоре́ние [ouskorenie] *n* acceleration

усло́вен [ousloven] *adj* conditional

усло́вие [ouslovie] *n* condition, stipulation

усложне́ние [ouslozhnenie] *n* complication

усложня́вам [ouslozhnyavam] v complicate

услу́га [ouslouga] f service, favor

услу́жвам [ouslouzhvam] v do a favor, render a service

усми́вка [ousmifka] f smile

усми́хвам се [ousmihvam se] v smile

успе́х [ouspeh] m success, marks, grades

успе́шен [ouspeshen] adj successful

уста́ [ousta] f mouth

у́стен [ousten] adj oral, mouth

у́стна [oustna] f lip

усто́йчив [oustoichif] adj steady, firm, stable

усто́йчивост [oustoichivost] f stability, firmness

утоля́вам [outolyavam] v satisfy, quench

уточня́вам [outochnyavam] v specify

у́тре [outre] adv tomorrow

ухо́ [ouho] n ear

у́ча [oucha] v learn, study, teach

уча́ствувам [ouchastvouvam] v participate, take part in

уча́стие [ouchastie] n participation, share

уча́стник [ouchasnik] m participant

уче́бник [ouchebnik] m textbook

у́чен [ouchen] m scholar

учени́к [ouchenik] m student

учи́лище [ouchilishte] n school

учи́тел [ouchitel] m teacher, schoolmaster

учти́в [ouchtif] adj polite, civil

учти́вост [ouchtivost] *f* politeness, courtesy
учу́двам [ouchoudvam] *v* surprise, astonish
учу́дване [ouchoudvane] *n* surprise, astonishment
уязви́м [ouyazvim] *adj* vulnerable

Ф

фа́брика [fabrika] *f* factory, mill
фа́за [faza] *f* phase, period, stage
факт [fakt] *m* fact
фа́ктор [faktor] *m* factor, agent
факту́ра [faktoura] *f* invoice, bill
факу́лтет [fakoultet] *m* faculty, department
фали́рам [faliram] *v* bankrupt
фали́т [falit] *m* bankruptcy, crash, failure
фалши́в [falshif] *adj* false, coined, forged
фанати́зъм [fanatizum] *m* fanaticism, bigotry
фанта́зия [fantaziya] *f* imagination, fancy
фантасти́чен [fantastichen] *adj* fantastical, fabulous
фар [far] *m* lighthouse, beacon, headlights
фаса́да [fasada] *f* front, facade
фасу́л [fasoul] *m* beans
фата́лен [fatalen] *adj* fatal
фа́уна [faouna] *f* fauna
фаши́зъм [fashizum] *m* fascism
февруа́ри [fevrouari] *m* February
фене́р [fener] *m* lantern

фенерче [fenerche] *n* flashlight, electric torch

фиба [fiba] *f* hairpin

фигура [figoura] *f* figure

физик [fizik] *m* physicist

физика [fizika] *f* physics, physique

физически [fizicheski] *adj* physical, bodily

физкултура [fiskoultoura] *f* physical education

филателист [filatelist] *m* stamp-collector

филе [file] *n* loin, fillet

филия [filiya] *f* slice

филм [film] *m* film, motion picture

философ [filosof] *m* philosopher

философия [filosofiya] *f* philosophy

филтър [filtur] *m* filter, strainer

филхармония [filharmoniya] *f* philharmonic orchestra

фин [fin] *adj* fine, delicate

финансист [finansist] *m* financier

фирма [firma] *f* firm, sign-board

флора [flora] *f* flora

флота [flota] *f* fleet, navy

фоайе [foaie] *n* foyer, lobby

фокус [fokous] *m* trick, stut

фолклор [folklor] *m* folklore

фон [fon] *m* background

фонд [fond] *m* fund

форма [forma] *f* form, shape

формален [formalen] *adj* formal

форма́лност [formalnost] *f* formality
форма́т [format] *m* size, format
фо́рмула [formoula] *f* formula
формуля́р [formoulyar] *m* form, blank
фо́тоапара́т [fotoaparat] *m* camera
фотогра́ф [fotograf] *m* photographer
фотографи́рам [fotografiram] *v* take a picture of
фотогра́фия [fotografiya] *f* photography, photo
фотьо́йл [fotyoil] *m* armchair, easy chair
фра́за [fraza] *f* phrase
фре́нски [frenski] *adj* French
фризьо́р [frizyor] *m* hairdresser
фронт [front] *m* front
фуни́я [founiya] *f* funnel
функциони́рам [founktsioniram] *v* function
фу́нкция [founktsiya] *f* function
фурма́ [fourma] *f* date
фу́рна [fourna] *f* bakery, oven
футбо́л [foutbol] *m* football, soccer
фъстъ́к [fustuk] *m* peanut

X

хабя́ [habya] *v* waste, spoil
хавли́я [havliya] *f* bathrobe, towel
хаза́рт [hazart] *m* gambling
хайве́р [haiver] *m* roe, caviar

халка́ [halka] *f* ring

хамба́р [hambar] *m* barn, granary

хао́с [haos] *m* chaos, mess

ха́пя [hapya] *v* bite

хара́ктер [harakter] *m* character, temper, disposition

характе́рен [harakteren] *adj* characteristic, peculiar

харе́свам [haresvam] *v* like, enjoy

хармо́ния [harmoniya] *f* harmony

харти́я [hartiya] *f* paper

ха́рча [harcha] *v* spend

хва́ля [hvalya] *v* praise, commend

хе́рния [herniya] *f* hernia, rupture

хигие́на [higiena] *f* hygiene, sanitation

хиля́да [hilyada] *num* thousand

хими́к [himik] *m* chemist

химика́л [himikal] *m* chemical

химика́лка [himikalka] *f* ball-point pen

хими́ческо чи́стене [himichesko chistene] *n* dry cleaning

хи́мия [himiya] *f* chemistry

химн [himn] *m* hymn, anthem

хиру́рг [hirourg] *m* surgeon

хирурги́я [hirourgiya] *f* surgery

хи́тър [hitur] *adj* sly, cunning, subtle

хлади́лник [hladilnik] *m* refrigerator, ice-box

хла́дък [hladuk] *adj* lukewarm, tepid

хлеба́рница [hlebarnitsa] *f* bakery

хлъзгав [hluzgaf] *adj* slippery
хлъзгам се [hluzgam se] *v* slip, slide
хляб [hlyab] *m* bread
ходя [hodya] *v* walk, go
холера [holera] *m* cholera
хор [hor] *m* chorus, choir
хора [hora] *noun pl* people
хоризонт [horizont] *m* horizon
хотел [hotel] *m* hotel
храброст [hrabrost] *f* bravery, courage
храбър [hrabur] *adj* brave, courageous
храм [hram] *m* temple
храна [hrana] *f* food, meal, board
хранене [hranene] *n* nutrition
храня [hranya] *v* feed, nourish
храст [hrast] *m* bush, shrub
християнин [hristiyanin] *m* Christian
Христос [hristos] *m* Christ
хубав [houbaf] *adj* nice, handsome, good-looking
хубост [houbost] *f* good looks, beauty
художник [houdozhnik] *m* artist, painter
хуманен [houmanen] *adj* humane
хуманизъм [houmanizum] *m* humanism
хуманитарен [houmanitaren] *adj* humanitarian
хумор [houmor] *m* humor
хълм [hulm] *m* hill
хъркам [hurkam] *v* snore

Ц

цар [tsar] *m* king
царевица [tsarevitsa] *f* maize, corn
царица [tsaritsa] *f* queen
царство [tsarstvo] *n* kingdom
цвекло [tsveklo] *n* beet
цвете [tsvete] *n* flower
цвят [tsvyat] *m* color, blossom
цел [tsel] *f* aim, purpose, object, end
целзий [tselzii] *adj* centigrade
целина [tselina] *f* celery
целувам [tselouvam] *v* kiss
целувка [tseloufka] *f* kiss
целя [tselya] *v* aim at
цена [tsena] *f* price, cost
ценен [tsenen] *adj* valuable
ценност [tsenost] *f* value, worth
център [tsentur] *m* center
ценя [tsenya] *v* value, estimate, appreciate
цивилен [tsivilen] *adj* civil, civilian
цивилизация [tsivilizatsiya] *f* civilization
циганин [tsiganin] *m* gypsy
цигара [tsigara] *f* cigarette
цигулар [tsigoular] *m* violinist
цигулка [tsigoulka] *f* violin, fiddle
цимент [tsiment] *m* cement
цинизъм [tsinizum] *m* obscentity, cynicism
цинк [tsink] *m* zinc

цип [tsip] *m* zip-fastener
цирк [tsirk] *m* circus
цита́т [tsitat] *m* quotation
ци́фра [tsifra] *f* figure
цъ́рква [tsurkva] *f* church
цъфтя́ [tsuftya] *v* bloom, blossom
цял [tsyal] *adj* entire, whole, all, full
ця́лост [tsyalost] *f* integrity, wholeness
ця́лостен [tsyalosten] *adj* entire, complete, overall

Ч

чадъ́р [chadur] *m* umbrella, parasol
чай [chai] *m* tea
ча́йка [chaika] *f* seagull
ча́йник [chainik] *m* teapot, tea-kettle
чака́лня [chakalnya] *f* waitingroom
ча́кам [chakam] *v* wait, expect
ча́нта [chanta] *f* bag, briefcase
чар [char] *m* charm, fascination
чарша́ф [charshaf] *m* sheet
час [chas] *m* hour, lesson, period
часо́вник [chasovnik] *m* clock, watch
част [chast] *f* part, portion, share
ча́стен [chasten] *adj* private
чек [chek] *m* check
че́ло [chelo] *n* forehead
че́люст [chelyust] *f* jaw

че́рвей [chervei] *m* worm
черве́н [cherven] *adj* red
черви́ло [chervilo] *n* lipstick
черво́ [chervo] *n* intestine, gut
че́рен [cheren] *adj* black
че́реп [cherep] *m* skull
черноко́ж [chernokozh] *adj* black, colored
черта́ [cherta] *f* line
черта́я [chertaya] *v* draw, trace
черте́ж [chertezh] *m* draft, sketch
черу́пка [cheroupka] *f* shell
чест [chest] *f* honor, credit
чест [chest] *adj* frequent, common
честву́вам [chestvouvam] *v* celebrate, commemorate
че́стен [chesten] *adj* honest, fair
че́стност [chestnost] *f* honesty
че́сто [chesto] *adv* often
че́сън [chesun] *m* garlic
чета́ [cheta] *v* read
че́твърт [chetvurt] *f* quarter
четвърти́т [chetvurtit] *adj* square
четвъ́ртък [chetvurtuk] *m* Thursday
че́тен [cheten] *adj* even
чети́во [chetivo] *n* reading
че́тири [chetiri] *num* four
четири́десет [chetirideset] *num* forty
четирина́десет [chetirinadeset] *num* fourteen
четириъ́гълник [chetiriugulnik] *m* quadrangle

чётка [chetka] *f* brush
чешма́ [cheshma] *f* tap
чин [chin] *m* desk, rank
чини́я [chiniya] *f* plate, dish
число́ [chislo] *n* number, figure
чист [chist] *adj* clean, neat
чиста́ч [chistach] *m* cleaner
чи́стене [chistene] *n* cleaning
чистота́ [chistota] *f* cleanliness
чи́стя [chistya] *v* clean
чита́тел [chitatel] *m* reader
чифт [chift] *m* pair, couple
член [chlen] *m* member
чове́к [chovek] *m* person, man
чове́шки [choveshki] *adj* human, humane
чора́п [chorap] *m* sock
чу́вам [chouvam] *v* hear, understand
чувстви́телен [choufstvitelen] *adj* sensitive
чу́вство [choufstvo] *n* feeling, emotion
чу́вствам [choufstvam] *v* feel
чу́до [choudo] *n* miracle, wonder
чу́дя се [choudya se] *v* wonder
чужби́на [chouzhbina] *f* abroad
чужд [chouzhd] *adj* alien, foreign
чужденéц [chouzhdenets] *m* foreigner
чук [chouk] *m* hammer
чу́кам [choukam] *v* knock, tap
чу́пя [choupya] *v* break
чу́шка [choushka] *f* pepper

Ш

шал [shal] *f* shawl

шама́р [shamar] *m* slap in the face

шампа́нско [shampansko] *n* champagne

шампио́н [shampion] *m* champion, title-holder

шампиона́т [shampionat] *m* championship

шампо́ан [shampoan] *m* shampoo

шанс [shans] *m* chance

ша́пка [shapka] *f* hat

шара́н [sharan] *m* carp

ша́рка [sharka] *f* measles

ша́хмат [shahmat] *m* chess

шев [shef] *m* seam, sewing, needlework

шега́ [shega] *f* joke, jest

шегу́вам се [shegouvam se] *v* joke

шедьо́вър [shedyovur] *m* masterpiece

шейна́ [sheina] *f* sledge, toboggan

ше́па [shepa] *f* handful

шепна́ [shepna] *v* whisper

шест [shest] *num* six

ше́ствие [shestvie] *n* procession, train

шестдесе́т [shestdeset] *num* sixty

шестна́десет [shestnadeset] *num* sixteen

шеф [shef] *m* chief, boss

шива́ч [shivach] *m* tailor

шип [ship] *m* thorn, spike

ширина́ [shirina] *f* width, breadth

широ́к [shirok] *adj* wide, broad, loose

шѝя [shiya] *v* sew
шѝя [shiya] *f* neck
шкаф [shkaf] *m* cupboard, locker
шлѝфер [shlifer] *m* raincoat
шоколад [shokolad] *m* chocolate
шосе́ [shose] *n* highway
шофьо́р [shofyor] *m* driver
шпио́нин [shpionin] *m* spy
шрифт [shrift] *m* type, font
шум [shoum] *m* noise, sound
шу́мен [shoumen] *adj* noisy, loud
шу́нка [shounka] *f* ham

Щ

щаб [shtab] *m* headquarters, staff
щанд [shtand] *m* counter, stall
ща́стие [shtastie] *n* happiness, luck
щастлѝв [shtastlif] *adj* happy, lucky, fortunate
ще [shte] *v* will, shall
ще́дрост [shtedrost] *f* generosity, lavishness
ще́дър [shtedur] *adj* generous, lavish
щета́ [shteta] *f* damage
щѝпя [shtipya] *v* pinch
щит [shtit] *m* shield
щом [shtom] *adv* as soon as, if

Ъ

ъ́гъл [ugul] *m* angle

Ю

юбиле́й [yubilei] *m* anniversary
юг [yug] *m* south
ю́жен [yuzhen] *adj* southern
ю́ли [yuli] *m* July
юмру́к [yumrouk] *m* fist
ю́ни [yuni] *m* June
ю́ноша [yunosha] *m* teenager
ю́ношески [yunosheski] *adj* teenage, juvenile
юриди́чески [yuridicheski] *adj* legal,
juridical
юри́ст [yurist] *m* lawyer, jurist
юти́я [yutiya] *v* iron

Я

я́бълка [yabulka] *f* apple
явле́ние [yavlenie] *n* phenomenon
я́года [yagoda] *f* strawberry
яд [yad] *m* anger
я́дрен [yadren] *adj* nuclear
ядро́ [yadro] *n* nucleus
я́зва [yazva] *f* ulcer

я́здя [yazdya] *v* ride
яйце́ [yaitse] *n* egg
яка́ [yaka] *f* collar
я́ке [yake] *n* jacket
ям [yam] *v* eat, have a meal
януа́ри [yanouari] *m* January
я́рък [yaruk] *adj* bright, brilliant
я́сен [yasen] *adj* clear, plain
я́стие [yastie] *n* dish
я́то [yato] *n* flock, flight

ENGLISH-BULGARIAN
DICTIONARY

ABBREVIATIONS USED IN THIS DICTIONARY

adj	adjective
adv	adverb
conj	conjunction
f	feminine
interj	interjection
m	masculine
n	neuter (Bulgarian-English Section)
n	noun (English-Bulgarian Section)
num	numeral
part	particle
pl	plural
prep	preposition
pron	pronoun
v	verb

A

abbreviation [ъбривиейшън] *n* съкраще́ние

ability [ъби́лити] *n* спосо́бност

able [е́йбъл] *adj* спосо́бен

abolish [ъбо́лиш] *v* према́хвам, унищожа́вам

about [ъба́ут] *adv* нао́коло, почти́; *prep* о́коло, из, по, за, отно́сно

above [абъ́в] *prep* над, по́вече от; *adv* го́ре

absent [а́-бсънт] *adj* отсъ́ствуващ

absolute [а́-бсълют] *adj* пъ́лен, неограниче́н

absurd [а́-бсърд] *adj* глу́пав, сме́шен

academical [ака́демикал] *adj* академи́чен, у́чен

academy [ака́-деми] *n* акаде́мия

accelerate [ъксе́лерейт] *v* ускоря́вам се

accent [а́-ксент] *n* ударе́ние, и́зговор

accept [ъксе́пт] *v* прие́мам, съглася́вам се

acceptable [ъксе́птъбъл] *adj* приемли́в

access [а́-ксес] *n* до́стъп

accessories [ъксе́сърис] *noun pl* принадле́жности

accident [а́-ксидент] *n* случа́йност, злополу́ка

accommodation [ъко́модейшън] *n* кварти́ра

accompany [акъ́мпани] *v* придружа́вам, съпрово́ждам

according to [акóрдинг ту] *prep* спорéд

account [акáунт] *n* смéтка, обяснéние; *v* дáвам смéтка, отчéт

accountant [акáунтънт] *n* счетоводи́тел

accuracy [áкюръси] *n* тóчност

accurate [áкюрът] *adj* тóчен

accusation [áкюзейшън] *n* обвинéние

accuse [акю́з] *v* обвиня́вам

ache [ейк] *n* бóлка; *v* боли́

achieve [ъчи́йв] *v* пости́гам, извъ́ршвам

achievement [ъчи́йвмънт] *n* постижéние

acid [á-сид] *n* киселинá

acquaint [ъкуéйнт] *v* запознáвам, осведомя́вам

acquaintance [ъкуéйнтънс] *n* запознáнство, познáт

acquit [ъкуи́т] *v* оправдáвам, освобождáвам

across [акрóс] *adv* напря́ко, отсрéща; *prep* през, отвъ́д, срещý

action [á-кшън] *n* дéйност, постъ́пка, сражéние

active [á-ктив] *adj* дéен, акти́вен

activity [акти́вити] *n* дéйност, акти́вност

actor [á-ктър] *n* арти́ст, актьóр

actress [á-ктрес] *n* актри́са, арти́стка

actually [á-кчуъли] *adv* наи́стина, в същност

acute [ъкю́т] *adj* óстър, бъ́рз, проница́телен

ad [а-д] *n* обявлéние

adapt [ъда́пт] *v* приспособя́вам, пригодя́вам

add [ад] *v* приба́вям, събира́м

addition [ъди́шън] *n* приба́вяне, събира́не

address [а-дре́с] *v* обръ́щам се, адреси́рам

adjective [а́-джектив] *n* прилага́телно и́ме

adjust [аджъ́ст] *v* нагла́сям, приспособя́вам

adjustment [аджъ́стмент] *n* пригодя́ване

administration [адми́нистре́йшън] *n* управле́ние, предписа́ние

admirable [а́-дмиръ́бъл] *adj* възхити́телен

admiration [а́дмире́йшън] *n* възхище́ние

admire [адма́йър] *v* възхища́вам се

admission [адми́шън] *n* вход, достъп, призна́ние

admit [ъдми́т] *v* пу́скам да вле́зе, призна́вам, допу́скам

adopt [адо́пт] *v* осиновя́вам, възприе́мам

adoption [адо́пшън] *n* осиновя́ване, възприе́мане

adult [а́дълт] *n* възрастен

advance [ъдва́нс] *v* напре́двам; *n* напре́дък, предпла́та

advanced [ъдва́нст] *adj* напре́днал, напре́дничав

advantage [ъдва́нтъдж] *n* преди́мство, по́лза

adventure [ъдве́нчър] *n* приключе́ние

adverb [а́-двъ́рб] *n* наре́чие

advice [ъдва́йс] *n* съве́т, изве́стие

advise [ъдва́йз] *v* съве́твам, известя́вам

adviser [ъдва́йзър] *n* съве́тник

aerial [е́риъл] *n* анте́на

affair [ъфе́р] *n* ра́бота, де́ло, въпро́с

affection [ъфе́кшън] *n* о́бич, привъ́рзаност

affectionate [ъфе́кшънът] *adj* любя́щ, привъ́рзан

afford [афо́рд] *v* позволя́вам си

afraid [ъфре́йд] *adj* изпла́шен, боя́щ се

after [а́фтър] *prep* след, по, спо́ред, за; *adv* по́сле

afternoon [а́фтърну́н] *n* следобе́д

again [ъге́йн] *adv* отно́во, пак

against [ъге́йнст] *prep* срещу́, проти́в, о

age [ейдж] *n* въ́зраст, век, перио́д; *v* старе́я

agency [е́йджънси] *n* аге́нция

agenda [ъдже́ндъ] *n* дне́вен ред

agent [е́йджънт] *n* фа́ктор, предста́вител, посре́дник

aggression [агре́шън] *n* агре́сия, нападе́ние

aggressive [агре́сив] *adj* агреси́вен

ago [аго́у] *adv* преди́

agony [а́-гъни] *n* аго́ния, си́лна мъка

agree [ъгри́] *v* съглася́вам се

agreement [ъгри́мънт] *n* съгла́сие, спого́дба

agricultural [а́-грикъ̀лчуръл] *adj* земеде́лски

agriculture [а́-грикъ̀лчър] *n* земеде́лие

aid [ейд] *v* пома́гам; *n* по́мощ, подкре́па

aim [ейм] *v* стремя́ се, прице́лвам се; *n* намере́ние, цел

air [е́ър] *n* въздух; *v* проветря́вам; *adj* възду́шен

airplane [е́ърплейн] *n* самоле́т

airport [е́ърпорт] *n* летище, аерога́ра

alarm [ала́рм] *n* трево́га; *v* трево́жа, безпоко́я

alcohol [а́-лкохол] *n* алкохо́л, спирт

alive [ъла́йв] *adj* жив, бо́дър, гъмжа́щ

all [ол] *adj* цял, все́ки, вси́чки

allow [ала́у] *v* позволя́вам, допу́скам

allowance [ала́уънс] *n* издръжка, отстъпка

alloy [а́лой] *n* сплав

almost [о́лмоуст] *adv* почти́

alone [ъло́ун] *adj* сам, еди́нствен

along [ъло́нг] *adv* напре́д; *prep* по, край

alphabet [а́лфабет] *n* а́збука

already [олре́ди] *adv* ве́че, преди́ това́

also [о́лсоу] *adv* също

although [олдо́у] *conj* при все че, въпреки́ че

always [о́луейз] *adv* ви́наги

amaze [ъмейз] *v* сли́свам, удивля́вам

amazement [ъме́йзмънт] *n* удивле́ние, си́лно учу́дване

ambassador [ъмба́-садър] *n* посла́ник

ambition [амби́шън] *n* амби́ция, честолюбие

ambitious [амби́шъс] *adj* амбицио́зен

ambulance [а́мбюлънс] *n* лине́йка

amount [ъмáунт] *v* възли́зам, равня́вам се;
n коли́чество, су́ма

amuse [ъмю́з] *v* забавля́вам

amusement [ъмю́змънт] *n* забавле́ние

amusing [ъмю́зинг] *adj* заба́вен

analyse [а́налайз] *v* анализи́рам

analysis [ана́лисис] *n* ана́лиз, разбо́р

ancient [е́йншънт] *adj* дре́вен

and [енд] *conj* и, а

angel [е́йнджъл] *n* а́нгел

anger [а́-нгър] *n* гняв

angle [а́-нгъл] *n* ъ́гъл

angry [а́-нгри] *adj* гне́вен, сърди́т

animal [а́-нимъл] *n* живо́тно

anniversary [а́ниве́рсари] *n* годи́шнина

announce [ънáунс] *v* съобща́вам,
известя́вам

announcement [ънáунсмънт] *n* съобще́ние

annual [а́-нюъл] *adj* годи́шен, ежего́ден

another [ана́дър] *adj* друг

answer [а́нсър] *n* о́тговор; *v* отгова́рям

ant [а-нт] *n* мра́вка

anxiety [ънкзáйъти] *n* безпоко́йство,
загри́женост, страх

anxious [а́-нкшъс] *adj* разтрево́жен, горя́щ
от жела́ние

any [е́ни] *pron* все́ки, ня́какъв

anybody [е́нибъди] *pron* все́ки, ня́кой

anything [е́нитинг] *pron* не́що, вси́чко

apartment [апа́ртмънт] *n* апартаме́нт, кварти́ра

apologize [апо́лоджайз] *v* извиня́вам се

apology [апо́лоджи] *n* извине́ние, защи́та

appear [апи́ър] *v* появя́вам се, изгле́ждам

appearance [апи́ърънс] *n* появя́ване, и́зглед, въ́ншност

appetizer [а́петайзър] *n* мезе́, аперити́в

applaud [ъпло́д] *v* ръкопля́скам, аплоди́рам

applause [ъпло́уз] *n* ръкопля́скане, аплодисме́нти

apple [а́-пъл] *n* я́бълка

appliance [апла́йънс] *n* у́ред, приспособле́ние

appoint [апо́йнт] *v* назнача́вам, определя́м

appointment [апо́йнтмънт] *n* назначе́ние, определе́на сре́ща

appreciation [апри́шиейшън] *n* цене́не, благода́рност

approach [апро́уч] *v* приближа́вам се; *n* подхо́д, приближа́ване

appropriate [апро́приът] *adj* подходя́щ

approve [апру́в] *v* одобря́вам

approximately [ъпро́ксимътли] *adv* приблизи́телно

April [е́йпръл] *n* апри́л

arc [арк] *n* дъга́

architect [а́ркитект] *n* архите́кт

architecture [а́ркитекчър] *n* архитекту́ра

area [е́риъ] *n* площ, о́бласт, ра́йон, о́бсег

arm [арм] *n* ръка́, оръжие; *v* въоръжа́вам

armament [а́рмамънт] *n* въоръже́ние

armchair [а́рмчеър] *n* кре́сло

army [а́рми] *n* войска́, а́рмия

around [ъра́унд] *adv* нао́коло

arrest [аре́ст] *v* аресту́вам, задържам

arrival [ара́йвъл] *n* присти́гане

arrive [ара́йв] *v* присти́гам

arrow [а́-роу] *n* стрела́

art [арт] *n* изку́ство, сръчност, хитрина́

artist [а́ртист] *n* худо́жник

artistic [арти́стик] *adj* худо́жествен, изя́щен

as [ъ-з] *conj* като́, ка́кто, докато́

ash [ъ-ш] *n* пе́пел

ash–tray [а́-щтрей] *n* пепелни́к

ask [аск] *v* пи́там, мо́ля, и́скам, ка́ня

asleep [ъсли́йп] *adv* спящ, заспа́л

assemble [ъсе́мбъл] *v* събѝрам, монти́рам

assembly [ъсе́мбли] *n* събра́ние

assist [аси́ст] *v* подпома́гам

assistance [аси́стънс] *n* по́мощ, съде́йствие

assistant [аси́стънт] *n* помо́щник

assure [ашу́ър] *v* уверя́вам

astonish [асто́ниш] *v* учу́двам

astonishing [асто́нишинг] *adj* удиви́телен

astonishment [асто́нишмънт] *n* учу́дване

at [ъ-т] *prep* при, на, в, у

attack [ата́-к] *v* напа́дам; *n* нападе́ние

attempt [ъте́мпт] *v* опи́твам се *n* о́пит

attend [ътéнд] *v* внимáвам, посещáвам
attic [á-тик] *n* тавáн
attorney [атърни] *n* пълномóщник, адвокáт
attract [атрá-кт] *v* привлúчам
attraction [атрá-кшън] *n* привлúчане, чар
attractive [атрá-ктив] *adj* привлекáтелен
auction [óкшън] *n* търг
audience [óдиънс] *n* пýблика
August [óгъст] *n* áвгуст
aunt [ант] *n* лéля, вýйна, стрúнка
author [óтър] *n* áвтор
authority [отóрити] *n* авторитéт, власт
automobile [óтомобúл] *n* автомобúл
available [ъвéйлъбъл] *adj* налúчен
avenue [áвеню] *n* алéя, булевáрд
avoid [ъвóйд] *v* избúгвам, странú
awake [ъуéйк] *v* бýдя, събýждам се
award [ъуóрд] *v* награждáвам *n* нагрáда
away [ъуéй] *adv* надалéче
awful [óфул] *adj* ужáсен
ax [а-кс] *n* брáдва

B

baby [бéйби] *n* бéбе
bachelor [бá-челър] *n* ергéн, бакалáвър
back [ба-к] *n* гръб, облегáло, óпако; *adv*
назáд, обрáтно; *v* подкрéпям
backbone [бá-кбоун] *n* гръбнáк

background [ба-кграунд] *n* фон, произход, среда

backward [ба-куърд] *adj* обратен, изостанал

bacon [бейкън] *n* бекон, сланина

bad [ба-д] *adj* лош, развален

badge [ба-дж] *n* значка, емблема

baggage [ба-гадж] *n* багаж

bake [бейк] *v* пека

baker [бейкър] *n* пекар, хлебар

balance [ба-ланс] *n* равновесие, баланс

balcony [ба-лкъни] *n* балкон

ball [бол] *n* топка, кълбо

bandage [ба-ндадж] *n* превръзка, бинт; *v* превързвам

bank [ба-нк] *n* банка

bank [ба-нк] *n* бряг

bankrupt [ба-нкръпт] *adj* фалирал, разорен

bankruptcy [ба-нкръпси] *n* фалит, банкрут

bar [бар] *n* преграда, адвокатура

barrel [ба-ръл] *n* бъчва

barrier [ба-риър] *n* препятствие, преграда, спънка

barter [бартър] *n* разменна търговия

base [бейс] *n* основа, база; *v* основавам

basic [бейсик] *adj* основен

basket [баскет] *n* кошница, кош

bath [бат] *n* баня, къпане

bathroom [батрум] *n* баня, тоалетна

battle [ба-тл] *n* битка, сражение

bay [бей] *n* за́лив

be [би] *v* съм, съществу́вам

beach [бийч] *n* мо́рски бряг, плаж

bean [бийн] *n* боб, фасу́л

beard [би́ърд] *n* брада́

beat [бийт] *v* би́я, у́дрям, побежда́вам

beautiful [бю́тифул] *adj* краси́в

beauty [бю́ти] *n* красота́, краса́вица

because [бико́уз] *conj* поне́же, защо́то

become [бику́м] *v* ста́вам, подхо́ждам

bed [бед] *n* легло́, кори́то, дъно, леха́

bedroom [бе́друм] *n* спа́лня

beef [бийф] *n* гове́ждо месо́

beer [би́ър] *n* би́ра

before [бифо́р] *adv* преди́

beg [бег] *v* про́ся, мо́ля

beggar [бе́гър] *n* про́сяк

begin [биги́н] *v* запо́чвам

beginner [биги́нър] *n* наче́ващ, нова́к

beginning [биги́нинг] *n* нача́ло

behave [бихе́йв] *v* държа́ се, постъ́пвам

behavior [бихе́йвиър] *n* поведе́ние, държа́не

belief [били́йф] *n* вя́ра, убежде́ние

believe [били́йв] *v* вя́рвам

bell [бел] *n* камба́на, звъне́ц

belong [било́нг] *v* принадлежа́

below [било́у] *prep* под; *adv* отдо́лу

belt [белт] *n* кола́н, по́яс

bench [бенч] *n* пе́йка, рабо́тна ма́са

bend [бенд] *v* наве́ждам, огъ́вам

beneath [бинийт] *prep* под; *adv* отдолу

beneficial [бенъфишъл] *adj* благотворен

benefit [бенъфит] *n* полза, изгода; *v* ползувам

beside [бисайд] *prep* край, до, извън

besides [бисайдз] *prep* освен

bet [бет] *v* обзалагам се; *n* бас, облог

betray [бетрей] *v* предавам, изневерявам

between [битуйн] *prep* между

beyond [бийонд] *prep* отвод, оттатък, извън, след

Bible [байбл] *n* Библия

bicycle [байсикъл] *n* велосипед

big [биг] *adj* голям, важен

bill [бил] *n* сметка, законопроект, афиш

biography [байографи] *n* биография

biology [байолъджи] *n* биология

bird [бърд] *n* птица

birth [бърт] *n* рождение, раждане

birthday [бъртдей] *n* рожден ден

biscuit [бискит] *n* бисквита

bishop [бишъп] *n* епископ

bite [байт] *v* хапя, захапвам

bitter [битър] *adj* горчив, озлобен

black [бла-к] *adj* черен

blade [блейд] *n* стрък, острие

blame [блейм] *v* обвинявам; *n* вина, упрек

blanket [бланкет] *n* одеяло

bleed [блийд] *v* кървя, пускам кръв

bless [блес] *v* благославям

blessing [блéсинг] *n* благодáт, благословия
blind [блайнд] *adj* сляп, безразсъден; *v* ослепявам, заслепéни
blindness [блáйнднис] *n* слепотá, заслепяване
blond [блонд] *adj* рус
blood [блъд] *n* кръв, проúзход, темперамéнт
blossom [блóсъм] *n* цвят; *v* цъфтя, разцъфвам
blouse [блáуз] *n* блýза
blue [блу] *adj* син, мрáчен, унúл
board [борд] *n* мáса, дъскá, хранá, съвéт
boarding—house [бóрдинг хáус] *n* пансиóн
boat [бóут] *n* лóдка, парахóд
body [бóди] *n* тяло, грýпа, мáса
boil [бойл] *v* вря, кипя, варя
bomb [бом] *n* бóмба *v* бомбардúрам
bone [бóун] *n* кост, кóкал
bonus [бóунъс] *n* извънрéдно възнаграждéние
book [бук] *n* кнúга; *v* запúсвам, купýвам
boot [бýут] *n* висóка обýвка, ботýш
booth [бýут] *n* бýдка, сергúя, кабúна
border [бóрдър] *n* грáница
bore [бóър] *v* пробúвам, досáждам
boredom [бóърдъм] *n* отегчéние, досáда
born [борн] *adj* родéн
boss [бос] *n* шеф
both [бот] *pron* и двáмата, и двéте

bother [бодър] *n* безпокойство; *v*
безпокоя, давам си труд

bottle [ботл] *n* бутилка, шише

bottom [ботъм] *n* дъно

boundary [баундъри] *n* граница, предел

bouquet [букей] *n* букет

box [бокс] *n* кутия, сандък, ложа

boy [бой] *n* момче

bracelet [брейслит] *n* гривна

bracket [бракит] *n* скоби, подпора

brain [брейн] *n* мозък, ум, интелект

branch [бранч] *n* клон, филиал

brandy [бра-нди] *n* ракия, коняк

bra [бра] *n* сутиен

brave [брейв] *adj* смел, храбър

bravery [брейвъри] *n* храброст

bread [бред] *n* хляб

break [брейк] *n* прекъсване, почивка

break [брейк] *v* чупя

breast [брест] *n* гърди

breath [брет] *n* дъх, дихание, полъх

breathe [брийд] *v* дишам, лъхам, шептя

brick [брик] *n* тухла

bride [брайд] *n* булка

bridge [бридж] *n* мост

brief [брийф] *adj* кратък

bright [брайт] *adj* светъл, ярък, умен

brightness [брайтнис] *n* блясък, яркост

bring [бринг] *v* нося, водя, довеждам

British [бритиш] *adj* британски

broadcast [бро́удкаст] *v* разпространя́вам

broker [бро́укър] *n* комисионе́р

brother [бра́дър] *n* брат

brother-in-law [бра́дър ин ло] *n* зет, де́вер, шу́рей

brown [бра́ун] *adj* кафя́в

brush [бръш] *n* че́тка

buck [бак] *n* до́лар, еле́н

bucket [бъкет] *n* ко́фа, ведро́

budget [бъджит] *n* бюдже́т

build [билд] *v* строя́, изгра́ждам

builder [би́лдър] *n* строи́тел

building [би́лдинг] *n* зда́ние, изгра́ждане

bulb [бълб] *n* лу́ковица, електри́ческа кру́шка

bun [бън] *n* кръ́гла ки́фла, кок

burn [бърн] *v* горя́, изга́рям

bury [бери] *v* зара́вям, погре́бвам

bus [бас] *n* автобу́с

bush [буш] *n* храст, гъстала́к

business [би́знис] *n* ра́бота, заня́тие, сде́лка

businessman [би́знисман] *n* търго́вец

butter [бъ́тър] *n* ма́сло

butterfly [бъ́търфлай] *n* пеперу́да

button [бъ́тън] *n* ко́пче, буто́н; *v* закопча́вам

buy [бай] *v* купу́вам

buyer [ба́йър] *n* купува́ч, заку́пчик

by [бай] *prep* до, при, с, чрез, покра́й

C

cab [ка-б] *n* файто́н, такси́

cabbage [ка́-бидж] *n* зе́ле

cable [ке́йбъл] *n* ка́бел, телегра́ма, ка́белна телеви́зия

café [кафе́] *n* кафене́, рестора́нт

cake [кейк] *n* кейк, то́рта

calculate [ка́-лкюлейт] *v* изчисля́вам, пресмя́там

calculation [ка́-лкюлейшън] *n* изчисле́ние, пресмя́тане, обми́сляне

calendar [ка́-лендър] *n* календа́р

call [кол] *v* ви́кам, нари́чам, посеща́вам; *n* пови́кване, посеще́ние

calm [кам] *adj* тих, споко́ен

calmness [ка́мнис] *n* тишина́, споко́йствие

camera [ка́-мера] *n* фотоапара́т, ка́мера

can [ка-н] *v* мо́га; *n* тенеки́ена кути́я

canal [ка́нал] *n* изку́ствен кана́л

cancer [ка́-нсър] *n* рак

candid [ка́-ндид] *adj* и́скрен, открове́н

candidate [ка́-ндидейт] *n* кандида́т

candle [ка́-ндъл] *n* свещ

canned [ка-нд] *adj* консерви́ран

canvas [ка́-нвас] *n* платни́ще, брезе́нт

capability [ке́йпъби́лити] *n* спосо́бност

capable [ке́йпъбъл] *adj* спосо́бен

capacity [капа́-сити] *n* вмести́мост, спосо́бност

capital [ка́-питал] *n* сто́лица, капита́л; *adj* гла́вен

car [кар] *n* кола́, автомоби́л, ваго́н

card [кард] *n* ка́рта за игра́, ка́ртичка

cardigan [ка́рдиган] *n* плете́на жиле́тка

care [ке́ър] *n* гри́жа, внима́ние; *v* гри́жа се, оби́чам

career [кари́ър] *n* карие́ра

careful [ке́ърфул] *adj* грижли́в, внима́телен

careless [ке́ърлис] *adj* неха́ен, лекоми́слен

carelessness [ке́ърлиснис] *n* неха́йство

cargo [ка́рго] *n* това́р

carpet [ка́рпет] *n* кили́м

carrier [ка́-риър] *m* самолетоно́сач

carrot [ка́-рът] *n* мо́рков

carry [ка́-ри] *v* но́ся, зана́сям, държа́ се

cartoon [карту́ун] *n* карикату́ра, мултипликацио́нен филм

case [кейс] *n* слу́чай, проце́с

cash [ка-ш] *n* пари́

cashier [ка-ши́ър] *n* касие́р

cat [ка-т] *n* ко́тка

catalog [ка́-талог] *n* катало́г

catch [ка-ч] *v* хва́щам, ловя́, дола́вям

cathedral [кати́драл] *n* катедра́ла

catholic [ка́-тълик] *adj* католи́чески

cattle [ка-тл] *n* доби́тък

cause [коз] *n* причи́на, ка́уза; *v* причиня́вам

cavity [ка́-вити] *n* кухина́, ду́пка

celebrate [се́лъбрейт] *v* че́ствувам, празну́вам, възхваля́вам

celebration [селъбре́йшън] *n* че́ствуване

celebrity [силе́брити] *n* изве́стност, знамени́тост

cell [сел] *n* кили́я, кле́тка

cellar [се́лър] *n* мазе́, и́зба

cemetery [се́митъри] *n* гро́бища

census [се́нсъс] *n* преброя́ване на населе́нието

central [се́нтрал] *adj* центра́лен, гла́вен

center [се́нтър] *n* це́нтър, среда́, сре́дище; *v* съсредоточа́вам

century [се́нчъри] *n* столе́тие, век

ceremony [се́ремъни] *n* о́бред, церемо́ния

certain [съ́ртън] *adj* си́гурен, уве́рен, несъмне́н

certainly [съ́ртънли] *adv* несъмне́но, разби́ра се

certificate [сърти́фикът] *n* удостовере́ние, свиде́телство

certify [съ́ртифай] *v* уве́реност

chain [чейн] *n* вери́га *v* окова́вам

chair [че́ър] *n* стол

chairman [че́ърмън] *n* председа́тел

challenge [ча́лъндж] *n* предизви́кателство; *v* призова́вам на борба́

champagne [шампе́йн] *n* шампа́нско

champion [ча́-мпиън] *n* шампио́н, защи́тник

championship [ча́-мпиъншип] *n* шампиона́т, защи́та

chance [ча-нс] *n* слу́чай, случа́йност; *v* слу́чвам се, риску́вам

change [чейндж] *n* промя́на, дре́бни пари́, ре́сто; *v* проме́ням се

channel [ча́-нъл] *n* кана́л, пото́к

chaos [ке́ъс] *n* ха́ос

character [ка́-ръктър] *n* хара́ктер, бу́ква, де́йствуващо лице́

characteristic [ка́-ръктери́стик] *adj* характе́рен

charge [чардж] *v* обвиня́вам, напа́дам; *n* обвине́ние

charity [ча́-рити] *n* благотвори́телност

charming [ча́рминг] *adj* чаро́вен, очарова́телен

chase [чейс] *v* го́ня, пресле́двам

cheap [чийп] *adj* е́втин, прост, долнока́чествен

cheat [чийт] *v* изма́мвам; *n* изма́ма, изма́мник

check [чек] *n* чек, прове́рка

cheek [чийк] *n* бу́за, безо́чливост

cheer [чи́ър] *v* аплоди́рам, насърча́вам

cheerful [чи́ърфул] *adj* бо́дър, жизнера́достен

cheese [чийз] *n* си́рене, кашкава́л
chemical [ке́микъл] *adj* хими́чески
chemist [ке́мист] *n* хими́к, апте́кар
chemistry [ке́мистри] *n* хи́мия
cherry [че́ри] *n* чере́ша
chess [чес] *n* ша́хмат
chest [чест] *n* сандъ́к, гръ́ден кош
chestnut [че́стнът] *n* ке́стен
chew [чу] *v* дъ́вча, предъ́вквам
chicken [чи́кън] *n* пи́ле, пи́лешко месо́
chief [чийф] *n* шеф, нача́лник, вожд; *adj* гла́вен
child [чайлд] *n* дете́
childhood [ча́йлдхуд] *n* де́тство, дети́нство
chimney [чи́мни] *n* коми́н, огни́ще
china [ча́йна] *n* порцела́н
chips [чипс] *n* вид пъ́ржени карто́фи
chocolate [чо́клът] *n* шокола́д
choice [чойс] *n* и́збор
choose [чу́уз] *v* изби́рам, реша́вам
Christ [крайст] *n* Христо́с
Christianity [кри́счиа́нити] *n* христия́нство
Christmas [кри́смъс] *n* Ко́леда
church [чърч] *n* църква
cigarette [сигъре́т] *n* цига́ра
cinema [си́нема] *n* ки́но
circle [съркъл] *n* кръг, окръжност; *v* кръжа́, обика́лям
circuit [съркит] *n* обико́лка, електри́ческа вери́га

circumstance [сёркъмстънс] *n* обстоя́телство

circus [сёркъс] *n* кръгъл площа́д, цирк

citizen [си́тизън] *n* гра́жданин, по́даник

citizenship [си́тизъншип] *n* гра́жданство, по́данство

city [си́ти] *n* град

civic [си́вик] *adj* гра́ждански

civilian [сиви́лиън] *adj* циви́лен

civilization [си́вилизе́йшън] *n* цивилиза́ция

claim [клейм] *v* претенди́рам, твърдя́; *n* иск, прете́нция

clamp [кла-мп] *n* ско́ба *v* затя́гам

clarity [кла́-рити] *n* яснота́

class [кла-с] *n* кла́са, уче́бен час *v* класифици́рам

classic [кла́-сик] *adj* класи́чески, образцо́в

classical [кла́-сикъл] *adj* класи́чески, съвърше́н

classification [кла́-сификейшън] *n* класифика́ция

classroom [кла́-срум] *n* кла́сна ста́я

claw [кло] *n* но́кът, ла́па

clean [клийн] *adj* чист, изку́сен

cleaner [кли́йнър] *n* сре́дство за почи́стване

clear [кли́ър] *adj* я́сен, би́стър, прозра́чен, чист; *v* очи́ствам, избистря́м

clearly [кли́ърли] *adv* я́сно, очеви́дно

clerk [кларк] *n* чино́вник

clever [кле́вър] *adj* у́мен, спосо́бен, изку́сен, хи́тър

climate [клáймът] *n* клúмат

climb [клайм] *v* кáчвам се, катéря се

clinic [клúник] *n* клúника

clip [клип] *n* скóба, клáмер; *v* защúпвам, пристягам

clock [клок] *n* часóвник

close [клóус] *adj* блúзък, тéсен, подрóбен

close [клóуз] *v* затвáрям, свършвам

closely [клóусли] *adv* отблúзо, внимáтелно

cloth [клот] *n* плат, покрúвка, парцáл

clothes [клóудз] *n* дрéхи

clothing [клóудинг] *n* облеклó

cloud [клáуд] *n* óблак; *v* заоблачáвам се, помрачáвам

cloudy [клáуди] *adj* óблачен, неясен, мътен

club [клаб] *n* клуб, тояга, пáлка

clutch [клъч] *v* сгрáбчвам; *n* лáпи, амбреáж

coach [кóуч] *n* колá, вагóн, треньóр; *v* обучáвам, тренúрам

coal [кóул] *n* въглища

coast [кóуст] *n* мóрски бряг, крайбрéжие

coat [кóут] *n* палтó, сакó, слой, мазúлка

cocktail [кóктейл] *n* коктéйл

cocoa [кóукоу] *n* какáо

coconut [кóукънът] *n* кокóсов óрех

coffee [кóфи] *n* кафé

coffin [кóфин] *n* ковчéг

coin [койн] *n* монéта

coincide [коуинсáйд] *v* съвпáдам
coincidence [кóуйнсидънс] *n* съвпадéние
cold [кóулд] *adj* студéн; *n* студ, простýда
coldness [кóулднис] *n* студенинá
collar [кóлър] *n* якá
colleague [кóлиг] *n* колéга
collect [кълéкт] *v* събúрам
collection [кълéкшън] *n* сбúрка, колéкция
college [кóлидж] *n* колéж, колéгия
colonel [кърнъл] *n* полкóвник
color [кáлър] *n* цвят, руменинá; *v*
оцветя́вам, изчервя́вам се
comb [кóум] *n* грéбен, чесáло; *v* рéша,
срéсвам
combine [къмбáйн] *v* съчетáвам,
комбинúрам
come [към] *v* úдвам
comedy [кóмеди] *n* комéдия
comfort [кáмфърт] *n* утéха, удóбство; *v*
утешáвам
comfortable [кáмфъртъбл] *adj* удóбен,
спокóен
comic [кóмик] *adj* смéшен, комúчен
comma [кóма] *n* запетáя
command [къмáнд] *v* заповя́двам, владéя,
контролúрам; *n* зáповед, комáнда
commander [къмáндър] *n* командúр
comment [кóмент] *n* критúческа белéжка,
коментáр; *v* коментúрам
commercial [къмъ́ршъл] *adj* търгóвски

commission [къми́шън] *n* коми́сия
commit [къми́т] *v* извършвам, преда́вам
commitment [къми́тмент] *n* задълже́ние, обвъ́рзване
committee [къми́ти] *n* коми́сия, комите́т
commodity [къмо́дити] *n* сто́ка
common [ко́мън] *adj* общ, обикнове́н
communicate [къмю́никейт] *v* съобща́вам, общу́вам
communication [къмюникейшън] *n* съобще́ние, комуника́ция
community [къмю́нити] *n* обшина́, о́бщност, общество́
company [къмпъни] *n* компа́ния, тру́па, ро́та
comparatively [къмпа́ративли] *adv* сравни́телно
compare [къмпе́ър] *v* сравня́вам
comparison [къмпа́рисън] *n* сравне́ние
compassion [къмпа-шън] *n* състрада́ние
compatible [къмпа-тибл] *adj* съвмести́м
compensate [ко́мпенсейт] *v* обезщетя́вам, компенси́рам
compensation [ко́мпенсейшън] *n* обезщете́ние, компенса́ция
compete [къмпи́йт] *v* състеза́вам се, конкури́рам
competence [ко́мпитънс] *n* компете́нтност
competent [ко́мпитънт] *adj* компете́нтен
complain [къмпле́йн] *v* опла́квам се

complaint [къмплейнт] *n* оплакване, жалба, болка

complete [къмплийт] *v* завършвам; *adj* пълен, завършен

component [къмпоунънт] *n* съставна част

composer [къмпоузър] *n* композитор

composition [композъишън] *n* съчинение, композиция, състав

comprehensive [комприхенсив] *adj* просторен, изчерпателен

comprise [къмпрайз] *v* обхващам, включвам

compromise [компръмайз] *v* правя компромис; *n* компромисно решение

compulsory [къмпълсъри] *adj* задължителен, принудителен

concentrate [консънтрейт] *v* съсредоточавам, сгъстявам

concentration [консънтрейшън] *n* съсредоточаване, струпване

concept [консъпт] *n* понятие, схващане, представа

concern [кънсърн] *v* касая се, засягам, интересувам се; *n* грижа, загриженост

concerning [кънсърнинг] *prep* относно

concert [консърт] *n* концерт, съгласие

condition [къндишън] *n* условие, положение, състояние

conduct [къндакт] *v* водя, провеждам, дирижирам

conduct [кондъкт] *n* поведение, водене

confederation [конфе́дъре́йшън] *n* съюз, конфедера́ция

conference [ко́нфъръис] *n* съвеща́ние, конфере́нция

confess [кънфе́с] *v* призна́вам, изпови́двам се

confession [кънфе́шън] *n* призна́ние, и́зповед

confidence [ко́нфидънс] *n* дове́рие, уве́реност, самонаде́яност, та́йна

confident [ко́нфидънт] *adj* уве́рен, самоуве́рен, смел

confirm [кънфъ́рм] *v* потвържда́вам

conflict [ко́нфликт] *n* сблъскване, конфли́кт

conflict [кънфли́кт] *v* сблъсквам се, противореча́

confuse [кънфю́з] *v* смуща́вам, обърквам

confusion [кънфю́жън] *n* бъркоти́я, смут, объркване

congratulate [кънгра́-чюле́йт] *v* поздравя́вам, честитя́

congratulation [кънгра́-чюле́йшън] *n* поздравле́ние

congress [ко́нгрес] *n* конгре́с

conjunction [кънджъ́нкшън] *n* съединя́ване, съюз

conscience [ко́ншънс] *n* съвест

conscientious [ко́ншиен́шъс] *adj* съзна́телен, добросъвестен

conscious [кóншъс] *adj* съзнáтелен

consecutive [кънсéкютив] *adj*
последовáтелен, порéден

consequence [кóнсикуенс] *n* слéдствие,
резултáт, значéние, вáжност

consider [кънсúдър] *v* счúтам, обмúслям,
разглéждам

considerable [кънсúдъръбл] *adj* значúтелен

consideration [кънсúдърéйшън] *n*
обмúсляне, съображéние, внимáние

consist [кънсúст] *v* състоя́ се, заключáвам
се

consonant [кóнсънънт] *n* съглáсна бýква;
adj съзвýчен, хармонúчен

constant [кóнстант] *adj* постоя́нен,
непоколебúм

constantly [кóнстантли] *adv* постоя́нно,
чéсто

constitution [кóнституюшън] *n* устрóйство,
организъм, конститýция

construct [кънстрѣкт] *v* строя́, градя́

construction [кънстрѣкшън] *n* строéж,
пострóйка, констрýкция

constructive [кънстрѣктив] *adj* градúвен,
полéзен

consult [кънсѣлт] *v* съвéтвам се, допúтвам
се

consultation [кóнсълтéйшън] *n* консултáция

consume [кънсю́м] *v* унищожáвам,
консумúрам

consumer [кънсю́мър] *n* потреби́тел,
консума́тор

consumption [кънсъ́мпшън] *n* употре́ба,
консума́ция, туберкуло́за

contact [ко́нта-кт] *n* до́пир, конта́кт

contain [кънте́йн] *v* съдържам, поби́рам,
възпи́рам

container [кънте́йнър] *n* съд

contemporary [кънте́мпъръри] *adj*
съвре́менен

contempt [кънте́мпт] *n* презре́ние,
пренебреже́ние

content [ко́нтент] *n* съдържа́ние,
вмести́мост

contest [кънте́ст] *v* състеза́вам се, спо́ря,
бо́ря се

contest [ко́нтест] *n* състеза́ние, борба́, спор

continent [ко́нтинънт] *n* контине́нт

continental [ко́нтине́нтъл] *adj*
контине́нтален, европе́йски

continuation [кънтинюе́йшън] *n* продълже́ние

continue [кънти́ню] *v* продължа́вам, тра́я,
прости́рам се

contract [ко́нтра-кт] *n* до́говор, контра́кт

contract [кънтра́-кт] *v* скли́чвам до́говор,
сви́вам се

contractor [кънтра́-ктър] *n* предприема́ч

contradict [ко́нтръди́кт] *v* противоречá

contradiction [ко́нтръди́кшън] *n*
противоре́чие, несъотве́тствие

contrary [ко́нтръри] *adj* противоположен;
adv проти́вно на

contrast [ко́нтраст] *n* противополо́жност,
контра́ст

contribute [кънтри́бют] *v* доприна́сям,
съде́йствувам

contribution [ко́нтрибю́шън] *n* при́нос,
уча́стие, сътру́дничество

control [кънтро́ул] *n* власт, надзо́р; *v*
управля́вам, контроли́рам, обузда́вам

convenience [кънви́ниънс] *n* удобство

convenient [кънви́ниънт] *adj* удо́бен

convention [кънве́ншън] *n* събра́ние,
конгре́с, споразуме́ние, усло́вност

conventional [кънве́ншънъл] *adj*
общоприе́т, усло́вен, обикнове́н

conversation [ко́нвърсе́йшън] *n* ра́зговор,
бесе́да

convict [кънви́кт] *v* осъждам

convict [ко́нвикт] *n* затво́рник

conviction [кънви́кшън] *n* осъждане,
убежде́ние

convince [кънви́нс] *v* убежда́вам

cook [ку́ук] *v* го́твя, сваря́вам; *n* готва́ч

cool [ку́ул] *adj* хла́ден, споко́ен; *v*
охла́ждам

cooperate [ко́упърейт] *v* сътру́днича,
съде́йствувам

cooperation [коуо́пърейшън] *n*
сътру́дничество, коопера́ция

coordinate [коуóрдинейт] *v* съгласýвам, координи́рам

cop [коп] *n* полицáй

copper [кóпър] *adj* мéден

copy [кóпи] *n* кóпие, брой, екземпля́р; *v* копи́рам, препи́свам

cord [корд] *n* връв, шнур, стрýна

cordial [кóрдиъл] *adj* сърдéчен

core [кор] *n* сърцевинá, същинá

cork [корк] *n* тáпа, корк

corn [корн] *n* зърно, царевица

corner [кóрнър] *n* ъгъл, кът

correct [кърéкт] *adj* прáвилен, тóчен; *v* попрáвям, кориги́рам

correction [кърéкшън] *n* попрáвка

correspondent [кóръспóндънт] *n* кореспондéнт; *adj* съотвéтен

corridor [кóридор] *n* коридóр

corrupt [кърáпт] *adj* поквáрен, продáжен; *v* поквáрявам, подкýпвам

corruption [кърáпшън] *n* поквáра, корýпция

cost [кост] *v* стрýвам; *n* ценá, стóйност

costly [кóстли] *adj* скъп

cotton [котн] *n* памýк

couch [кáуч] *n* дивáн, кушéтка

cough [коф] *v* кáшлям; *n* кáшлица

council [кáунсъл] *n* съвéт, съвещáние

count [кáунт] *v* броя́, счи́там

counter [кáунтър] *n* тезгя́х, щанд

country [кънтри] *n* страна́, прови́нция

couple [къпл] *n* дво́йка, чифт; *v* свързвам

courage [къридж] *n* сме́лост, хра́брост

courageous [къре́йджъс] *adj* смел, хра́бър

course [корс] *n* ход, курс, я́стие

court [корт] *n* двор, съд, те́нис игри́ще

cousin [къзън] *n* братовче́д

cover [къвър] *v* покри́вам, обхва́щам; *n* покри́вка, похлупа́к, прикри́тие

cow [ка́у] *n* кра́ва

crack [кра-к] *n* пукнати́на; *v* пу́квам, чу́пя

cracked [кра-кт] *adj* пу́кнат

craftsman [кра́фтсман] *n* занаятчи́я

crate [крейт] *n* ща́йга

crazy [кре́йзи] *adj* луд, побъ́ркан, сма́хнат

cream [крийм] *n* смета́на, крем

create [крие́йт] *v* творя́, създа́вам

creature [кри́чър] *n* създа́ние

credit [кре́дит] *n* дове́рие, креди́т

creditor [кре́дитър] *n* креди́тор

crime [крайм] *n* престъпле́ние

criminal [кри́минъл] *adj* престъ́пен, кримина́лен; *n* престъ́пник

critic [кри́тик] *n* крити́к

critical [кри́тикъл] *adj* крити́чески, крити́чен

crop [кроп] *n* реко́лта, жъ́тва

cross [крос] *n* кръст, кръсто́сване

crossing [кро́синг] *n* преси́чане, пресе́чка

crowd [крауд] *n* тълпа́, мно́жество; *v* тру́пам се, тълпя́ се

crown [краун] *n* вене́ц, коро́на; *v* увенча́вам, короня́свам, завършвам

cruel [кру́ъл] *adj* жесто́к

cruelty [кру́ълти] *n* жесто́кост

crush [кръш] *v* сма́чквам, сма́звам, унищожа́вам

cry [край] *v* ви́кам, пла́ча; *n* вик, плач

crystal [кри́стъл] *adj* криста́лен

cube [кюб] *n* куб

cubic [кю́бик] *adj* куби́чески

cucumber [кю́къмбър] *n* кра́ставица

cuff [къф] *n* манше́т, ръкаве́л

cultivate [къ́лтивейт] *v* обрабо́твам, култиви́рам

cultivation [къ́лтивейшън] *n* обрабо́тване, отгле́ждане

cultural [къ́лчъръл] *adj* культу́рен

culture [къ́лчър] *n* култу́ра

cup [къп] *n* порцела́нова ча́ша

cupboard [къ́бърд] *n* бюфе́т, шкаф

cure [кю́ър] *n* лек, леку́ване; *v* излеку́вам

curiosity [кюрио́сити] *n* любопи́тство, ря́дкост

curious [кю́риъс] *adj* любопи́тен, стра́нен

current [къ́рънт] *adj* теку́щ; *n* струя́, тече́ние, ток

curse [кърс] *n* прокля́тие, ругатня́; *v* кълна́, руга́я

curtain [къртън] *n* завеса, перде
cushion [кушън] *n* възглавница за сядане
custom [кѣстъм] *n* навик, обичай, мито
customer [кѣстъмър] *n* клиент
cut [кът] *v* режа, броя, сека; *n* порязване, кройка
cycle [сайкъл] *n* цикъл, велосипед
cynical [синикъл] *adj* скептичен, циничен
cynicism [синисизм] *n* неверие в доброто, цинизъм

D

dad [да-д] *n* татко
daily [дейли] *adj* ежедневен
dairy [деъри] *n* млечни произведения
damage [да-мъдж] *n* вреда, щета, повреда; *v* повреждам
dance [да-нс] *v* танцувам; *n* танц
dancer [да-нсър] *n* танцьор, танцьорка
danger [дейнджър] *n* опасност
dangerous [дейнджърѣс] *adj* опасен
dark [дарк] *adj* тъмен, черен; *n* тъмнина, мрак
darkness [даркнис] *n* тъмнина, мрак, невежество
data [дейта] *noun pl* данни
date [дейт] *n* дата, среща; *v* датирам

daughter [до́тър] *n* дъщеря́

daughter-in-law [до́тър ин ло] *n* снаха́

day [дей] *n* ден, деноно́щие

dead [дед] *adj* мъ́ртъв, безчу́вствен

deaf [деф] *adj* глух

deal [дийл] *v* да́вам, търгу́вам, занима́вам се; *n* сде́лка, дял

dealer [дий́лър] *n* търго́вец

dear [ди́ър] *adj* мил, драг, скъп

debt [дет] *n* дълг

decade [де́кейд] *n* десетиле́тие

deceased [диси́йст] *adj* поко́ен, умря́л

deceit [диси́йт] *n* изма́ма

December [дисе́мбър] *n* деке́мври

decency [ди́сънси] *n* благоприли́чие

decent [ди́сънт] *adj* прили́чен, подходя́щ, задоволи́телен

decide [диса́йд] *v* реша́вам

decision [диси́жън] *n* реше́ние

decisive [диса́йсив] *adj* реши́телен, реша́ващ

declaration [де́клърейшън] *n* изявле́ние, деклара́ция

declare [дикле́ър] *v* заявя́вам, деклари́рам

decline [дикла́йн] *v* отка́звам, запа́дам, влоша́вам се

decorate [де́кърейт] *v* украся́вам, декори́рам

decoration [де́кърейшън] *n* укра́са, украше́ние, меда́л

decrease [дикрийс] *v* намаля́вам
decrease [ди́крийс] *n* намаля́ване, намале́ние
deep [дийп] *adj* дълбо́к
deer [ди́ър] *n* еле́н
defeat [дифи́йт] *v* побежда́вам, би́я, прова́лям
defect [дифе́кт] *n* недоста́тък, дефе́кт
defective [дифе́ктив] *adj* дефе́ктен, непъ́лен
defense [дифе́нс] *n* защи́та, отбра́на
defend [дифе́нд] *v* защища́вам, браня́
defendant [дифе́ндънт] *n* обвиня́ем, отве́тник
define [дифа́йн] *v* определя́м, очерта́вам
definition [де́финишън] *n* определе́ние, дефини́ция
degree [дигри́й] *n* сте́пен, гра́дус
delegate [де́лигит] *n* делега́т
delegation [де́лигейшън] *n* делега́ция
deliberate [дели́бърът] *adj* уми́шлен, преднаме́рен
delicate [де́ликът] *adj* не́жен, изя́щен, кре́хък
delicious [дели́шъс] *adj* прекра́сен, вку́сен, сла́дък
delight [дила́йт] *v* ра́двам, очаро́вам, възхища́вам *n* насла́да, възхище́ние
delightful [дила́йтфул] *adj* възхити́телен
delivery [дели́въри] *n* доста́вка, изна́сяне

demand [диманд] *v* и́скам; *n* и́скане, търсене

democracy [димо́кръси] *n* демокра́ция

democratic [де́мъкра́тик] *adj* демократи́чен

demonstrate [де́мънстрейт] *v* дока́звам, демонстри́рам

demonstration [де́мънстре́йшън] *n* манифеста́ция

denial [дина́йъл] *n* о́тказ, опроверже́ние

dense [денс] *adj* гъст, плътен

density [де́нсити] *n* гъстота́, плътност

dental [де́нтъл] *adj* зъбен

dentist [де́нтист] *n* зъболе́кар

deny [дина́й] *v* отри́чам, отка́звам, опроверга́вам

depart [дипа́рт] *v* замина́вам, тръгвам

department [дипа́ртмънт] *n* отде́л, факулте́т

departure [дипа́рчър] *n* замина́ване, тръгване

depend [дипе́нд] *v* зави́ся, разчи́там

dependence [дипе́ндънс] *n* зави́симост, подчине́ние, дове́рие

deposit [дипо́зит] *v* вла́гам, утая́вам, депози́рам; *n* влог, на́нос, ута́йка

depth [депт] *n* дълбочина́

deputy [де́пюти] *n* заме́стник

derive [дира́йв] *v* извли́чам, получа́вам, произли́зам

describe [дискра́йб] *v* опи́свам

description [дискри́пшън] *n* описа́ние, сорт, вид

desert [дезърт] *n* пусти́ня; *adj* пуст, пусти́нен

design [диза́йн] *n* план, чертёж *v* скици́рам, зами́слям

designer [диза́йнър] *n* проекта́нт

desire [диза́йър] *v* жела́я; *n* жела́ние

desk [деск] *n* бюро́, чин

despair [диспе́ър] *v* отча́йвам се; *n* отча́яние

desperate [де́спърът] *adj* отча́ян, безразсъ́ден, безнадёжден

despite [диспа́йт] *prep* въпреки́

dessert [дизъ́рт] *n* десе́рт

destination [де́стине́йшън] *n* местоназначе́ние, предназначе́ние

destiny [де́стини] *n* предопределе́ние, съдба́

destroy [дистро́й] *v* разруша́вам, унищожа́вам

destruction [дистръ́кшън] *n* разруше́ние, ги́бел

destructive [дистръ́ктив] *adj* разруши́телен, унищожи́телен

detail [ди́тейл] *n* подро́бност

detect [дите́кт] *v* откри́вам

deteriorate [дити́риърейт] *v* влоша́вам

determination [дитъ́рмине́йшън] *n* определе́ние, реши́телност

determine [дитъ́рмин] *v* определя́м, реша́вам

develop [дивéлъп] *v* разви́вам, проявя́вам, усъвърше́нствувам

development [дивéлъпмънт] *n* разви́тие, разво́й, събитие

device [дива́йс] *n* план, за́мисъл, сре́дство, приспособле́ние

devil [де́въл] *n* дя́вол

devote [диво́ут] *v* посвеща́вам, отда́вам

devotion [диво́ушън] *n* пре́даност, любов

dew [дю] *n* роса́

diagram [да́йъграм] *n* диагра́ма

dialect [да́йълект] *n* диале́кт, наре́чие

dialogue [да́йълъг] *n* диало́г

diameter [дайми́тър] *n* диаме́тър

diamond [да́йъмънд] *n* диама́нт, каро́

diary [да́йъри] *n* дне́вник

dice [дайс] *noun pl* за́рове

dictate [дикте́йт] *v* дикту́вам

dictation [дикте́йшън] *n* дикто́вка

dictionary [ди́кшънъри] *n* ре́чник

die [дай] *v* уми́рам

diet [да́йът] *n* храна́, дие́та

differ [ди́фър] *v* различа́вам, изразя́вам несъгла́сие

difference [ди́фърънс] *n* ра́злика, спор, несъгла́сие

different [ди́фърънт] *adj* разли́чен, друг, отде́лен

difficult [ди́фикълт] *adj* тру́ден, мъчен, те́жък

difficulty [дификълти] *n* трудност, мъчнотия

dig [диг] *v* копая, ровя

digestion [дайджесчън] *n* храносмилане

dignity [дигнити] *n* достойнство

dimension [дименшън] *n* измерение, размер

dine [дайн] *v* обядвам, вечерям

dinner [динър] *n* обед, вечеря

diplomacy [диплоумъси] *n* дипломация

direct [дайрект] *adj* пряк, непосредствен; *v* ръководя, отправям, насочвам

direction [дайрекшън] *n* посока

directly [дайректли] *adv* пряко, направо, веднага

director [дайректър] *n* директор, режисьор

dirt [дърт] *n* мръсотия, смет, пръст

dirty [дърти] *adj* мръсен

disappear [дисапиър] *v* изчезвам

disappearance [дисъпиърънс] *n* изчезване

disappoint [дисъпойнт] *v* разочаровам

disappointment [дисъпойнтмънт] *n* разочарование

disarmament [дисармамънт] *n* разоръжаване

disaster [дизастър] *n* нещастие, бедствие

discipline [дисиплин] *n* дисциплина

discount [дискаунт] *n* намаление

discover [дискавър] *v* откривам, разкривам

discovery [дискавъри] *n* откритие, разкриване

discuss [дискъс] *v* разисквам, обсъждам

discussion [дискъшън] *n* разискване, обсъждане

disease [дизийз] *n* болест

disgust [дисгъст] *n* отвращение, погнуса; *v* отвращавам, възмущавам

dish [диш] *n* чиния, съд, ястие, блюдо

disk [диск] *n* диск, грамофонна плоча

display [дисплей] *v* излагам, показвам; *n* изложба, излагане

disregard [дисрегард] *v* пренебрегвам; *n* пренебрежение

distance [дистънс] *n* разстояние, далечина

distant [дистънт] *adj* далечен

distinguish [дистингуиш] *v* различавам, разграничавам

distinguished [дистингуишт] *adj* виден, изтъкнат

distribute [дистрибют] *v* разпределям, раздавам

distribution [дистрибюшън] *n* разпределение, разпространение

district [дистрикт] *n* район, област, околия

disturb [дистърб] *v* безпокоя, смущавам

dive [дайв] *v* гмуркам се, спускам се; *n* гмуркане, спускане

divide [дивайд] *v* разделям

division [дивижън] *n* деление, дивизия

divorce [диворс] *n* развод

do [ду] *v* правя, върша

doctor [доктър] *n* доктор, лекар

document [дókюмънт] *n* докумéнт

dog [дог] *n* кýче

doll [дол] *n* кýкла

domestic [домéстик] *adj* домáшен

donkey [дóнки] *n* магáре

door [дор] *n* вратá

double [дабл] *adj* двóен; *v* удвоя́вам

doubt [дáут] *v* съмня́вам се; *n* съмнéние

down [дáун] *adv* дóлу; *adj* нанадóлен

dozen [дáзън] *n* дузи́на

draw [дро] *v* привли́чам, чертáя, рисýвам

drawer [дрóър] *n* чекмеджé

drawing [дрóинг] *n* рисýнка

dream [дрийм] *v* сънýвам, мечтáя; *n* мечтá

dress [дрес] *v* обли́чам, украся́вам, пригóтвям *n* рóкля, облеклó

drink [дринк] *v* пи́я; *n* питиé

drive [драйв] *v* кáрам, шофи́рам, вóзя се; *n* кампáния

driver [дрáйвър] *n* колáр, шофьóр

drought [дрáут] *n* сýша

drown [дрáун] *v* удáвям, заглушáвам

drug [драг] *n* лекáрство, опиáт

dry [драй] *adj* сух, изсушéн

duck [дък] *n* пáтица

duration [дюрéйшън] *n* времетрáене

during [дю́ринг] *prep* през, по време

dust [дъст] *n* прах

dusty [дъ́сти] *adj* прáшен

duty [дю́ти] *n* дълг, ми́то

E

each [ийч] *adj* всéки
eagle [ѝйгъл] *n* орéл
ear [ѝър] *n* ухó
early [ѐрли] *adv* рáно; *adj* рáнен
earn [ърн] *v* припечéлвам, заслужáвам
earring [ѝъринг] *n* обицá
earth [ърт] *n* земя́, пръст
earthquake [ѐрткуейк] *n* земетресéние
ease [ииз] *n* леснинá, спокóйствие; *v*
облекчáвам, отпýскам се
easily [ѝйзили] *adv* лéсно
east [ийст] *n* ѝзток
Easter [ѝйстър] *n* Велѝкден
eastern [ѝйстърн] *adj* ѝзточен
easy [ѝзи] *adj* лéсен, свобóден, приятен
eat [ийт] *v* ям
economic [ѝкънóмик] *adj* стопáнски,
икономѝчески
economy [икóнъми] *n* стопáнство,
икономѝка
edge [едж] *n* край, ръб, острие́
edition [едѝшън] *n* издáние
editor [ѐдитър] *n* редáктор
educate [ѐдюкейт] *v* образóвам, възпитáвам
education [ѐдюкéйшън] *n* образовáние,
възпитáние

educational [éдюкéйшънъл] *adj*
образователен, възпитателен
effect [ифéкт] *n* последствие, вещи
effective [ифéктив] *adj* действителен,
резултатен, ефектен
efficiency [ифишиънси] *n* експедитивност
efficient [ифишънт] *adj* резултатен,
ефикасен
effort [éфърт] *n* усилие
egg [ег] *n* яйце
eight [ейт] *num* óсем
eighteen [ейтийн] *num* осемнáдесет
eighty [éйти] *num* осемдесéт
either [áйдър] *pron* един от двáма
elbow [éлбоу] *n* лáкът
elderly [éлдърли] *adj* възстáр
election [илéкшън] *n* избор
electric [илéктрик] *adj* електрически
electricity [електрисити] *n* електричество
element [éлмънт] *n* елемéнт, част, стихия
elephant [éлъфънт] *n* слон
elevator [елъвéйтър] *n* асансьóр
eleven [илéвън] *num* единáдесет
else [елс] *adv* иначе, друг, óще
embassy [éмбъси] *n* посóлство
embrace [имбрéйс] *v* прегръщам,
обхвáщам; *n* прегрúдка
emergency [имъ́рджънси] *n* непредвидено
обстоятелство, извънрéдно положéние
emigrate [éмигрейт] *v* изсéлвам се

emotion [имо́ушън] *n* чу́вство, емо́ция

emotional [имо́ушънъл] *adj* емоциона́лен, темпераме́нтен

emphasis [е́мфъсис] *n* набля́гане,ударе́ние

emphasize [е́мфъсайз] *v* набля́гам

empire [е́мпайър] *n* импе́рия

employ [импло́й] *v* нае́мам на ра́бота, използу́вам

employee [е́мплойи] *n* слу́жещ

employer [импло́йър] *n* работода́тел

employment [емпло́ймънт] *n* ра́бота, слу́жба

empower [емпа́уър] *v* упълномоща́вам

empty [е́мпти] *adj* пра́зен; *v* изпра́звам

encore [ънко́р] *intej* бис

encyclopedia [енса́йклопи́дия] *n* енциклопе́дия

end [енд] *n* край, цел; *v* завъ́ршвам

endanger [инде́йнджър] *v* застраша́вам

endure [инди́ър] *v* пона́сям, издържам, тра́я

enemy [е́нъми] *n* неприя́тел, враг

energy [е́нърджи] *n* ене́ргия

engage [инге́йдж] *v* ангажи́рам, сгодя́вам

engagement [инге́йджмънт] *n* задълже́ние, годе́ж

engine [е́нджин] *n* маши́на, локомоти́в

engineer [е́нджини́ър] *n* инжене́р

enjoy [инджо́й] *v* наслажда́вам се, ра́двам се

enjoyment [инджо́ймънт] *n* насла́да, удово́лствие

enough [инъф] *adj* доста́тъчен; *adv* доста́тъчно

enter [е́нтър] *v* вли́зам, постъ́пвам

enterprise [е́нтърпрайз] *n* предприя́тие, предприемчи́вост

entertain [е́нтъртéйн] *v* забавля́вам, ка́ня го́сти

entertainment [е́нтъртéйнмънт] *n* забавле́ние

entire [ента́йър] *adj* цял

entrance [е́нтрънс] *n* вход, вли́зане

entry [е́нтри] *n* вли́зане, впи́сване

envelope [е́нвълоуп] *n* плик

environment [енва́йърмънт] *n* среда́, око́лна среда́

envy [е́нви] *n* за́вист; *v* зави́ждам

episode [е́писоуд] *n* епизо́д

equality [екуо́лити] *n* ра́венство

equation [екуéйшън] *n* уравне́ние

equip [екуи́п] *v* снабдя́вам, екипи́рам

equipment [екуи́пмънт] *n* снабдя́ване, съоръже́ния

erase [ирéйз] *v* изтри́вам, зали́чавам

err [ер] *v* греша́

error [е́рър] *n* гре́шка, заблу́да

essence [е́снс] *n* същина́

establish [еста́блиш] *v* установя́вам, създа́вам

establishment [еста́блишмънт] *n* създа́ване, заведе́ние, институ́т

evaporate [ева́пърейт] *v* изпаря́вам се

evaporation [евáпърейшън] *n* изпарéние

eve [ийв] *n* вéчер, навечéрие

even [ѝвън] *adj* рáвен, чéтен; *adv* дáже, дорѝ

evening [ѝвнинг] *n* вéчер

event [ивéнт] *n* събѝтие, слýчай

ever [éвър] *adv* нѝкога, вѝнаги

every [éври] *adj* всéки

everybody [éврибъди] *pron* всéки, всѝчки

everyday [éвридей] *adj* всекиднéвен, обикновéн

evidence [éвидънс] *n* доказáтелство, показáния

evil [ѝвъл] *adj* лош, зъл *n* зло

exact [игзáкт] *adj* тóчен; *v* изѝсквам

exactly [игзáктли] *adv* тóчно

examination [игзáминéйшън] *n* ѝзпит, прéглед, проýчване

examine [игзáмин] *v* разглéждам, изпѝтвам, проýчвам

example [игзáмпъл] *n* примéр

excellent [éксълънт] *adj* отлѝчен, превъзхóден

except [иксéпт] *prep* освéн, с изключéние на; *v* изключвам

exception [иксéпшън] *n* изключéние, възражéние

exchange [иксчéйндж] *n* размѝна, бóрса; *v* размéням

excite [иксáйт] *v* възбýждам, вълнýвам

excitement [иксáйтмънт] *n* възбу́да, вълне́ние

excuse [икскю́з] *v* извиня́вам

excuse [икскю́с] *n* извине́ние

exhibit [игзи́бит] *v* изла́гам, проявя́вам; *n* експона́т

exhibition [ѐкзиби́шън] *n* изло́жба

exile [ѐксайл] *n* изгна́ние, изгна́ник; *v* пра́щам в изгна́ние

exist [игзи́ст] *v* съществу́вам

existence [игзи́стънс] *n* съществу́ване

exit [ѐкзит] *n* изли́зане, и́зход

expand [икспа́нд] *v* разширя́вам, разви́вам

expansion [икспа́ншън] *n* разшире́ние

expect [икспѐкт] *v* оча́квам, предпола́гам

expedition [ѐкспиди́шън] *n* експеди́ция, бързина́, то́чност

expenditure [икспѐндичър] *n* разно́ски, ра́зход

expense [икспѐнс] *n* разно́ски

expensive [икспѐнсив] *adj* скъп

experience [икспи́риънс] *n* о́пит, преживя́ване

experiment [икспѐримънт] *n* пра́вя о́пит

experiment [икспѐримънт] *n* о́пит

expert [ѐкспърт] *adj* вещ; *n* експѐрт

explain [икспле́йн] *v* обясня́вам

explanation [ѐксплънѐйшън] *n* обясне́ние

explode [икспло́уд] *v* експлоди́рам, избу́хвам, обо́рвам

exploration [ékсплорéйшън] *n* изслéдване, проýчване

explore [иксплóр] *v* изслéдвам, проýчвам

explorer [иксплóрър] *n* изследовáтел

explosion [иксплóужън] *n* експлóзия, избýхване

export [експóрт] *v* изнáсям

export [éкспорт] *n* и́знос

expression [икспрéшън] *n* и́зраз, изражéние

extend [икстéнд] *v* простирам, продължáвам, разширя́вам

extension [икстéншън] *n* продължéние, разширя́ване

exterior [екстириър] *adj* въ́ншен

external [екстъ́рнъл] *adj* въ́ншен

extra [éкстра] *adj* допълни́телен

extreme [икстри́йм] *adj* крáен; *n* крáйност

eye [ай] *n* окó; *v* глéдам, наблюдáвам

F

fabric [фá-брик] *n* тъкáн, плáт

face [фейс] *n* лицé; *v* обърнат съм с лицé към

fact [фа-кт] *n* факт, обстоя́телство

factor [фá-ктър] *n* фáктор, агéнт

factory [фá-ктъри] *n* фáбрика

faculty [фá-кюлти] *n* факултéт, спосóбност, дáрба

fail [фéйл] *v* пропáдам, не сполýчвам

failure [фéйлиър] *n* неуспéх, пропáдание, фалѝт

faint [фéйнт] *n* припáдък; *adj* слаб; *v* припáдам, ослáбвам

faith [фейт] *n* вя́ра

faithful [фéйтфул] *adj* вéрен, тóчен

fall [фол] *v* пáдам, стѝхвам; *n* пáдане, валéж, éсен, водопáд

false [фолс] *adj* погрéшен, лъжлѝв, фалшѝв

fame [фейм] *n* слáва, извéстност

family [фá-мили] *n* семéйство, род

famous [фéймъс] *adj* прочýг, извéстен

fan [фа-н] *n* ветрѝло, запаля́нко; *v* вéя, раздýхвам

fantastic [фантá-стик] *adj* фантастѝчен

fantasy [фá-нтъси] *n* въображéние, фантáзия

far [фар] *adv* далéч; *adj* далéчен

farewell [фéъруéл] *interj* сбóгом; *adj* сбогýване

farm [фарм] *n* фéрма, стопáнство

farmer [фáрмър] *n* земедéлец, чифликчѝя

farming [фáрминг] *n* земедéлие

fashion [фá-шън] *n* мóда, стил, нáчин

fashionable [фá-шънъбл] *adj* мóден

fast [фаст] *adj* бърз; *adv* бързо, здрáво

fat [фа–т] *adj* дебе́л, тлъст; *n* тлъстина́, мазнина́

fatal [фе́йтъл] *adj* съдбоно́сен, па́губен

fate [фейт] *n* съдба́, ги́бел

father [фа́дър] *n* баща́

fault [фолт] *n* гре́шка, дефе́кт, вина́

favor [фе́йвър] *n* благоскло́нност, услу́га, по́лза

fear [фи́ър] *n* страх; *v* страху́вам се

feather [фе́дър] *n* перо́, перуши́на

feature [фи́чър] *n* черта́, осо́беност

February [фе́брюри] *n* февруа́ри

feel [фийл] *v* чу́вствувам, смя́там

feeling [фи́йлинг] *n* чу́вство, усе́щане, отноше́ние

fellow [фе́лоу] *n* чове́к, друга́р

female [фи́мейл] *adj* же́нски

fertile [фъ́ртайл] *adj* плодоро́ден, плодови́т

fertility [фъртѝлити] *n* плодоро́дност

fertilizer [фъртила́йзър] *n* изку́ствен тор

festival [фе́стивъл] *n* празненство́, фестива́л, пра́зник

fever [фи́въvr] *n* тре́ска, температу́ра

few [фю] *adj* ма́лко

fiancé [фиа́нсе] *n* годени́к

fiancée [фиа́нсей] *n* годени́ца

fiction [фи́кшън] *n* белетри́стика, изми́слица

field [фийлд] *n* поле́, ни́ва, о́бласт

fifteen [фифти́йн] *num* петна́десет

fifty [фѝфти] *num* петдесе́т

fig [фиг] *n* смоки́ня

fight [файт] *v* би́я се, бо́ря се; *n* бой, борба́

fighter [фа́йтър] *n* боре́ц

figure [фѝгър] *n* фигу́ра, ци́фра; *v* изобразя́вам, представя́м си

fill [фил] *v* пъ́лня, изпъ́лвам, пломби́рам

film [филм] *n* филм, тъ́нък слой

filter [фѝлтър] *n* фѝлтър; *v* филтри́рам

final [фа́йнъл] *adj* кра́ен, заключи́телен; *n* фина́лен мач, после́ден и́зпит

finally [фа́йнъли] *adv* на́й-по́сле, напъ́лно

finance [файна́нс] *n* фина́нси, до́ходи; *v* финанси́рам

financial [файна́-ншъл] *adj* фина́нсов

find [файнд] *v* нами́рам

fine [файн] *adj* ху́бав, фин; *adv* чуде́сно

finger [фѝнгър] *n* пръст

fire [фа́йър] *n* о́гън, пожа́р, въодушеве́ност; *v* стре́лям, запа́лвам

fireplace [фа́йърплейс] *n* огни́ще, ками́на

fireworks [фа́йъруъркс] *noun pl* фойерве́рки

firm [фърм] *adj* твъ́рд, постоя́нен, си́гурен; *adv* твъ́рдо, непоколеби́мо; *n* фѝрма

first [фърст] *adj* пръв; *adv* на́й-напре́д, за първи пъ́т

fish [фиш] *n* ри́ба *v* ловя́ ри́ба

fist [фист] *n* юмру́к

five [файв] *num* пет

fix [фикс] *v* прикре́пвам, опреде́лям, попра́вям

flag [фла-г] *n* зна́ме

flame [флейм] *n* пла́мък

flat [фла-т] *adj* пло́сък, ра́вен; *n* пло́скост, апартаме́нт

flavor [фле́йвър] *n* вкус; *v* подпра́вям

flesh [флеш] *n* месо́, плът

flood [флад] *n* наводне́ние, пото́п; *v* наводня́вам, зали́вам

floor [флор] *n* под, ета́ж

flour [фла́уър] *n* брашно́

flourish [флъ́риш] *v* цъфтя́, процъфтя́вам, разма́хвам

flow [фло́у] *v* тека́, ле́я се, произти́чам; *n* тече́ние, при́лив

flower [фла́уър] *n* цве́те, цъфте́не

fluid [флу́ид] *adj* те́чен, газообра́зен; *n* те́чност

fly [флай] *n* муха́; *v* летя́

focus [фо́къс] *n* фо́кус; *v* съсредоточа́вам се

fold [фо́улд] *v* сгъ́вам; *n* гъ́нка

folder [фо́улдър] *n* па́пка

folk [фо́ук] *n* наро́д, хо́ра

follow [фо́лоу] *v* сле́двам, върви́ след, разби́рам

food [фу́уд] *n* храна́

fool [фу́ул] *n* глупа́к, шут; *v* изма́мвам

foolish [фу́улиш] *adj* глу́пав

foot [фу́ут] *n* крак, похо́дка

for [фор] *prep* за, в по́лза на, по
причи́на на

forbid [форби́д] *v* забраня́вам

force [форс] *n* си́ла, войска́

forecast [фо́ркаст] *n* предска́зване,
прогно́за

forehead [фо́рид] *n* че́ло

foreign [фо́рън] *adj* чуждестра́нен, въ́ншен

foreigner [фо́рънър] *n* чужденéц

forest [фо́рист] *n* гора́

forget [фърге́т] *v* забра́вям

forgive [фърги́в] *v* проща́вам

fork [форк] *n* ви́лица, ви́ла, разклоне́ние

form [форм] *n* фо́рма, вид, клас; *v*
образу́вам, офо́рмям

formal [фо́рмъл] *adj* форма́лен,
официа́лен

formality [форма́лити] *n* форма́лност,
официа́лност

formula [фо́рмюла] *n* фо́рмула

fortunate [фо́рчънът] *adj* щастли́в

fortune [фо́рчън] *n* сполу́ка, бога́тство,
бъ́деще

forty [фо́рти] *num* чети́ридесет

forward [фо́руърд] *adj* прéден; *adv*
напрéд, ната́тък *v* подпома́гам, изпра́щам

four [фор] *num* че́тири

fourteen [фо́ртийн] *num* четирина́десет

fox [фокс] *n* лиси́ца

frame [фрейм] *n* ра́мка; *v* офо́рмям, приспособя́вам

framework [фре́ймуърк] *n* констру́кция, ра́мки, структу́ра

frank [фра-нк] *adj* и́скрен, прям

frankly [фра́-нкли] *adv* и́скрено, открове́но

fraud [фрод] *n* изма́ма

free [фри] *adj* свобо́ден, безпла́тен; *v* освобожда́вам

freedom [фри́йдъм] *n* свобода́

freight [фрейт] *n* пре́воз, това́р

frequent [фри́куънт] *adj* чест, многокра́тен

frequently [фри́куънтли] *adv* че́сто

fresh [фреш] *adj* пре́сен, свеж, нов

freshness [фре́шнис] *n* све́жест

Friday [фра́йди] *n* пе́тък

friend [френд] *n* прия́тел

friendly [фре́ндли] *adv* прия́телски

friendship [фре́ндшип] *n* прия́телство, дру́жба

fright [фрайт] *n* страх, упла́ха, плаши́ло

frighten [фра́йтън] *v* изпла́швам

frog [фрог] *n* жа́ба

from [фром] *prep* от, из

front [франт] *n* пре́дна част, фронт

fruit [фрут] *n* плод

fruitful [фру́тфул] *adj* плодоро́ден, плодоно́сен

fruitless [фру́тлис] *adj* безпло́ден, безполе́зен

fry [фрай] *v* пържа

fuel [фю́ъл] *n* гори́во; *v* снабдя́вам с гори́во

fulfil [фулфи́л] *v* изпълня́вам, извъ́ршвам, задоволя́вам

full [фул] *adj* пъ́лен, цял

fully [фу́ли] *adv* напъ́лно

fun [фън] *n* шега́, заба́ва

funeral [фю́нъръл] *n* погребе́ние

funny [фъ́ни] *adj* сме́шен, стра́нен

furniture [фъ́рничър] *n* мебелиро́вка

further [фъ́рдър] *adv* по́-ната́тък; *v* съде́йствувам, придви́жвам

fuse [фюз] *adj* бушо́н

future [фю́чър] *n* бъ́деще; *adj* бъ́дещ

G

gain [гейн] *v* пече́ля, изби́рзвам; *n* печа́лба

gallery [га́-лъри] *n* гале́рия

game [гейм] *n* игра́, ди́веч

gang [га-нг] *n* гру́па, ба́нда

garage [гара́ж] *n* гара́ж; *v* гари́рам

garbage [га́рбидж] *n* смет

garden [га́рдън] *n* гради́на

garlic [га́рлик] *n* че́сън

gas [га–с] *n* бензи́н, газ

gasoline [га́–сълин] *n* бензи́н

gate [ге́йт] *n* по́рта, врата́

gay [гей] *adj* ве́сел

gender [дже́ндър] *n* род

general [дже́неръл] *adj* общ, обикнове́н, главен; *n* генера́л

generally [дже́нерълли] *adv* о́бщо взе́то, обикнове́но

generation [дженеръ́йшън] *n* поколе́ние

generosity [дже́нъро́сити] *n* ще́дрост

generous [дже́нъръс] *adj* ще́дър

gentle [дже́нтл] *adj* не́жен, благоро́ден, уме́рен

gently [дже́нтли] *adv* внима́телно, не́жно, ле́ко

genuine [дже́нюин] *adj* и́стински, неподпра́вен

geography [джио́гръфи] *n* геогра́фия

gesture [дже́счър] *n* жест

get [гет] *v* взе́мам, доби́вам, пече́ля, получа́вам

giant [джа́йънт] *n* велика́н, гига́нт

gift [гифт] *n* пода́рък, да́рба

gifted [ги́фтид] *adj* талантли́в, надаре́н

girl [гърл] *n* моми́че

give [гив] *v* да́вам, подаря́вам

glad [гла–д] *adj* ра́достен, дово́лен

gladly [гла́–дли] *adv* охо́тно, с удово́лствие

gland [гла–нд] *n* жлеза́

glass [глас] *n* стъкло́
globe [гло́уб] *n* кълбо́, гло́бус
glory [гло́ри] *n* сла́ва; *v* горде́я се, лику́вам
glove [глав] *n* ръкави́ца
glue [глу] *n* лепи́ло; *v* лепя́
go [го́у] *v* оти́вам, вървя́, дви́жа се
goal [го́ул] *n* цел, гол, врата́
goat [го́ут] *n* коза́
God [год] *n* бог, го́спод
gold [го́улд] *n* зла́то; *adj* зла́тен
good [гуд] *adj* добър, ху́бав; *n* добро́, сто́ка
good-bye [гудба́й] *interj* сбо́гом, дови́ждане; *n* сбогу́ване
good night [гу́днайт] *interj* ле́ка нощ
gospel [го́спъл] *n* ева́нгелие, ве́рую
gossip [го́сип] *n* клюка
government [га́върмънт] *n* прави́телство, управле́ние
governor [га́върнър] *n* губерна́тор
grace [грейс] *n* гра́ция, изя́щност, привлека́телност, благоволе́ние
grade [грейд] *n* сте́пен, клас
graduate [гра́-джюейт] *v* завъ́ршвам учи́лище и́ли университе́т
graduation [гра́-джюе́йшън] *n* завъ́ршване на университе́т
grammar [гра́мър] *n* грама́тика
grandfather [гра́ндфадър] *n* дя́до
grandmother [гра́ндма́дър] *n* ба́ба

grandson [грáндсън] *n* внук

grass [грас] *n* тревá, пáсбище

gratitude [грáтитюд] *n* благодáрност, признáтелност

grave [грейв] *n* гроб; *adj* сериóзен

great [грейт] *adj* голя́м, велѝк

greed [грийд] *n* áлчност, лакомѝя

green [грийн] *adj* зелéн, незря́л

greet [грийт] *v* поздравя́вам

greeting [грѝтинг] *n* пóздрав

grey [грей] *adj* сив, побеля́л

grief [грийф] *n* скръб, печáл

grill [грил] *n* скáра за печéне на месó; *v* пекá на скáра

grocer [грóусър] *n* бакáлин

ground [грáунд] *n* земя́, пóчва

grow [грóу] *v* растá, стáвам, отглéждам

guaranteee [гá-рантѝ] *n* гарáнция, поръчѝтелство; *v* обезпечáвам

guard [гард] *v* пáзя, защищáвам; *n* охрáна

guest [гест] *n* гост, клиéнт

guide [гайд] *v* ръководя́

guilt [гилт] *n* винá

guilty [гѝлти] *adj* винóвен

guitar [гѝтар] *n* китáра

gum [гъм] *n* венéц, клей, лепѝло

gun [гън] *n* оръ́дие, пýшка, пистолéт

guy [гай] *n* човéк, момчé

gypsy [джѝпси] *adj* цѝгански

H

habit [ха́-бит] *n* на́вик

hail [хейл] *n* граду́шка

hair [хе́ър] *n* коса́

hairdresser [хе́ърдре́сър] *n* фризьо́р

half [хаф] *n* полови́на

hall [хол] *n* за́ла, хол

ham [ха-м] *n* шу́нка, бут

hammer [ха́-мър] *n* чук

hand [ха-нд] *n* ръка́, по́черк, часо́вникова
стре́лка; *v* пода́вам, връ́чвам

handkerchief [ха́-ндкърчиф] *n* но́сна кърпа

handle [ха́-ндъл] *n* дръжка, ръчка; *v*
пи́пам, бора́вя управля́вам

handsome [ха́-ндсъм] *adj* ху́бав, ще́дър

hang [ха-нг] *v* вися́, зака́чвам, обе́свам

hanger [ха́-нгър] *n* закача́лка за дре́хи

happen [ха́-пън] *v* слу́чва се, ста́ва,
попа́дам

happiness [ха́-пинис] *n* ща́стие

happy [ха́-пи] *adj* щастли́в, успе́шен

hard [хард] *adj* твъ́рд, кора́в, те́жък,
тру́ден; *adv* си́лно, уси́лено

hardware [ха́рдуеър] *n* железари́я

harm [харм] *n* вреда́; *v* увре́ждам, вредя́

harmful [ха́рмфул] *adj* вре́ден

harmless [ха́рмлис] *adj* безвре́ден

harvest [ха́рвъст] *n* жътва, реко́лта

hat [ха-т] *n* ша́пка

hate [хейт] *v* мра́зя; *n* омра́за

hatred [хе́йтрид] *n* омра́за

have [ха-в] *v* и́мам, нала́га ми се, тря́бва

he [хи] *pron* той

head [хед] *n* глава́, връх; *v* оглавя́вам, стоя́ начело́ на

headache [хе́дейк] *n* главобо́лие

health [хелт] *n* здра́ве, здравеопа́зване

healthy [хе́лти] *adj* здрав, здравосло́вен

hear [хи́ър] *v* чу́вам, изслу́швам

hearing [хи́ъринг] *n* слух, изслу́шване

heart [харт] *n* сърце́, душа́, ку́па

heat [хийт] *n* горещина́, гняв, разга́р

heater [хи́йтър] *n* нагрева́тел, отопли́тел

heaven [хевн] *n* небе́

heavy [хе́ви] *adj* те́жък, си́лен

heel [хийл] *n* пета́, ток

height [хайт] *n* височина́, възвише́ние

heir [е́ър] *n* насле́дник

hell [хел] *n* ад

hello [хъло́у] *interj* здраве́й, а́ло

help [хелп] *v* пома́гам; *n* по́мощ

hemisphere [хе́мисфиър] *n* полукълбо́

her [хъ] *pron* не́я, не́ин

here [хи́ър] *adv* тук, е́то

hereditary [хире́дитъри] *adj* насле́дствен

heredity [хире́дити] *n* насле́дственост

heritage [хе́ритидж] *n* насле́дство

hero [хи́роу] *n* геро́й

heroic [хирóик] *adj* герои́чен
hesitate [хéзитейт] *v* колеба́я се
hesitation [хéзитéйшън] *n* колеба́ние
hide [хайд] *n* кóжа
high [хай] *adj* висóк, възви́шен, отли́чен, си́лен
hill [хил] *n* хълм, кýпчина пръст
him [хим] *pron* нéго, го
hint [хинт] *n* нáмек; *v* загáтвам
hip [хип] *n* бедрó, ши́пка
hire [хáйър] *v* наéмам
his [хиз] *pron* нéгов
historic [хистóрик] *adj* истори́чески
history [хи́стъри] *n* истóрия
hit [хит] *v* ýдрям, улýчвам; *n* ýдар, успéх
hold [хóулд] *v* държá
hole [хóул] *n* дýпка
holiday [хóлидей] *n* прáзник, вака́нция, óтпуска, почи́вка
hollow [хóлоу] *adj* кух, прáзен, хлътнал; *n* хралýпа, вдлъбнатинá
holy [хóули] *adj* свят, свещéн
home [хóум] *n* дом; *adj* домáшен, вътрешен
homeless [хóумлис] *adj* бездóмен
honest [óнист] *adj* чéстен, откровéн, прям
honesty [óнисти] *n* чéстност, откровéност
honey [хáни] *n* пчéлен мед
honor [óнър] *n* чест, пóчит, отли́чия; *v* почи́там, удостоя́вам

hook [хук] *n* ку́ка, сърп; *v* зака́чвам, хва́щам

hope [хо́уп] *n* наде́жда; *v* надя́вам се

hopeless [хо́уплис] *adj* безнаде́жден

horizon [хъра́йзън] *n* хоризо́нт

horizontal [хо́ризо́нтъл] *adj* хоризонта́лен

horrible [хо́рибл] *adj* ужа́сен

horrify [хо́рифай] *v* ужася́вам

horror [хо́рър] *n* у́жас

horse [хорс] *n* кон, кавале́рия

hose [хо́уз] *n* марку́ч, чора́пи

hospital [хо́спитъл] *n* бо́лница

hospitality [хо́спита́лити] *n* гостоприе́мство

host [хо́уст] *n* домаки́н, стопа́нин

hostile [хо́стайл] *adj* неприя́телски, враждѐбен, вра́жески

hostility [хости́лити] *n* враждѐбност

hot [хот] *adj* горе́щ, лют

hotel [хоуте́л] *n* хоте́л

hour [а́уър] *n* час

hourly [а́урли] *adj* ежеча́сен; *adv* ежеча́сно, все́ки час

house [ха́ус] *n* къ́ща, ка́мара

housewife [ха́усуайф] *n* домаки́ня, стопа́нка

housing [ха́узинг] *n* кварти́ра, жи́лище

how [ха́у] *adv* как

however [хауѐвър] *adv* ка́кто и да е, ко́лкото и; *conj* оба́че, при все това́

human [хю́мън] *adj* чове́шки

humane [хюме́йн] *adj* чове́чен, хума́нен

humanity [хюма́-нити] *n* чове́чество, хума́нност

humid [хюмид] *adj* вла́жен

humidity [хюми́дити] *n* вла́га, вла́жност

humor [хю́мър] *n* ху́мор, настрое́ние

hunger [ха́нгър] *n* глад, си́лно жела́ние

hungry [ха́нгри] *adj* гла́ден

hunt [хънт] *v* тъ́рся, пресле́двам, хо́дя на лов; *n* тъ́рсене, лов

hunter [хъ́нтър] *n* лове́ц

hunting [хъ́нтинг] *n* лов

hurricane [хъ́рикейн] *n* урага́н

hurry [хъ́ри] *v* бъ́рзам; *n* бъ́рзане, бързина́

hurt [хърт] *v* нараня́вам, наскърбя́вам, боля́; *n* бо́лка, ра́на

husband [ха́збънд] *n* съпру́г

hut [хът] *n* коли́ба, хи́жа, бара́ка

hydrogen [ха́йдръджън] *n* водоро́д

hygiene [ха́йджин] *n* хигие́на

hymn [хим] *n* химн

hyphen [ха́йфън] *n* тире́

hypocrisy [хипо́кръси] *n* лицеме́рие

I

I [ай] *pron* аз

ice [айс] *n* лед, сладоле́д

ice—cream [а́йскрийм] *n* сладоле́д

icon [áйкън] *n* икóна, изображéние
idea [áйдиа] *n* идéя, предстáва
ideal [айдѝъл] *adj* идеáлен; *n* идеáл
identity [айдéнтити] *n* самолѝчност,
еднáквост
idiom [ѝдиъм] *n* идиóм, гóвор, нарéчие
idol [áйдъл] *n* ѝдол, божествó
if [иф] *conj* акó, далѝ
ignite [игнáйт] *v* възпламенявам
ignorance [ѝгнърънс] *n* невéжество,
незнáние
ignorant [ѝгнърънт] *adj* невéж, несвéдущ
ignore [игнóр] *v* не зачѝтам, пренебрéгвам
ill [ил] *adj* бóлен, лош
illegal [илѝгъл] *adj* незакóнен,
противозакóнен
illiterate [илѝтърит] *adj* неграмóтен
illness [ѝлнис] *n* бóлест
illustrate [ѝлъстрейт] *v* илюстрѝрам
illustration [ѝлъстрéйшън] *n* илюстрáция,
рисýнка, примéр
image [ѝмидж] *n* óбраз, изображéние
imagination [имá-джинéйшън] *n* въображéние
imagine [имá-джин] *v* предстáвям си,
въобразявам си, предполáгам
immediate [имѝдиът] *adj* незабáвен,
непосрéдствен
immediately [имѝдиътли] *adv* веднáга,
незабáвно

immigrant [и́мигрънт] *n* пресе́лник, имигра́нт

immigration [и́мигре́йшън] *n* пресе́лничество, имигра́ция

immunity [имю́нити] *n* неприкоснове́ност, имуните́т

impatience [импе́йшънс] *n* нетърпе́ние

impatient [импе́йшънт] *adj* нетърпели́в

impetus [и́мпетъс] *n* у́стрем, тла́сък, импу́лс

implication [и́мпликейшън] *n* уча́стие, на́мек

imply [импла́й] *v* зага́твам, наме́квам

import [импо́рт] *v* вна́сям

import [и́мпорт] *n* внос

importance [импо́ртънс] *n* ва́жност, значе́ние

important [импо́ртънт] *adj* ва́жен, значи́телен

impose [импо́уз] *v* нала́гам

impossible [импо́сибл] *adj* невъзмо́жен

impression [импре́шън] *n* отпеча́тък, впечатле́ние

impressive [импре́сив] *adj* внуши́телен

improve [импру́в] *v* подобря́вам

improvement [импру́вмънт] *n* подобре́ние

impulse [и́мпълс] *n* тла́сък, подбу́да

in [ин] *prep* в, у, през

inability [и́нъби́лити] *n* неспосо́бност

incident [и́нсидънт] *n* слу́чка, произше́ствие, епизо́д, инциде́нт; *adj* прису́щ

include [инклу́д] *v* включвам

income [и́нкъм] *n* при́ход, до́ход

incompetent [инко́мпътънт] *adj* некомпете́нтен, неспосо́бен

inconvenience [и́нкънви́ниънс] *n* неудо́бство

inconvenient [и́нкънви́ниънт] *adj* неудо́бен, ненавре́менен

increase [инкри́с] *v* увелича́вам

increase [и́нкрис] *n* увеличе́ние, нара́стване, расте́ж

independence [и́ндипе́ндънс] *n* незави́симост

independent [и́ндипе́ндънт] *adj* незави́сим

index [и́ндекс] *n* указа́тел, и́ндекс

indictment [инда́йтмънт] *n* обвини́телен акт

indifference [инди́фърънс] *n* безразли́чие, равноду́шие

indignant [инди́гнънт] *adj* възмуте́н

indignation [и́ндигне́йшън] *n* възмуще́ние, негодува́ние

individual [и́ндиви́джуъл] *adj* едини́чен, отде́лен; *n* лице́, индиви́д

individuality [и́ндивиджуа́-лити] *n* индивидуа́лност

industry [и́ндъстри] *n* проми́шленост, прилежа́ние

inevitable [ине́витъбл] *adj* неизбе́жен, немину́ем

infant [и́нфънт] *n* бе́бе, дете́

infect [инфе́кт] *v* зарази́вам

infection [инфе́кшън] *n* зара́за, инфе́кция

inflation [инфле́йшън] *n* наду́ване, инфла́ция

influence [и́нфлуънс] *n* влия́ние, въздействие; *v* влия́я, въздействувам

influential [инфлуе́ншъл] *adj* влия́телен

inform [инфо́рм] *v* уведомя́вам, информи́рам

information [инфърме́йшън] *n* све́дения, съобще́ние, информа́ция

innocence [и́нъсънс] *n* неви́нност

innocent [и́нъсънт] *adj* неви́нен

innovation [иноуве́йшън] *n* нововъведе́ние, нова́торство

insane [инсе́йн] *adj* безу́мен, неразу́мен

insanity [инса́-нити] *n* безу́мие, лу́дост

insect [и́нсект] *n* насеко́мо

inside [инса́йд] *n* вътрешност; *adj* вътрешен; *adv* вътре

insist [инси́ст] *v* настоя́вам, наблягам

inspect [инспе́кт] *v* разгле́ждам, инспекти́рам

inspection [инспе́кшън] *n* разгле́ждане, инспекти́ране

inspire [инспа́йър] *v* вдъхвам, внуша́вам, подти́квам

install [инсто́л] *v* настаня́вам, инстали́рам

installation [инстъле́йшън] *n* инстала́ция

installment [инсто́лмънт] *n* вно́ска, част

instead [инсте́д] *adv* вме́сто

instinct [и́нстинкт] *n* инсти́нкт

institute [и́нститют] *n* институ́т; *v*
учредя́вам

institution [инститю́шън] *n* учрежде́ние,
учредя́ване

instruction [инстръ́кшън] *n* обуче́ние,
наставле́ния, директи́ви

instructor [инстръ́ктър] *n* инстру́ктор,
учи́тел

instrument [и́нструмънт] *n* инструме́нт,
оръ́дие

insufficient [инсъфи́шънт] *adj* недоста́тъчен

insulate [и́нсюлейт] *v* изоли́рам

insult [и́нсълт] *n* оби́да, оскърбле́ние

insult [инсъ́лт] *v* оби́ждам, оскърбя́вам

insurance [иншу́ърънс] *n* застрахо́вка

insure [иншу́ър] *v* осигуря́вам, застрахо́вам

intellect [и́нтилект] *n* интеле́кт, ум

intellectual [интиле́кчуъл] *adj* у́мствен,
интелектуа́лен

intelligence [инте́лиджънс] *n*
интелиге́нтност, ум, разузна́ване

intelligent [инте́лиджънт] *adj*
интелиге́нтен, у́мен, сми́слен

intensity [инте́нсити] *n* си́ла, напреже́ние

intensive [инте́нсив] *adj* напре́гнат,
интензи́вен

intention [инте́ншън] *n* намере́ние, цел

interest [и́нтрест] *n* интере́с,
заинтересо́ваност, ли́хва; *v* заинтересу́вам

interesting [и́нтрестинг] *adj* интере́сен

interior [интириър] *n* вътрешност, интериóр

internal [интърнъл] *adj* вътрешен

international [интърнá-шънъл] *adj* международен

interpret [интърприт] *v* превéждам ýстно, тълкýвам

interpreter [интърпритър] *n* преводáч

interrupt [интъръпт] *v* прекъсвам

interruption [интъръпшън] *n* прекъсване

interval [интървъл] *n* промеждýтък, интервáл, пáуза

interview [интървю] *n* интервю; *v* интервюи́рам

intestine [интéстин] *n* червá

intimacy [интимъси] *n* инти́мност

intimate [интимът] *adj* бли́зък, инти́мен

into [инту] *prep* в

introduce [интрадюс] *v* въвéждам, предстáвям, запознáвам

introduction [интрадъкшън] *n* въведéние, ýвод, запознáване

invasion [инвéйжън] *n* нашéствие

invent [инвéнт] *v* изобретя́вам, изми́слям

invention [инвéншън] *n* изобретéние

inventor [инвéнтър] *n* изобретáтел

invest [инвéст] *v* инвести́рам

investment [инвéстмънт] *n* вложéние, инвести́ция

investor [инвéстър] *n* вложи́тел, инвести́тор

invisible [инви́зибл] *adj* неви́дим

invitation [инвитéйшън] *n* покáна
invite [инвáйт] *v* кáня, покáнвам
invoice [инвóйс] *n* фактýра
involve [инвóлв] *v* въвлúчам, замéсвам
iron [áйън] *n* желя́зо, ютúя
irrigate [úригейт] *v* напоя́вам
irrigation [úригéйшън] *n* напоя́ване
island [áйлънд] *n* óстров
isolation [áйсълéйшън] *n* изолáция, уединéние
issue [úшю] *n* резултáт, край, изтúчане, спóрен въпрóс, издáние; *v* издáвам, разбúрам, произлúзам
itch [ич] *n* сърбéж; *v* сърбú ме
ivory [áйвъри] *n* слóнова кост

J

jacket [джá-кит] *n* жакéт, сакó, корá
jail [джейл] *n* затвóр; *v* затвáрям
jam [джа-м] *n* мармалáд, конфитюр; *v* задръствам
January [джá-нюъри] *n* януáри
jaw [джо] *n* чéлюст
jazz [джа-э] *n* джаз
jealous [джéлъс] *adj* ревнúв, завистлúв
jealousy [джéлъси] *n* рéвност, зáвист
jeans [джийнз] *noun pl* панталóни, джúнси, дънки

jet [джет] *n* стру́я; *adj* реакти́вен
Jew [джу] *n* евре́ин
jewel [джу́ъл] *n* скъпоце́нност, бижу́
job [джоб] *n* ра́бота, слу́жба
join [джойн] *v* свъ́рзвам, присъединя́вам
joint [джойнт] *n* ста́ва; *adj* съвме́стен
joke [джо́ук] *n* шега́; *v* шегу́вам се
journal [джъ́рнъл] *n* списа́ние, дне́вник
journalism [джъ́рнълизм] *n* журнали́зъм
journalist [джъ́рнълист] *n* журнали́ст
journey [джъ́рни] *n* пъту́ване, пътеше́ствие
joy [джой] *n* ра́дост
judge [джъдж] *n* съдия́, познава́ч; *v* съдя́,
преценя́вам
judicial [джуди́шъл] *adj* съде́бен
juice [джус] *n* сок
July [джула́й] *n* юли
jump [джъмп] *v* ска́чам; *n* скок
June [джун] *n* юни
jungle [джъ́нгъл] *n* джу́нгла
jury [джу́ри] *n* съде́бни заседа́тели, жу́ри
just [джъст] *adj* справедли́в, ве́рен, то́чен,
заслу́жен; *adv* то́чно, са́мо
justice [джъ́стис] *n* справедли́вост,
правосъ́дие, съдия́

K

keep [кийп] *v* па́зя, държа́, спа́звам,
продължа́вам

key [ки] *n* ключ, клави́ш
kid [кид] *n* дете́; *v* шегу́вам се
kidney [ки́дни] *n* бъбрек
kill [кил] *v* уби́вам
kind [кайнд] *n* вид, сорт, съ́щност; *adj* любе́зен, мил
kindness [ка́йнднис] *n* любе́зност, не́жност
king [кинг] *n* крал, цар
kingdom [ки́нгдъм] *n* кра́лство, ца́рство
kiss [кис] *v* целу́вам; *n* целу́вка
kitchen [ки́чън] *n* ку́хня
knee [ний] *n* коля́но
knife [найф] *n* нож
knob [ноб] *n* то́пка, дръжка
knock [нок] *v* чу́кам, тро́пам; *n* почу́кване, у́дар
know [но́у] *v* зна́я, позна́вам
knowledge [но́лидж] *n* зна́ние, нау́ка

L

label [ле́йбъл] *n* етике́т
laboratory [лъбо́рътъри] *n* лаборато́рия
labor [ле́йбър] *n* труд, ра́бота; *v* тру́дя се
lace [лейс] *n* данте́ла
lack [ла-к] *n* ли́пса, недо́стиг, ну́жда; *v* ли́псва ми
ladder [ла́-дър] *n* стъ́лба
lady [ле́йди] *n* да́ма

lag [ла-г] *v* изоста́вам
lake [лейк] *n* е́зеро
lamb [ла-м] *n* а́гне, а́гнешко месо́
lamp [ла-мп] *n* ла́мпа
land [ла-нд] *n* земя́, су́ша, страна́; *v* приземя́вам се
landscape [ла́-ндскейп] *n* пейза́ж
lane [лейн] *n* але́я, у́личка
language [ла́-нгуидж] *n* ези́к, го́вор
large [лардж] *adj* голя́м, е́дър, ще́дър
last [ласт] *adj* после́ден, ми́нал; *v* тра́я, продължа́вам
lasting [ла́стинг] *adj* тра́ен, продължи́телен
late [лейт] *adj* късен, закъсня́л, поко́ен, би́вш; *adv* късно
latitude [ла́-титюд] *n* геогра́фска ширина́
laugh [лаф] *v* сме́я се; *n* смях
laughter [ла́фтър] *n* смях
laundry [ло́ндри] *n* пера́лня, пране́
lavatory [ла́вътъри] *n* тоале́тна
law [ло] *n* зако́н, пра́во
lawyer [ло́йър] *n* юри́ст, адвока́т
layer [ле́йър] *n* пласт, слой
lazy [ле́йзи] *adj* лени́в, мързели́в
lead [лед] *n* оло́во
lead [лийд] *v* ръково́дя, предво́ждам, во́дя
leader [ли́йдър] *n* вода́ч, вожд, ръководи́тел
leadership [ли́йдършип] *n* вода́чество, ръково́дство

leaf [лийф] *n* лист

lean [лийн] *adj* слаб, мършав; *v* навеждам се, облягам се

learn [лърн] *v* уча, научавам

lease [лийс] *n* наем; *v* наемам

leather [лéдър] *n* обработена кожа

leave [лийв] *v* оставям, напускам, заминавам; *n* отпуска

lecture [лéкчър] *n* лекция; *v* поучавам, мъмря

left [лефт] *adj* ляв

leg [лег] *n* крак, бут, крачол

legal [лúгъл] *adj* законен, юридически

legislation [лéджислéйшън] *n* законодателство

legislature [лéджислейчър] *n* законодателна власт

lemon [лéмън] *n* лимон

lemonade [лéмънейд] *n* лимонада

lend [ленд] *v* давам назаем, придавам

length [ленгт] *n* дължина

lens [ленс] *n* леща

lentil [лéнтил] *n* леща

less [лес] *adj* по-малък; *adv* по-малко *prep* без

lesson [лéсън] *n* урок, поука

let [лет] *v* позволявам, оставям, давам под наем

letter [лéтър] *n* буква, писмо

level [лéвъл] *n* равни́ще, ниво́; *adj*
хоризонта́лен, ра́вен

liberate [ли́бърейт] *v* освобожда́вам

liberation [ли́бърéйшън] *n* освобожде́ние

liberty [ли́бърти] *n* свобода́, во́лност

library [ла́йбръри] *n* библиоте́ка

licence [ла́йсънс] *n* позволе́ние,
разреши́телно

lick [лик] *v* ли́жа, би́я

lid [лид] *n* похлупа́к, капа́к, клепа́ч

lie [лай] *n* лъжа́; *v* лъ́жа

lie [лай] *v* лежа́, прости́рам се

life [лайф] *n* живо́т

lift [лифт] *v* вди́гам

light [лайт] *n* светлина́; *adj* свéтъл, блед

light [лайт] *v* осветя́вам, запа́лвам; *adj* лек

lightning [ла́йтнинг] *n* светка́вица

like [лайк] *adj* подо́бен; *prep* като́; *v*
харéсвам, оби́чам, и́скам, жела́я

limb [лим] *n* кра́йник, клон

line [лайн] *n* ли́ния, черта́, връв, жи́ца,
реди́ца, направле́ние

link [линк] *n* връзка, звено́; *v* свързвам,
съединя́вам

lion [ла́йън] *n* лъв

lip [лип] *n* у́стна; *adj* нейскрен

lipstick [ли́пстик] *n* черви́ло за у́стни

liquid [ли́куид] *n* тéчност; *adj* тéчен

liquor [ли́кър] *n* алкохо́лно питиé

list [лист] *n* спи́сък; *v* пра́вя спи́сък

listen [лисън] *v* слушам
listner [лисънър] *n* слушател
literary [литъръри] *adj* литературен
literature [литръчър] *n* литература
little [литъл] *adj* малък; *adv* малко
live [лив] *v* живея
liver [ливър] *n* черен дроб
load [лоуд] *n* товар; *v* товаря
loan [лоун] *n* заем
lobby [лоби] *n* фоайе
local [лоукъл] *adj* местен
locate [лоукейт] *v* разполагам, намирам мястото
location [лоукейшън] *n* разположение, място
lock [лок] *n* ключалка; *v* заключвам, скопчвам
lodging [лоджинг] *n* квартира, жилище
logic [лоджик] *n* логика
logical [лоджикъл] *adj* логически
lonely [лоунли] *adj* самотен
long [лонг] *adj* дълг
longitude [лонгитюд] *n* географска дължина
look [лук] *v* гледам, изглеждам; *n* поглед, изражение
loose [луус] *adj* свободен, хлабав, нехаен, разхлабен
loosen [лусън] *v* разхлабвам, освобождавам
lose [луз] *v* губя, изгубвам, изпускам
loss [лос] *n* загуба

lot [лот] *n* жре́бий, съдба́, мно́го
loud [ла́уд] *adj* си́лен, гръмогла́сен
love [лъв] *n* любо́в; *v* оби́чам, любя́
lovely [лъ́вли] *adj* ху́бав, прекра́сен
lover [лъ́вър] *n* любо́вник, люби́тел
low [ло́у] *adj* ни́сък, тих, низш, вулга́рен
loyal [ло́йъл] *adj* лоя́лен, ве́рен
luck [лък] *n* късме́т, ща́стие
lucky [лъ́ки] *adj* щастли́в, с късме́т
luggage [лъ́гидж] *n* бага́ж
lunch [лънч] *n* о́бед
lung [лънг] *n* бял дроб
luxury [лъ́кжъри] *n* разко́ш, лукс

M

machine [мъши́йн] *n* маши́на
machinery [мъши́йнъри] *n* маши́ни,
машинари́я, механи́зъм
mad [ма-д] *adj* луд, обезумя́л, вбесе́н
madam [ма́-дъм] *n* госпожа́
madness [ма́-днис] *n* лу́дост
magazine [ма́-гъзи́йн] *n* списа́ние
magic [ма́-джик] *n* маги́я
magnet [ма́-гнит] *n* магни́т
magnetic [магне́тик] *adj* магни́тен,
привлека́телен
mail [мейл] *n* по́ща; *v* изпра́щам по
по́щата

main [мейн] *adj* гла́вен

mainly [ме́йнли] *adv* гла́вно, преди́мно

maintenance [ме́йнтънънс] *n* поддръ́жка, издръ́жка

major [ме́йджър] *n* майо́р, пълноле́тен чове́к

majority [мъджо́рити] *n* болшинство́, мнозинство́, пълноле́тие

make [мейк] *v* пра́вя, произве́ждам

male [мейл] *n* мъж

mammal [ма́-мъл] *n* боза́йник, млекопита́ещо живо́тно

man [ма-н] *n* мъж, чове́к

manage [ма́-нидж] *v* управля́вам, успя́вам, спра́вям се

management [ма́-ниджмънт] *n* ръково́дство, упра́ва

manager [ма́-ниджър] *n* упра́вител, дире́ктор

mankind [ма-нка́йнд] *n* чове́чество, мъже́

manner [ма́-нър] *n* на́чин, държа́не, обно́ски, нра́ви

manual [ма́-нюъл] *adj* ръче́н, физи́чески; *n* наръ́чник

manufacture [ма́-нюфа́кчър] *v* произве́ждам, фабрику́вам; *n* произво́дство

manufacturer [ма́-нюфа́кчърър] *n* фабрика́нт, производи́тел

many [мѐни] *adv* мно́го; *n* мно́жество, голя́м брой

map [ма–п] *n* геогра́фска ка́рта

March [март] *n* март

marine [мърѝйн] *adj* мо́рски; *n* фло́та

mark [марк] *n* бѐлег, следа́, бележка; *v* беле́жа, оценя́вам

market [ма́ркит] *n* паза́р; *v* търгу́вам

marriage [ма́–ридж] *n* жени́тба, сва́тба

marry [ма́–ри] *v* оже́нвам се, омъ́жвам се

mask [маск] *n* ма́ска; *v* маски́рам, прикри́вам

mat [ма–т] *n* рого́зка, покри́вка

match [ма–ч] *n* кибри́т

match [ма–ч] *n* жени́тба, мач; *v* подхо́ждам

material [мътѝриъл] *n* материа́л, плат

maternity [мътъ́рнити] *n* ма́йчинство

mathematics [ма́–тема́–тикс] *n* матема́тика

matter [ма́–тър] *n* вещество́, съ́щност, въпро́с

maximum [ма́–ксимъм] *adj* максима́лен

May [мей] *n* май

may [мей] *v* мо́га, разрешено́, мо́же, не́ка

maybe [мѐйби] *adv* мо́же би

mayor [мѐйър] *n* кмет

meal [мийл] *n* я́дене

mean [мийн] *v* зна́ча, възнамеря́вам, и́скам да ка́жа

meaning [мѝйнинг] *n* значе́ние; *adj* изрази́телен, многозначи́телен

measure [мѐжър] *n* мя́рка; *v* ме́ря, измѐрвам

measurement [мѐжърмънт] *n* мя́рка, разме́ри, измѐрване

meat [мийт] *n* месо́

mechanic [мика́-ник] *n* техни́к, меха́ник

mechanism [мѐкънизм] *n* механи́зъм, апара́т

medal [мѐдъл] *n* меда́л

medical [мѐдикъл] *adj* медици́нски

medicine [мѐдисин] *n* лека́рство, медици́на

medieval [мѐдии́въл] *adj* средновеко́вен

meet [мийт] *v* сре́щам, запозна́вам се

meeting [мѝйтинг] *n* събра́ние, сре́ща

melody [мѐлъди] *n* мело́дия

melon [мѐлън] *n* пъпеш

melt [мелт] *v* топя́, стопя́вам

member [мѐмбър] *n* член

membership [мѐмбършип] *n* чле́нство, чле́нове

memory [мѐмъри] *n* па́мет, спо́мен

mental [мѐнтъл] *adj* у́мствен, психи́чески

mention [мѐншън] *v* спомена́вам; *n* спомена́ване

menu [мѐню] *n* меню́, лист за я́стия

merchandise [мъ́рчъндайс] *n* сто́ка

merchant [мъ́рчънт] *n* търго́вец на е́дро, съдържа́тел на магази́н

mercy [мъ́рси] *n* ми́лост, състрада́ние

merge [мърдж] *v* сме́свам, сли́вам

message [ме́сидж] *n* съобще́ние, посла́ние, ми́сия, поръче́ние

metal [ме́тъл] *n* мета́л

method [ме́тъд] *n* на́чин, спо́соб, ме́тод, систе́ма

microphone [ма́йкръфоун] *n* микрофо́н

middle [ми́дъл] *n* среда́; *adj* сре́ден

midnight [ми́днайт] *n* полуно́щ

mild [майлд] *adj* мек, благ, лек

milk [милк] *n* мля́ко; *v* доя́

million [ми́лиън] *num* милио́н

millionaire [ми́лиънне́ър] *n* милионе́р

mind [майнд] *n* ум, мне́ние; *v* внима́вам, гри́жа се

mine [майн] *n* ми́на; *v* копа́я, мини́рам

miner [ма́йнър] *n* миньо́р

mineral [ми́нъръл] *n* минера́л, ру́да; *adj* минера́лен

minimum [ми́нимъм] *n* ми́нимум

minister [ми́нистър] *n* мини́стър, посла́ник, свеще́ник

ministry [ми́нистри] *n* министе́рство, духо́венство

minute [ми́нит] *n* мину́та, протоко́л на заседа́ние

miracle [ми́ръкъл] *n* чу́до

mirror [ми́рър] *n* огледа́ло

mischief [ми́счиф] *n* па́кост, неми́рство, па́лавост

miserable [ми́зъръбъл] *adj* жа́лък, неща́стен

misery [мизъри] *n* нищета, мизерия, нещастие

miss [мис] *v* пропускам, не улучвам, липсва ми

Miss [мис] *n* госпожица

missing [мисинг] *adj* липсващ, отсъствуващ, загубен

mission [мишън] *n* задача, мисия

mistake [мистейк] *n* грешка; *v* греша, бъркам

Mister [мистър] *n* господин

misunderstand [мисъндърста̀-нд] *v* разбирам погрешно

misunderstanding [мисъндърста̀-ндинг] *n* недоразумение, неразбирателство

mix [микс] *v* смесвам

mixture [миксчър] *n* смес

model [мо̀дъл] *n* образец, модел

modern [мо̀дърн] *adj* нов, съвременен, модерен

modest [мо̀дест] *adj* скромен

modesty [мо̀дисти] *n* скромност, умереност

moist [мойст] *adj* влажен

moisten [мойсън] *v* навлажнявам

moisture [мойсчър] *n* влага, влажност

moment [мо̀умънт] *n* момент, миг

monastery [мо̀нъстри] *n* манастир

Monday [мъ̀нди] *n* понеделник

money [мъ̀ни] *n* пари

monkey [мъ̀нки] *n* маймуна

monopoly [мънóпъли] *n* монопóл

month [мънт] *n* мéсец

monthly [мѝнтли] *adj* мéсечен

monument [мóнюмънт] *n* пáметник

mood [мýуд] *n* настроéние, наклонéние

moon [мýун] *n* лунá, мéсец

moral [мóръл] *adj* нрáвствен, морáлен; *n* поýка

morality [морáлити] *n* морáл, нрáвственост

more [мор] *adj* пóвече

most [мóуст] *adj* нáй-мнóго, пóвечето; *adv* нáй-мнóго

mostly [мóустли] *adv* предѝмно, глáвно

mother [мáдър] *n* мáйка

mother-in-law [мáдър ин ло] *n* свекѝрва, тъща

motion [мóушън] *n* движéние, предложéние

motor [мóутър] *n* мотóр, двигáтел

motorist [мóутърист] *n* автомобилѝст

mountain [мáунтин] *n* планинá

mourn [морн] *v* жалéя, оплáквам

mourning [мóрнинг] *n* скръб, трáур

mouse [мáус] *n* мѝшка

mouth [мáут] *n* устá, ýстие, óтвор

move [мýув] *v* двѝжа, мéстя, вълнýвам, трóгвам; *n* ход, постѝпка

movement [мýувмънт] *n* движéние

movie [мýви] *n* кѝно

much [мач] *adj* голямо колѝчество, мнóго

mud [мъд] *n* кал

multiply [мѐлтиплай] *v* умножа́вам, размножа́вам

murder [мѐрдър] *n* уби́йство; *v* уби́вам

murderer [мѐрдърър] *n* уби́ец

muscle [мѐсъл] *n* му́скул

muscular [мѐскюлър] *adj* му́скулен, му́скулест

museum [мюзи́ъм] *n* музе́й

mushroom [мѐшрум] *n* гѐба

music [мю́зик] *n* му́зика

musical [мю́зикъл] *adj* музика́лен; *n* опере́та

musician [мюзѝшън] *n* музика́нт

must [мъст] *v* тря́бва, длѐжен съм да

mutton [мѐтън] *n* о́внешно месо́

mutual [мю́чуъл] *adj* взаи́мен, общ

my [май] *pron* мой

myself [майсѐлф] *pron* аз самѝят, себе си

N

nail [нѐйл] *n* но́кът, гвозде́й, пиро́н; *v* закова́вам

naive [наѝв] *adj* наѝвен

naked [нѐйкид] *adj* гол

name [нейм] *n* и́ме, репута́ция; *v* нари́чам, назова́вам

narrow [на́-роу] *adj* те́сен, ограниче́н; *v* стеснявам

nation [не́йшън] *n* наро́д, на́ция

national [на́-шънъл] *adj* наро́ден, национа́лен, държа́вен

natural [на́-чуръл] *adj* есте́ствен, приро́ден, вроде́н

nature [не́йчър] *n* приро́да, естество́, хара́ктер

naval [не́йвъл] *adj* фло́тски, мо́рски

navy [не́йви] *n* фло́та, мари́на

near [ни́ър] *prep* близо́ до, при, почти́; *adj* бли́зък; *v* приближа́вам

near-by [ни́ърбай] *adj* набли́зо

nearly [ни́ърли] *adv* почти́

necessary [не́сесъри] *adj* необходи́м, ну́жен

neck [нек] *n* врат, ши́я

necklace [не́клис] *n* огъ́рлица, герда́н

need [нийд] *n* ну́жда; *v* нужда́я се

needle [нийдл] *n* игла́

negative [не́гътив] *adj* отрица́телен; *n* отрица́ние, негати́в

neglect [нигле́кт] *v* пренебре́гвам; *n* пренебреже́ние, небре́жност

negligence [не́глиджънс] *n* небре́жност, немарли́вост

negligent [не́глиджънт] *adj* небре́жен, неха́ен, немарли́в

negro [ни́гроу] *n* не́гър

neighbor [не́йбър] *n* съсе́д, бли́жен

neighborhood [нéйбърхуд] *n* окóлност, махалá

neither [нáйдър] *adv* нúто; *pron* нúто едúният, нúто дрýгият

nephew [нéфю] *n* плéменник

nervous [нъ́рвъс] *adj* нéрвен, раздразнúтелен

nervousness [нъ́рвъснис] *n* нéрвност

nest [нест] *n* гнездó

net [нет] *n* мрéжа; *v* улáвям в мрéжа

network [нéтуърк] *n* мрéжа

neutral [ню́тръл] *adj* неутрáлен

never [нéвър] *adv* нúкога

new [ню] *adj* нов

news [нюз] *n* новинá

newspaper [ню́зпейпър] *n* вéстник

next [нект] *adj* слéдващ, съсéден; *adv* след товá; *prep* до

nice [найс] *adj* хýбав, приятен

niece [нийс] *n* плéменница

night [найт] *n* нощ

nightgown [нáйтгаун] *n* нóщница

nine [найн] *num* дéвет

nineteen [нáйнтийн] *num* деветнáдесет

ninety [нáйнти] *num* деветдесéт

no [нóу] *adj* нúкакъв

noise [нойз] *n* шум; *v* разгласявам

noisy [нóйзи] *adj* шýмен

none [нън] *adj* нúкакъв

nonsense [нóнсънс] *n* глýпости

normal [нóрмъл] *adj* обикновéн, нормáлен
north [норт] *n* сéвер; *adj* сéверен
northern [нóрдърн] *adj* сéверен
nose [нóуз] *n* нос; *v* подýшвам
note [нóут] *n* знак, белéжка, нóта; *v* белéжа, забеля́звам
notebook [нóутбук] *n* тетрáдка
notion [нóушън] *n* идéя, предстáва
noun [нáун] *n* съществи́телно и́ме
novel [нóвъл] *n* ромáн
novelist [нóвълист] *n* романи́ст
November [новéмбър] *n* ноéмври
now [нáу] *adv* сегá
number [нѣмбър] *n* число́, брой, нóмер
numerous [юомъръс] *adj* многобрóен
nun [нън] *n* монахи́ня
nurse [нърс] *n* меди́цинска сестрá
nut [нът] *n* óрех, гáйка
nutrition [нютри́шън] *n* хрáнене, хранá

O

oak [óук] *n* дъб
oath [óут] *n* клéтва
obey [обéй] *v* покоря́вам се, подчиня́вам се
object [óбджикт] *n* предмéт, обéкт, цел, намерéние, допълнéние

object [ъбджéкт] *v* възразявам, противопоставям се

objection [ъбджéкшън] *n* възражéние

obligation [óблигéйшън] *n* задължéние

obligatory [облѝгътъри] *adj* задължѝтелен

obscure [ъбскю́ър] *adj* неясен, смътен, скрит, неизвéстен

obscurity [ъбскю́рити] *n* смътност, неизвéстност

observe [ъбзъ́рв] *v* наблюдáвам, забелязвам, спáзвам

observer [ъбзъ́рвър] *n* наблюдáтел

obtain [ъбтéйн] *v* получáвам, придобѝвам

obvious [óбвиъс] *adj* очевѝден, явен

occasion [ъкéйжън] *n* слу́чай, пóвод, причѝна

occasionally [ъкéйжънъли] *adv* понякога, от врéме на врéме

occupation [óкюпéйшън] *n* занимáние, занятие

occupy [óкюпай] *v* заéмам, окупѝрам

occur [ъкъ́р] *v* случвам се, ѝдва ми наум

occurrence [ъкъ́рънс] *n* слу́чка, произшéствие

ocean [óушън] *n* океáн

October [ъктóубър] *n* октóмври

odd [од] *adj* нечéтен, тек, осóбен, стрáнен, случáен

odor [óудър] *n* миризмá, аромáт, репутáция

of [ов] *prep* на, за, с, от

off [оф] *prep* от, на разстоя́ние от, извъ́н

offense [ъфе́нс] *n* наруше́ние, просту́пка, провине́ние, оскърбле́ние

offend [ъфе́нд] *v* оскърбя́вам, дра́зня

offer [о́фър] *v* предла́гам; *n* предложе́ние

office [о́фис] *n* слу́жба, длъжност, канто́ра

official [ъфи́шъл] *adj* служе́бен, официа́лен; *n* служи́тел

often [о́фън] *adv* че́сто

oil [ойл] *n* ма́сло, петро́л

O.K. [оуке́й] *adv* добре́; *adj* пра́вилен, в изпра́вност

old [о́улд] *adj* стар, дре́вен

olive [о́лив] *n* масли́на

omission [оми́шън] *n* изпу́скане, про́пуск

omit [оми́т] *v* пропу́скам, изпу́щам

on [он] *prep* на, върху́, по, в, за, от

once [уа́нс] *adv* веднъ́ж, еди́н път, ня́кога

one [уа́н] *adj* еди́н, еди́нствен; *n* чове́к

onion [ъ́ниън] *n* лук

only [о́унли] *adj* еди́нствен; *adv* са́мо, еди́нствено

open [о́упън] *adj* отво́рен, откри́т; *v* отва́рям, откри́вам

opener [о́упънър] *n* отвара́чка

openly [о́упънли] *adv* откри́то, открове́но

opera [о́упъра] *n* о́пера

operation [о́пъре́йшън] *n* де́йствие, опера́ция

operator [о́пърейтър] *n* меха́ник, опера́тор
opinion [ъпи́ниън] *n* мне́ние
opponent [ъпо́унънт] *n* проти́вник
opportunity [о́пъртю́нити] *n* възмо́жност, удо́бен слу́чай
oppose [ъпо́уз] *v* противопоста́вям, противоде́йствувам
opposite [о́пъзит] *adj* противополо́жен, насре́щен, обра́тен
opposition [о́пъзи́шън] *n* противоде́йствие, съпротивле́ние
oppression [ъпре́шън] *n* поти́скане, гнет
oppressive [ъпре́сив] *adj* поти́скащ, гнетя́щ
oppressor [ъпре́сър] *n* поти́сник, тира́нин
optimism [о́птимизм] *n* оптими́зъм
or [ор] *conj* или́
oral [о́ръл] *adj* у́стен
orange [о́риндж] *n* портока́л; *adj* ора́нжев
orchestra [о́ркистра] *n* орке́стър
order [о́рдър] *n* ред, наре́ждане, за́повед, поръ́чка; *v* запове́двам, поръ́чвам
ordinary [о́динъри] *adj* обикнове́н, всекидне́вен
ore [ор] *n* ру́да
organ [о́ргън] *n* о́рган
organic [орга́-ник] *adj* органи́чен, органи́чески
organism [о́ргънизм] *n* органи́зъм
organization [о́ргънайзе́йшън] *n* организа́ция
organize [о́ргънайз] *v* организи́рам

origin [о́риджин] *n* про́изход, и́зточник, нача́ло

original [ори́джинъл] *adj* първонача́лен, оригина́лен, самоби́тен

ornament [о́рнъмънт] *n* украше́ние, орна́мент

orphan [о́рфън] *n* сира́к

orthodox [о́ртъдокс] *adj* праворе́рен, общоприе́т, правосла́вен

other [а́дър] *adj* друг

our [а́уър] *pron* наш

ourselves [ауърсе́лвз] *pron* ни́е сами́те

out [а́ут] *prep* вън, навън

outer [а́утър] *adj* вътешен

outline [а́утлайн] *n* очерта́ние, конту́ри; *v* скици́рам

output [а́утпут] *n* произво́дство, проду́кция

outside [а́утса́йд] *n* въшна страна́, въшност; *adj* въшен; *adv* отвън, навън

oval [о́увъл] *adj* елипсови́ден, о́бъл

oven [ъ́вън] *n* пещ, фу́рна

over [о́увър] *adv* наго́ре, по́вече; *prep* над, през, из, по, за, свръх

overlook [о́увърлу́к] *v* надзира́вам, недогле́ждам

owe [о́у] *v* дължа́

owner [о́унър] *n* со́бственик

ownership [о́унършип] *n* со́бственост, притежа́ние

oxide [о́ксайд] *n* о́кис
oxygen [о́ксиджън] *n* кислоро́д

P

pace [пейс] *n* кра́чка, върве́ж, ско́рост, темп; *v* вървя́, кра́ча
pack [па-к] *n* паке́т, вързо́п, глу́тница; *v* опако́вам
page [пейдж] *n* страни́ца
pain [пейн] *n* бо́лка, мъ́ка
painful [пе́йнфул] *adj* боле́знен, мъчи́телен
paint [пейнт] *n* боя́; *v* боя́дисвам, рису́вам
painter [пе́йнтър] *n* худо́жник, бояджи́я
painting [пе́йнтинг] *n* живопи́с, рису́нка, карти́на
pair [пе́ър] *n* чифт, дво́йка; *v* чифто́свам
pal [па-л] *n* прия́тел
palace [па́-лъс] *n* дворе́ц, пала́т
pale [пейл] *adj* бле́ден
palm [палм] *n* длан, па́лма
pan [па-н] *n* тига́н, тава́, те́нджера
panic [па́-ник] *n* па́ника; *v* паники́освам
pants [па-нтс] *noun pl* панталони́
paper [пе́йпър] *n* харти́я, докуме́нт, ве́стник, докла́д, сту́дия
paradise [па́-ръдайс] *n* рай
paragraph [па́-ръграф] *n* парагра́ф, нов ред, алине́я

parallel [па-рълел] *adj* успореден; *n* паралел *v* сравнявам

paralysis [пърáлисис] *n* парализа, парализиране

parcel [пáрсъл] *n* пакéт, колéт; *v* пакетирам, разделям

pardon [пáрдън] *n* прóшка, извинéние; *v* прощáвам

parent [пéрънт] *n* родител

park [парк] *n* парк; *v* гарирам

parliament [пáрлъмънт] *n* парламéнт

parrot [пá-рът] *n* папагáл

part [парт] *n* част, дял, рóля, странá; *v* деля, разделям

participant [партисипънт] *n* учáстник

participate [партисипейт] *v* учáствувам

participation [партисипéйшън] *n* учáстие

particular [пъртикюлър] *adj* чáстен, специáлен, осóбен; *n* подрóбност

particularly [пъртикюлъли] *adv* осóбено, специáлно, подрóбно

partner [пáртнър] *n* партньóр, съдрýжник

party [пáрти] *n* грýпа, пáртия, странá, забáва

pass [пас] *v* минáвам, подáвам, прокáрвам; *n* прóход

passenger [пá-сънджър] *n* пътник, пасажéр

passion [пá-шън] *n* страст

passport [пáспърт] *n* паспóрт

past [паст] *n* ми́нало; *adj* ми́нал; *adv* край, покра́й, след

patch [па–тч] *n* кръпка, петно́; *v* кърпя

patent [пе́йтънт] *n* пате́нт

path [пат] *n* пъте́ка, път

patience [пе́йшънс] *n* търпе́ние

patient [пе́йшънт] *n* пацие́нт; *adj* търпели́в

patriot [пе́йтриът] *n* патрио́т

pause [поз] *n* па́уза; *v* спи́рам

pavement [пе́йвмънт] *n* пава́ж, тротоа́р

pay [пей] *v* пла́щам; *n* запла́та, запла́щане

pea [пий] *n* грах

peace [пийс] *n* мир, поко́й, споко́йствие

peaceful [пи́йсфул] *adj* ми́рен, тих, споко́ен, миролюби́в

peach [пийч] *n* пра́сковa

peak [пийк] *n* връх

peanut [пи́йнът] *n* фъстък

pear [пе́ър] *n* кру́ша

pearl [пърл] *n* пе́рла, би́сер

peasant [пе́зънт] *n* се́лянин

pedestrian [педе́стриън] *n* пешехо́дец

peel [пийл] *v* бе́ля, обе́лвам; *n* кора́

pen [пен] *n* перо́, писа́лка

penalty [пе́нълти] *n* наказа́ние, са́нкция

pencil [пе́нсъл] *n* мо́лив

peninsula [пини́нсюла] *n* полуостров

people [пи́пъл] *n* хо́ра, наро́д; *v* населя́вам

pepper [пе́пър] *n* пипе́р, чу́шка

percent [пърсе́нт] *n* проце́нт, на сто

perception [пърсéпшън] *n* възприемане, възприятие

perfect [пъ́рфект] *adj* съвършéн, цял, завършен

perfect [пърфéкт] *v* усъвършéнствувам

perform [пърфóрм] *v* изпълня́вам, извършвам

performance [пърфóрмънс] *n* изпълнéние, представлéние

performer [пъфóрмър] *n* изпълни́тел

perfume [пъ́рфюм] *n* парфю́м

perhaps [пъха́-пс] *adv* мóже би

period [пи́ридд] *n* периóд, тóчка

permanent [пъ́рмънънт] *adj* постоя́нен

permission [пърми́шън] *n* разрешéние

permit [пърми́т] *v* разреша́вам, позволя́вам

permit [пъ́рмит] *n* позволи́телно

persecute [пъ́рсикют] *v* преслéдвам

persecution [пърсикю́шън] *n* преслéдване

person [пъ́рсън] *n* лицé, човéк

personal [пъ́рсънъл] *adj* ли́чен

personality [пърсъна́лити] *n* ли́чност

personnel [пърсънéл] *n* персона́л, ли́чен съста́в

persuade [пърсуéйд] *v* убежда́вам, приду́мвам, скла́ням

pet [пет] *n* любúмо живóтно, гáленик

phase [фейз] *n* фáза

phenomenon [фенóмънън] *n* явлéние

philosopher [филóсъфър] *n* философ

philosophy [филóсъфи] *n* филосóфия
photograph [фóутъграф] *n* снѝмка
photographer [фътóгръфър] *n* фотогрáф
photography [фътóгръфи] *n* фотогрáфия
phrase [фрейз] *n* фрáза; *v* изразя́вам с
дýми
physician [физѝшън] *n* лéкар
physics [фѝзикс] *n* фѝзика
pianist [пѝънист] *n* пианѝст
piano [пиáноу] *n* пиáно
pick [пик] *v* берá, избѝрам, крадá
picnic [пѝкник] *n* ѝзлет; *v* прáвя ѝзлет
picture [пѝкчър] *n* картѝна, снѝмка, кѝно;
v престáвям, изобразя́вам
pie [пай] *n* плóдов сладкѝш, пай
piece [пийс] *n* парчé, къс, част
pig [пиг] *n* прасé, свиня́
pile [пайл] *n* куп, клáда; *v* трýпам,
натрýпвам
pill [пил] *n* хáпче
pillow [пѝлоу] *n* възглáвница
pilot [пáйлът] *n* пилóт; *v* пилотѝрам
pin [пин] *n* топлѝйка, карфѝца; *v*
забóждам
pine [пайн] *n* бор
pipe [пайп] *n* трѝбá, свѝрка, лулá
pistol [пѝстъл] *n* пистолéт
pity [пѝти] *n* мѝлост, жáлост, състрадáние
place [плейс] *n* мя́сто, мéстност, къща; *v*
постáвям, настаня́вам

plain [плейн] *adj* я́сен, прост, обикнове́н; *n* равнина́

plan [пла-н] *n* план; *v* плани́рам

plane [плейн] *n* пло́скост, самоле́т; *adj* пло́сък, ра́вен

plant [плант] *n* расте́ние, заво́д; *v* садя́, поста́вям

plastic [пла́стик] *adj* пласти́чен, от пла́стмаса; *n* пла́стмаса

plateau [пла́тоу] *n* плато́

play [плей] *v* игра́я, свиря́; *n* игра́, пие́са

player [пле́йър] *n* игра́ч, актьо́р, свира́ч

playground [пле́йграунд] *n* игри́ще

pleasant [пле́зънт] *adj* прия́тен

please [плийз] *v* задоволя́вам, ра́двам, и́скам, мо́ля

pleasure [пле́жър] *n* удово́лствие, ра́дост

plenty [пле́нти] *n* изоби́лие, мно́го, мно́жество

plot [плот] *n* къс земя́, за́говор; *v* загово́рнича

plug [плъг] *n* запуша́лка, ще́псел; *v* запу́швам

plum [плъм] *n* сли́ва

plumber [плъ́мър] *n* водопрово́дчик

plural [плу́ръл] *adj* мно́жествен; *n* мн. число́

plus [плъс] *prep* плюс

pneumonia [нюмо́униъ] *n* пневмо́ния

pocket [пóкит] *n* джоб; *v* слáгам в джóба си

poem [пóуем] *n* стихотворéние, поéма

poet [пóует] *n* поéт

poetry [пóуетри] *n* поéзия

point [пойнт] *n* тóчка, връх, цел, същинá; *v* посóчвам, сóча

poison [пóйзън] *n* отрóва; *v* отрáвям, трóвя

poisonous [пóйзънъс] *adj* отрóвен

police [пълѝйс] *n* полѝция

policeman [пълѝйсмън] *n* полицáй

policy [пóлиси] *n* полѝтика, полѝца

polish [пóлиш] *v* изглáждам, полѝрам; *n* бóя, лак

polite [пълáйт] *adj* учтѝв, изѝскан

political [пълѝтикъл] *adj* полѝтически

politician [пóлитѝшън] *n* полѝтик

politics [пóлитикс] *n* полѝтика

poll [пóул] *n* брой на гласовéте; *v* гласýвам

pollute [пълю́т] *v* замърсявам, поквáрям

pollution [пълю́шън] *n* замърсявáне

pool [пýул] *n* басéйн, вир, лóква

poor [пýър] *adj* бéден, недостáтъчен

pope [пóуп] *n* пáпа

popular [пóпюлър] *adj* нарóден, популярен

popularity [пóпюла-рити] *n* популярност

population [пóпюлéйшън] *n* населéние

pork [порк] *n* свѝнско месó

port [порт] *n* пристáнище

portable [пóртъбл] *adj* портати́вен
portrait [пóртрит] *n* портре́т
pose [пóуз] *v* пози́рам, поста́вям; *n* пóза, престру́вка
position [пъзи́шън] *n* положе́ние, пози́ция, дли́жност
positive [пóзитив] *adj* положи́телен, си́гурен
possess [пъзéс] *v* притежа́вам, владе́я
possession [пъзéшън] *n* притежа́ние, владе́ние
possibility [пóсиби́лити] *n* възмо́жност
possible [пóсибл] *adj* възмо́жен
post [пóуст] *n* пост, дли́жност; *v* поста́вям
post [пóуст] *n* пóща; *v* изпра́щам по пóщата
poster [пóустър] *n* афи́ш, плака́т
pot [пот] *n* те́нджера, съд, сакси́я
potato [пътéйтоу] *n* карто́ф
pottery [пóтъри] *n* грънча́рство, грънци́, кера́мика
poultry [пóултри] *n* дома́шни пти́ци
pound [па́унд] *v* би́я, у́дрям
pour [пор] *v* нали́вам, ле́я се
poverty [пóвърти] *n* бе́дност
powder [па́удър] *n* прах, пу́дра, бару́т
power [па́уър] *n* си́ла, власт, ене́ргия
powerful [па́уърфул] *adj* могъщ, си́лен, мóщен

practical [пра́-ктикъл] *adj* практи́чен,
практи́чески

practice [пра́-ктис] *n* пра́ктика, обича́й

practise [пра́-ктис] *v* практику́вам,
упражня́вам се

pray [прей] *v* мо́ля

prayer [пре́йър] *n* моли́тва

preach [прийч] *v* пропове́двам,
препоръ́чвам

precaution [прико́ушън] *n* предпа́зна мя́рка

precinct [при́синкт] *n* полице́йски уча́стък

precise [приса́йс] *adj* то́чен, преци́зен

precision [приси́жън] *n* то́чност, преци́зност

predecessor [при́дисе́сър] *n* предше́ственик

predict [приди́кт] *v* предска́звам

prediction [приди́кшън] *n* предсказа́ние

prefer [прифъ́р] *v* предпочи́там

preference [пре́фърънс] *n* предпочита́ние

pregnant [пре́гнънт] *adj* бре́менна

prejudice [пре́джудис] *n* предубежде́ние,
предразсъ́дък

preliminary [прили́минъри] *adj*
предвари́телен, подготви́телен

preparation [пре́пъре́йшън] *n* подгото́вка,
препара́т

preparatory [припа́-ръту́ри] *adj*
подготви́телен, предвари́телен

prepare [припе́ър] *v* приго́твям, подго́твям

preposition [пре́пъзи́шън] *n* предло́г

prescribe [прискра́йб] *v* предпи́свам

prescription [прискри́пшън] *n* предписа́ние, реце́пта

presence [пре́зънс] *n* присъствие, вид, външност

present [пре́зънт] *adj* присъствуващ, настоя́щ; *n* пода́рък

present [призе́нт] *v* предста́вям, подаря́вам

preservation [пре́зървéйшън] *n* запа́зване

preserve [призъ́рв] *v* запа́звам, консерви́рам; *n* конфитю́р

presidency [пре́зидънси] *n* председа́телство

president [пре́зидънт] *n* председа́тел, президе́нт

press [прес] *n* пре́са; *v* пресо́вам, прити́скам, гла́дя

pressure [пре́шър] *n* на́тиск, наля́гане

pretend [прите́нд] *v* претенди́рам, престру́вам се

pretext [при́текст] *n* прете́кст, предло́г

pretty [при́ти] *adj* ху́бав, прия́тен; *adv* до́ста

prevent [приве́нт] *v* предотвратя́вам, осуетя́вам, пре́ча

prevention [приве́ншън] *n* предотвратя́ване

previous [при́виъс] *adj* преди́шен, предвари́телен

prey [прей] *n* пля́чка, же́ртва; *v* крада́, огра́бвам

price [прайс] *n* цена́

pride [прайд] *n* го́рдост, себелюбие

priest [прийст] *n* свеще́ник

primary [пра́ймъри] *adj* първонача́лен, гла́вен

primitive [при́митив] *adj* първоби́тен, примити́вен

prince [принс] *n* принц

princess [при́нсес] *n* принце́са

principal [при́нсипъл] *adj* гла́вен; *n* дире́ктор

principle [при́нсипъл] *n* при́нцип

print [принт] *n* печа́т, отпеча́тък, шрифт, басма́; *v* печа́там, щампо́свам

printer [при́нтър] *n* печата́р

priority [прайо́рити] *n* преди́мство

prison [при́зън] *n* затво́р

prisoner [при́зънър] *n* затво́рник

private [пра́йвит] *adj* ча́стен, ли́чен; *n* войни́к, ре́дник

privately [пра́йвътли] *adv* та́йно, повери́телно, насаме́

privilege [при́вилидж] *n* привиле́гия

prize [прайз] *n* награ́да, пре́мия; *v* ценя́

probability [про́бъби́лити] *n* вероя́тност

probable [про́бъбл] *adj* вероя́тен

problem [про́блъм] *n* въпро́с, пробле́м, зада́ча

procedure [проуси́джър] *n* процеду́ра

proceed [проуси́йд] *v* продължа́вам, напре́двам

process [про́усес] *n* проце́с; *v* обрабо́твам

produce [пръдю́с] *v* произве́ждам, предста́вям, причиня́вам

producer [пръдю́сър] *n* производи́тел, режисьо́р

product [про́дъкт] *n* произведе́ние, проду́кт

production [пръдъ́кшън] *n* произво́дство, постано́вка

profession [профе́шън] *n* профе́сия

professional [профе́шънъл] *adj* професиона́лен

professor [пръфе́сър] *n* профе́сор

profile [про́уфайл] *n* про́фил

profit [про́фит] *n* печа́лба, изго́да; *v* извли́чам печа́лба

profitable [про́фитъбл] *adj* изго́ден, до́ходен

program [про́уграм] *n* програ́ма

progress [про́угрес] *n* напре́дване, напре́дък, прогре́с

progress [проугре́с] *v* напре́двам

prohibit [проухи́бит] *v* забраня́вам, пре́ча

project [проудже́кт] *v* проекти́рам, хвърлям, изпъквам

project [про́уджект] *n* издатина́, проже́кция

prominent [про́минънт] *adj* изда́ден, забележи́телен, ви́ден

promise [про́мис] *n* обеща́ние; *v* обеща́вам

promising [про́мисинг] *adj* обеща́ващ, наде́жден

promote [прємо́ут] *v* повиша́вам,
подпома́гам

promotion [прємо́ушън] *n* повише́ние,
промо́ция

pronoun [про́унаун] *n* местоиме́ние

pronounce [прєна́унс] *v* произна́сям,
обявя́вам

pronunciation [прєнъ̀нсие́йшън] *n*
произноше́ние

proof [пру́уф] *n* доказа́телство,
изпита́ние, коректу́ра; *adj* импрегни́ран

propeller [прєпе́лър] *n* пе́рка, витло́

proper [про́пър] *adj* со́бствен, подходя́щ,
прили́чен

properly [про́пърли] *adv* прили́чно,
подходя́що

property [про́пърти] *n* со́бственост,
сво́йство

proportion [прєпо́ршън] *n* пропо́рция

proposal [прєпо́узъл] *n* предложе́ние

propose [прєпо́уз] *v* предла́гам,
възнамеря́вам

prose [про́уз] *n* про́за

prosecute [про́сикют] *v* продължа́авам,
пресле́двам

prosecution [про́сикю̀шън] *n* съде́бно
пресле́дване

prosper [про́спър] *v* преуспя́вам

prosperity [проспе́рити] *n* благополу́чие,
преуспя́ване

protect [пръте́кт] *v* пазя, закри́лям

protection [пръте́кшън] *n* покрови́телство, закри́ла

protest [проуте́ст] *v* заявя́вам, протести́рам

protest [про́утест] *n* проте́ст

proud [пра́уд] *adj* горд, надме́нен

prove [пру́ув] *v* дока́звам, ока́звам се

proverb [про́връб] *n* посло́вица, погово́рка

provide [пръва́йд] *v* снабдя́вам, предви́ждам

province [про́винс] *n* о́бласт, прови́нция

provincial [пръви́ншъл] *adj* провинциа́лен

provoke [пръво́ук] *v* предизви́квам

public [пъ́блик] *n* обще́ственост, хо́ра, пу́блика; *adj* обще́ствен

publication [пъблике́йшън] *n* публику́ване, публика́ция, изда́ние

publicity [пъбли́сити] *n* гла́сност, рекла́ма

publish [пъ́блиш] *v* публику́вам, изда́вам

publisher [пъ́блишър] *n* изда́тел

pull [пул] *v* дъ́рпам, те́гля

pulse [пълс] *n* пулс; *v* пулси́рам, би́я

pump [пъмп] *n* по́мпа‿ *v* по́мпя

punctual [пъ́нкчуъл] *adj* то́чен

punctuality [пънкчуа́лити] *n* то́чност

puncture [пъ́нкчър] *n* спу́скване на гу́ма; *v* пу́квам

punish [пъ́ниш] *v* нака́звам

punishment [пъ́нишмънт] *n* наказа́ние

pupil [пю́пъл] *n* учени́к

puppet [пъпит] *n* ку́кла
purchase [пъ́рчъс] *v* купу́вам; *n* поку́пка
pure [пю̀р] *adj* чист
purity [пю̀рити] *n* чистота́
purple [пъ́рпъл] *adj* лила́в, мо́рав
purpose [пъ́рпъс] *n* намере́ние, цел
purse [пърс] *n* портмоне́
push [пуш] *v* бу́там, тла́скам; *n* тла́скане
put [пут] *v* сла́гам, поста́вям

Q

qualification [куъ̀лифике́йшън] *n*
квалифика́ция, ограниче́ние
qualify [куо́лифай] *v* квалифици́рам,
определя́м
quality [куо́лити] *n* ка́чество
quantity [куо́нтити] *n* коли́чество
quarrel [куо́ръл] *n* кавга́, сва́да; *v* ка́рам се
queen [куи́йн] *n* цари́ца, крали́ца
question [куе́счън] *n* въпро́с, пробле́м; *v*
разпи́твам, оспо́рвам
quick [куи́к] *adj* бърз, жив, пъргав
quiet [куа́йът] *adj* безшу́мен, тих,
споко́ен; *n* споко́йствие
quit [куи́т] *v* напу́скам, спи́рам
quite [куа́йт] *adv* съвсе́м, напъ́лно
quotation [куоуте́йшън] *n* цита́т
quote [куо́ут] *v* цити́рам, коти́рам

R

rabbit [ра́-бит] *n* за́ек
race [рейс] *n* надбя́гване; *v* надбя́гвам се
race [рейс] *n* ра́са
radiation [рейдие́йшън] *n* излъчване, радиа́ция
radiator [ре́йдиейтър] *n* радиа́тор
radio [ре́йдиоу] *n* ра́дио
rail [рейл] *n* парапе́т, закача́лка, ре́лса
railroad [ре́йлроуд] *n* желе́зница, жп. ли́ния
railway [ре́йлуей] *n* желе́зница, жп. ли́ния
rain [рейн] *n* дъжд; *v* вали́ дъжд
raise [рейз] *v* вди́гам, повиша́вам, отгле́ждам
raisin [ре́йзин] *n* стафи́да
rally [ра́-ли] *n* събра́ние, ми́тинг
random [ра́-ндъм] *n* случа́йност; *adj* случа́ен, произво́лен
rape [рейп] *v* изнаси́лвам; *n* изнаси́лване
rapid [ра́-пид] *adj* бърз, стръ́мен
rare [ре́ър] *adj* ря́дък, необикнове́н
rarity [ре́ърити] *n* ря́дкост, разреде́ност
rash [ра-ш] *n* и́зрив, о́брив
raspberry [ра́збъри] *n* мали́на
rat [ра-т] *n* плъх
rate [рейт] *n* разме́р, сто́йност, ско́рост, сте́пен, съотноше́ние, та́кса

rather [ра́дър] *adv* по–ско́ро, доста́, твъ́рде

ratio [ре́йшиоу] *n* съотноше́ние, пропо́рция

raw [ро] *adj* суро́в, необрабо́тен

razor [ре́йзър] *n* бръсна́ч, самобрисна́чка

reach [рийч] *v* посяга́м, прости́рам, дости́гам; *n* о́бсег

react [риа́–кт] *v* реаги́рам, въздѐйствувам

reaction [риа́–кшън] *n* реа́кция

read [рийд] *v* чета́, у́ча

readiness [ре́динис] *n* гото́вност, охо́та, бързина́

reading [ри́йдинг] *n* че́тене, четиво́, тълкува́ние

ready [ре́ди] *adj* гото́в, скло́нен, бърз, навре́менен

real [ри́ъл] *adj* действи́телен, и́стински

reality [риа́–лити] *n* действи́телност, реа́лност

realize [ри́ълайз] *v* осъществя́вам, разби́рам

really [ри́ъли] *adv* действи́телно, найстина́

reason [ри́йзън] *n* причи́на, основа́ние, ра́зум

receipt [риси́йт] *n* получа́ване, квита́нция, постъпле́ния

receive [риси́йв] *v* получа́вам, прие́мам

recent [ри́сънт] *adj* неотда́внашен, нов, съвре́менен

recipe [ре́сипи] *n* реце́пта, предписа́ние

recipient [риси́пиънт] *n* получа́тел; *adj* възприемчи́в

recognition [рекъгни́шън] *n* разпозна́ване, призна́ние

recognize [ре́къгнайз] *v* разпозна́вам, различа́вам, призна́вам

recommend [рекъме́нд] *v* препоръ́чвам, повери́вам

recommendation [рекъмендейшън] *n* препоръ́ка

record [рико́рд] *v* запи́свам, отбеля́звам

record [ре́къɒд] *n* докуме́нт, реко́рд, грамофо́нна пло́ча

recover [рикъ́въɒ] *v* съвзе́мам се, възвръ́щам си

recovery [рикъ́въɒи] *n* съвзе́мане, възстанови́ване

red [ред] *adj* червѐн

reduce [риди́ɒс] *v* намаля́вам, понижа́вам

reduction [риди́кшън] *n* намаля́ване, съкраще́ние

refer [рифъ́ɒ] *v* отпра́вям, насо́чвам, спомена́вам

referee [рефъри́] *n* ре́фер, съдия́

reference [ре́фъɒънс] *n* спомена́ване, спра́вка

reflection [рифле́кшън] *n* отраже́ние, размишле́ние

reform [рифо́ɒм] *v* преустро́йвам; *n* преобразова́ние, рефо́рма

refresh [рифре́ш] *v* опресня́вам, освежа́вам

refreshment [рифрѐшмънт] *n* освежа́ване, заку́ска

refugee [рѐфюджѝ] *n* бежане́ц, емигра́нт

refund [рифъ́нд] *v* възстановя́вам

refuse [рифю́з] *v* отка́звам

regard [рига́рд] *v* счи́там, уважа́вам

regarding [рига́рдинг] *prep* отно́сно

region [ри́джън] *n* о́бласт, райо́н, сфе́ра

regret [ригре́т] *v* съжаля́вам; *n* съжале́ние, разка́яние

regular [ре́гюлър] *adj* редо́вен, постоя́нен, пра́вилен

regularly [ре́гюлъли] *adv* редо́вно, постоя́нно, съвъ́ршено

rehearsal [рихъ́рсъл] *n* репети́ция

rehearse [рихъ́рс] *v* репети́рам, преповта́рям

reject [риджѐкт] *v* отка́звам, отхвъ́рлям

rejection [риджѐкшън] *n* о́тказ, отхвъ́рляне

relation [риле́йшън] *n* отноше́ние, връ́зка, родни́на

relatively [ре́лътивли] *adv* относи́телно

relax [рила́-кс] *v* отпу́щвам, почи́вам се

relaxation [ри́ла-ксе́йшън] *n* отпу́щане, почи́вка

release [рили́йс] *v* освобожда́вам, пу́скам

reliable [рила́йъбл] *adj* си́гурен, наде́жден

reliance [рила́йнс] *n* дове́рие, упова́ние

relief [рили́йф] *n* облекче́ние, успокое́ние, по́мощ

relieve [рилийв] *v* облекчáвам, подпомáгам, смéням

religion [рилийджън] *n* релѝгия, вя́ра

religious [релѝджъс] *adj* религиóзен, вéрующ

reluctance [рилъ́ктънс] *n* нежелáние, неохóта

reluctant [рилъ́ктънт] *adj* неохóтен, неподатлѝв

rely [рилáй] *v* разчѝтам,ослáням се

remain [римéйн] *v* остáвам, стоя́; *n* остáнки, развалинѝ

remark [римáрк] *v* забеля́звам; *n* забелéжка

removal [римýвъл] *n* премéстване, отстраня́ване, уволня́ване

remove [римýв] *v* премéствам, отстраня́вам, уволня́вам

renew [риню́] *v* подновя́вам, възобновя́вам

renewal [риню́ъл] *n* подновя́ване, възобновя́ване

rent [рент] *n* нáем, рéнта; *v* наéмам, дáвам под нáем

repair [рипéър] *v* попрáвям

repeat [рипѝйт] *v* повтáрям, рецитѝрам

repetition [рéпитишън] *n* повторéние

replace [риплéйс] *v* възтановя́вам, замéням

reply [риплáй] *v* отговáрям, отвръ́щам; *n* óтговор

report [рипóрт] *v* съобщáвам, доклáдвам; *n* доклáд, гръм

reporter [рипо́ртър] *n* до́писник, репортьо́р

represent [ре́призе́нт] *v* предста́вям, представля́вам, опи́свам

representative [ре́призе́нтатив] *n* предста́вител

reproduce [ри́пръдю́с] *v* възпроизве́ждам

reproduction [ри́пръдъ́кшън] *n* възпроизве́ждане, репроду́кция

reptile [ре́птайл] *n* влечу́го

republic [рипъ́блик] *n* репу́блика

republican [рипъ́бликън] *n* република́нец

reputation [ре́пютейшън] *n* и́ме, репута́ция

request [рикуе́ст] *n* и́скане, молба́, тъ́рсене; *v* изи́сквам

require [рикуа́йър] *v* и́скам, изи́сквам, нужда́я се

requirement [рикуа́йърмънт] *n* изи́скване, ну́жда

research [рисъ́рч] *n* изсле́дване, проу́чване; *v* проу́чвам

reserve [ризъ́рв] *v* запа́звам; *n* запа́с, сдъ́ржаност

reside [риза́йд] *v* живе́я, пребива́вам

residence [ре́зидънс] *n* местожи́телство, резиде́нция

resident [ре́зидънт] *n* жи́тел

residential [ре́зиде́ншъл] *adj* жи́лищен

resign [риза́йн] *v* изли́зам в оста́вка, оттегля́м се

resignation [резигнейшън] *n* оставка, примирение

resist [ризист] *v* съпротивлявам се, устоявам

resistance [ризистънс] *n* съпротива, отпор

respect [риспект] *n* уважение, отношение; *v* почитам

respectability [риспектъбилити] *n* почтеност

respectable [риспектъбл] *adj* почтен, приличен

respective [риспектив] *adj* съответен

respiration [респирейшън] *n* дишане

respond [риспонд] *v* отговарям, реагирам

response [риспонс] *n* отговор, отзив

responsibility [риспонсибилити] *n* отговорност

responsible [риспонсибл] *adj* отговорен

rest [рест] *n* почивка, покой; *v* почивам

rest [рест] *n* остатък

restaurant [рестъран] *n* ресторант

restrict [ристрикт] *v* ограничавам

restriction [ристрикшън] *n* ограничение

result [ризълт] *v* последвам, произтичам; *n* последица, резултат

retail [ритейл] *n* продажба на дребно

retire [ритайър] *v* оттеглям, излизам в оставка

retired [ритайърд] *adj* пенсиониран

retirement [ритайърмънт] *n* оставка, оттегляне

return [ритѐрн] *v* връщам; *n* връщане

revenge [ривѐндж] *v* отмъщавам; *n* отмъщение

revenue [рѐвиню] *n* приход, постъпления

review [ривю̀] *v* разглеждам, рецензирам; *n* преглед, рецензия

revise [ривайз] *v* преглеждам, поправям

revolution [рѐвълюшън] *n* въртене, революция

reward [риуо́рд] *n* награда; *v* възнаграждавам

rhyme [райм] *n* рима, стихотворение

rib [риб] *n* ребро

ribbon [рибън] *n* панделка, лента

rice [райс] *n* ориз

rich [рич] *adj* богат, разкошен

richness [ричнис] *n* богатство

rid [рид] *v* освобождавам, избавям

ride [райд] *v* яздя, возя се

rifle [райфъл] *n* пушка

right [райт] *adj* прав, верен, десен; *n* дясно; *adv* вярно, право

ring [ринг] *n* пръстен, ринг, кръг; *v* звъня

rise [райз] *v* ставам, издигам се, изгрявам

risk [риск] *n* опасност, риск; *v* рискувам

risky [риски] *adj* опасен, рискован

rival [райвъл] *n* съперник, конкурент; *v* съпернича, конкурирам

rivalry [райвълри] *n* съперничество

river [ривър] *n* река

road [ро́уд] *n* шосе́, път

roast [ро́уст] *v* пека́; *n* пе́чено месо́

rob [роб] *v* гра́бя, огра́бвам

robber [ро́бър] *n* кра́дец

robbery [ро́бъри] *n* грабе́ж

rock [рок] *n* скала́, канара́

rocket [ро́кит] *n* раке́та

rodent [ро́удънт] *n* гриза́ч

role [ро́ул] *n* ро́ля

Roman [ро́умън] *adj* ри́мски

romance [роума́-нс] *n* рома́нтика, рома́нс

romantic [роума́-нтик] *adj* романти́чен

roof [ру́уф] *n* по́крив, подсло́н

room [ру́ум] *n* ста́я, мя́сто

rooster [ру́стър] *n* пете́л

root [ру́ут] *n* ко́рен

rope [ро́уп] *n* въже́

rose [ро́уз] *n* ро́за; *adj* ро́зов

rot [рот] *n* гни́ене; *v* гни́я

rotate [роуте́йт] *v* въртя́

rotation [роуте́йшън] *n* върте́не, кръговра́т

rough [ръф] *adj* груб, бу́рен, необрабо́тен

round [ра́унд] *adj* кръгъл; *n* кръг, обико́лка, тур *v* закръгля́м; *prep* зад, о́коло

route [рут] *n* път, маршру́т

row [ро́у] *n* реди́ца, ред

royal [ро́йъл] *adj* кра́лски, великоле́пен

royalty [ро́йълти] *n* кра́лска осо́ба, а́вторски хонора́р

rub [ръб] *v* трия, търкам

rubber [ръбър] *n* гума, каучук

rubbish [ръбиш] *n* боклук, смет, глупости

rude [руд] *adj* груб, неучтив

rug [ръг] *n* килим

ruin [руин] *v* разрушавам, разорявам; *n* гибел, развалина

rule [рул] *v* управлявам, решавам; *n* правило, власт

ruler [рулър] *n* владетел, линия

rum [ръм] *n* ром

rumor [румър] *n* слух, мълва; *v* пръскам слух

run [рън] *v* тичам, движа се

runner [рънър] *n* бегач, пратеник

rural [рурал] *adj* селски

rush [ръш] *v* втурвам се, спускам се, прибързвам, нахлувам

rust [ръст] *v* ръждясвам; *n* ръжда

rusty [ръсти] *adj* ръждясел, ръждив, извехтял

S

sack [са-к] *n* чувал *v* уволнявам

sacred [сейкрид] *adj* свещен

sad [са-д] *adj* тъжен, мрачен

safe [сейф] *adj* невредим, сигурен; *n* сейф

safety [сейфти] *n* сигурност, безопасност

sail [сейл] *n* корабно платно, морско пътуване; *v* пътувам по море

sailor [сейлър] *n* моряк

saint [сейнт] *n* светец

salad [са-лъд] *n* салата

salary [са-лъри] *n* заплата

sale [сейл] *n* продажба

salesman [сейлэмън] *n* продавач

salt [солт] *n* сол; *v* посолявам

salty [солти] *adj* солен

same [сейм] *adj* същ

sample [са-мпл] *n* мостра; *v* изпробвам

sanction [са-нкшън] *n* одобрение, санкция; *v* одобрявам

sand [са-нд] *n* пясък

sandal [са-ндъл] *n* сандал

sandwich [са-ндуич] *n* сандвич; *v* притискам

sanitation [са-нитейшън] *n* здравеопазване

Santa Claus [санта клоз] *n* Дядо Мраз

sarcasm [сарка-эм] *n* сарказъм

satire [са-тайър] *n* сатира

satisfaction [са-тисфа-кшън] *n* задоволство, удовлетворение

satisfactory [са-тисфа-ктъри] *adj* задоволителен

satisfy [са-тисфай] *v* задоволявам, убеждавам

Saturday [са-търди] *n* събота

saucer [со́усър] *n* чини́йка за ча́ша

sausage [со́сидж] *n* сала́м, наде́ница

save [сейв] *v* спася́вам, спестя́вам; *prep* осве́н

saving [се́йвинг] *adj* пестели́в; *n* спестя́вания

say [сей] *v* ка́звам

scale [скейл] *n* мащаб, ска́ла, везни́

scandal [ска́-ндъл] *n* сканда́л, клю́ка

scandalize [ска́-ндълайз] *v* шоки́рам

scare [ске́ър] *v* пла́ша; *n* па́ника

scene [сийн] *n* сце́на, гле́дка

scenery [си́йнъри] *n* деко́ри, приро́да

sceptic [ске́птик] *n* скепти́к

school [скул] *n* учи́лище, шко́ла; *v* обуча́вам

schoolboy [ску́лбой] *n* учени́к

schoolgirl [ску́лгърл] *n* учени́чка

science [са́йънс] *n* нау́ка

scientific [са́йънти́фик] *adj* нау́чен

scientist [са́йънтист] *n* у́чен

scissors [си́зърс] *noun pl* но́жици

score [скор] *n* сме́тка, резулта́т, музика́лна партиту́ра

scratch [скра-ч] *v* дра́скам; *n* драскоти́на

scream [скрийм] *v* пи́скам; *n* пи́сък

screen [скрийн] *n* параван, екра́н

screw [скру] *n* винт, витло́; *v* зави́нтам

sculptor [скъ́лптър] *n* ску́лптор

sculpture [скъ́лпчър] *v* ва́я; *n* скулпту́ра

sea [сий] *n* море
seal [сийл] *n* печа́т, тюле́н; *v* запеча́тавам
search [сърч] *v* тъ́рся; *n* тъ́рсене, претъ́рсване
season [си́йзън] *n* сезо́н, годи́шно вре́ме; *v* подпра́вям
seat [сийт] *n* мя́сто, седа́лище
second [се́кънд] *a* вто́ри; *n* секу́нда
secret [си́крит] *adj* та́ен; *n* та́йна
secretary [се́кръттъри] *n* секрета́р
seduce [сидю́с] *v* прелъстя́вам, привли́чам
see [сий] *v* ви́ждам, разби́рам
seed [сийд] *n* се́ме
seek [сийк] *v* тъ́рся, ди́ря
seem [сийм] *v* изгле́ждам
select [силе́кт] *v* подби́рам
selection [силе́кшън] *n* подбо́р, селе́кция
self [селф] *pron* сам, се́бе си
selfish [се́лфиш] *adj* егоисти́чен
selfishness [се́лфишнис] *n* егои́зъм
sell [сел] *v* прода́вам, изма́мвам
senate [се́нит] *n* сена́т
senator [се́нътър] *n* сена́тор
send [сенд] *v* изпра́щам
senior [си́ниър] *adj* стар, ста́рши
sensation [сенсе́йшън] *n* усе́щане, сенза́ция
sensational [сенсе́йшънъл] *adj* сензацио́нен
sense [сенс] *n* чу́вство, сетиво́, ра́зум, значе́ние
sensible [се́нсъбл] *adj* разу́мен

sentence [сѐнтънс] *n* изрече́ние, присъ́да;
v осъ́ждам

separate [сѐпърит] *adj* отде́лен

separate [сѐпърейт] *v* разде́лям

separation [сѐпърѐйшън] *n* отделя́не,
раздя́ла

September [септѐмбър] *n* септе́мври

series [си́рийз] *n* се́рия, реди́ца

serious [си́риъс] *adj* серио́зен

sermon [съ́рмън] *n* про́повед

servant [съ́рвънт] *n* слуга́, прислу́жник

serve [сърв] *v* служа́ на, серви́рам

service [съ́рвис] *n* слу́жба, услу́га,
серви́ране

session [сѐшън] *n* заседа́ние, се́сия

set [сет] *v* заля́звам, поста́вям,
втвърдя́вам; *n* серви́з, апара́т

seven [сѐвън] *num* се́дем

seventeen [сѐвънти́йн] *num* седемна́десет

seventy [сѐвънти] *num* седемдесе́т

several [сѐвъръл] *adj* ня́колко, разли́чен

sew [со́у] *v* ши́я, заши́вам

sex [секс] *n* пол, секс

shadow [ша́доу] *n* ся́нка; *v* засе́нчвам,
следя́

shake [шейк] *v* кла́тя се, разколеба́вам

shaky [шѐйки] *adj* неси́гурен, колебли́в

shall [шал] *v* ще

shame [шейм] *n* срам, позо́р; *v* засра́мвам

shape [шейп] *n* фо́рма, о́браз, калъ́п; *v* оформя́м

share [ше́ър] *n* дял, пай, уча́стие, а́кция; *v* поде́лям

sharehold [ше́ърхо́улдър] *n* акционе́р

shark [шарк] *n* аку́ла

sharp [шарп] *adj* о́стър, си́лен, у́мен

sharpen [ша́рпън] *v* о́стря

shave [шейв] *v* бръ́сна се

she [ши] *pron* тя

sheep [шийп] *n* овца́

sheet [шийт] *n* лист, чарша́ф

shelf [шелф] *n* поли́ца, рафт

shell [шел] *n* черу́пка, ги́лза; *v* обстре́лвам

shield [шийлд] *n* щит; *v* закри́лям

shine [шайн] *v* гре́я, блистя́

ship [шип] *n* ко́раб; *v* експеди́рам

shipment [ши́пмънт] *n* пра́тка, експеди́ране

shirt [шърт] *n* ри́за

shiver [ши́вър] *v* трепе́ря; *n* тръ́пка

shoe [шу] *n* обу́вка, подко́ва

shoot [шу́ут] *v* стре́лям, изра́ствам

shop [шоп] *n* магази́н, работи́лница, цех; *v* пазару́вам

shopping [шо́пинг] *n* пазару́ване

shore [шор] *n* бряг

short [шорт] *adj* къс, кра́тък, ни́сък

shoulder [шо́улдър] *n* ра́мо

shout [ша́ут] *v* ви́кам; *n* вик

shovel [шъ́въл] *n* лопа́та

show [шо́у] *v* пока́звам; *n* изло́жба, представле́ние

shower [ша́уър] *n* преваля́ване, душ

shut [шът] *v* затва́рям

shy [шай] *adj* срамежли́в, стесни́телен

shyness [ша́йнис] *n* свенли́вост

sick [сик] *adj* бо́лен, повръща́щ

side [сайд] *n* страна́

sight [сайт] *n* зре́ние, гле́дка, забележи́телности

sign [сайн] *n* знак, при́знак, на́дпис; *v* да́вам знак, подпи́свам

signal [си́гнъл] *n* сигна́л, знак; *v* сигнализи́рам

signature [си́гнъчър] *n* по́дпис

significance [сигни́фикънс] *n* значе́ние

significant [сигни́фикънт] *adj* значи́телен, ва́жен

silence [са́йлънс] *n* мълча́ние, тишина́

silent [са́йлънт] *adj* мълчали́в, тих

silk [силк] *adj* копри́нен

silver [си́лвър] *n* сребро́

similar [си́милър] *adj* подо́бен, схо́ден

similarity [си́мила-рити] *n* при́лика, схо́дство

simple [си́мпъл] *adj* прост, обикнове́н, открове́н, глу́пав

sin [син] *n* грях; *v* прегреша́вам

since [синс] *prep* от; *conj* отка́кто, тъй като́

sincere [синси́ър] *adj* и́скрен

sincerity [синсе́рити] *n* и́скреност

sing [синг] *v* пе́я, възпя́вам

singer [си́нгър] *n* певе́ц

sink [синк] *v* потъ́вам, спа́дам; *n* ми́вка

sir [сър] *n* господи́не

siren [са́йрън] *n* сире́на

sister [си́стър] *n* сестра́

sit [сит] *v* седя́

situation [си́чюе́йшън] *n* местоположе́ние, длъ́жност

six [сикс] *num* шест

sixteen [си́кстийн] *num* шестна́десет

sixty [си́ксти] *num* шестдесе́т

size [сайз] *n* разме́р, но́мер

skate [скейт] *n* кънка́; *v* пързя́лям се с кънки́

skeleton [ске́литън] *n* скеле́т, ски́ца

ski [ский] *v* ка́рам ски

skill [скил] *n* сръ́чност, уме́ние

skin [скин] *n* ко́жа

skirt [скърт] *n* пола́

skull [скъл] *n* че́реп

sky [скай] *n* небе́

slang [сла́-нг] *n* сленг, жарго́н

slap [сла-п] *v* пля́скам; *n* плесни́ца

slave [слейв] *n* роб

sleep [слийп] *v* спя; *n* сън

sleeve [слийв] *n* ръка́в, му́фа

slice [слайс] *n* ре́зен, фили́я; *v* ре́жа

slight [слайт] *adj* незначи́телен, слаб

slim [слим] *adj* стро́ен, слаб

slip [слип] *v* хлъ́згам

slipper [сли́пър] *n* че́хъл

slow [сло́у] *adj* ба́вен

small [смол] *adj* ма́лък, дре́бен

smart [смарт] *adj* елега́нтен, у́мен

smell [смел] *v* мири́ша; *n* миризма́

smile [смайл] *v* усми́хвам; *n* усми́вка

smoke [смо́ук] *n* пу́шек; *v* пу́ша

smoker [смо́укър] *n* пуша́ч

smooth [сму́ут] *adj* гла́дък, ра́вен

snack [сна-к] *n* ле́ка заку́ска

snake [снейк] *n* змия́

sneeze [сни́йз] *v* ки́хам

snore [снор] *v* хъ́ркам; *n* хъ́ркане

snow [сно́у] *n* сняг; *v* вали́ сняг

so [со́у] *adv* така́, то́лкова; *conj* така́ че

soap [со́уп] *n* сапу́н; *v* сапуни́свам

sober [со́убър] *adj* тре́звен, серио́зен

soccer [со́кър] *n* фу́тбол

socialism [со́ушълизм] *n* социали́зъм

socialist [со́ушълист] *adj* социалисти́чески

society [съса́йъти] *n* обществó, дру́жество, компа́ния

sock [сок] *n* къс чора́п, сте́лка

soda [со́уда] *n* со́да, гази́рана вода́

sofa [со́уф] *n* канапе́

soft [софт] *adj* мек, тих, не́жен, лек

softness [со́фтнис] *n* ме́кост, не́жност

soil [сойл] *n* по́чва; *v* изца́пвам
soldier [со́улджър] *n* войни́к
sole [со́ул] *n* подме́тка; *adj* еди́нствен
solid [со́лид] *adj* твърд, здрав
solve [солв] *v.* разреша́вам
some [съм] *pron* ня́кой, ня́какъв, ня́колко
somebody [съмбъди] *pron* ня́кой
something [съмтинг] *pron* не́що
son [сън] *n* син
song [сонг] *n* пе́сен
son-in-law [сън ин ло] *n* зет
soon [су́ун] *adv* ско́ро, ведна́га
sorrow [со́роу] *n* тъга́; *v* тъгу́вам
sorry [со́ри] *adj* жа́лък, изпи́тващ съжале́ние
soul [со́ул] *n* душа́
sound [са́унд] *n* звук, шум; *v* звуча́; *adj* здрав, си́лен
soup [су́уп] *n* су́па
sour [са́уър] *adj* кисел, раздразни́телен
south [са́ут] *n* юг
southern [са́дърн] *adj* ю́жен
sow [со́у] *v* се́я
space [спейс] *n* простра́нство, ко́смос
spare [спе́ър] *v* щадя́, иконома́свам; *adj* оскъ́ден, резе́рвен
spark [спарк] *n* и́скра
sparrow [спа́-роу] *n* врабче́
speak [спийк] *v* гово́ря

speaker [спѝйкър] *n* орѐтор, говорѝтел, спѝкер

speaking [спѝйкинг] *adj* говорещ

special [спѐшъл] *adj* особен, специѐлен

specialist [спѐшълист] *n* специалѝст

species [спѝйшийз] *n* вид, порода

specific [спесѝфик] *adj* специфѝчен, определён

spectator [спектѐйтър] *n* зрѝтел

speech [спѝйч] *n* говор, реч

speed [спѝйд] *n* бързинѐ, скорост

spell [спел] *v* прочѝтам буква по буква

spelling [спѐлинг] *n* правопѝс

spend [спенд] *v* хѐрча, израсходвам

sphere [сфѝър] *n* сфѐра, кълбо, област

spice [спайс] *n* подпрѐвка за ѝстие

spider [спѐйдър] *n* паяк

spill [спил] *v* разлѝвам

spinach [спѝнидж] *n* спанѐк

spine [спайн] *n* гръбнѐк, бодѝл

spirit [спѝрит] *n* дух, прѝзрак, смѐлост, спирт

spit [спит] *v* плюя

spite [спайт] *n* злоба

split [сплит] *v* цѐпя; *n* разцеплѐние

spoil [спойл] *v* развѐлям, разглѐзвам; *n* плячка

spokesman [споуксмън] *n* говорѝтел

sponge [спъндж] *n* гъба

spoon [спуун] *n* лъжѝца

sport [спорт] *n* спорт

spot [спот] *n* петно́, мя́сто

spouse [спа́уз] *n* съпру́г

spray [спрей] *v* пръ́скам

spread [спред] *v* разсти́лам, прости́рам; *n* разпростране́ние

spring [спринг] *v* ска́чам; *n* пружи́на, и́звор, про́лет

spy [спай] *v* шпиони́рам; *n* шпио́нин

square [скуе́ър] *n* квадра́т, площа́д

squeeze [скуи́йз] *v* сти́скам, изце́ждам

stability [стъби́лити] *n* устойчи́вост

stable [стейбл] *adj* устойчи́в

stadium [сте́йдиъм] *n* стадио́н

staff [стаф] *n* щаб, персона́л

stage [стейдж] *n* сце́на, фа́за, ета́п; *v* поста́вям

stair [сте́ър] *n* стъпа́ло, стъ́лба

staircase [сте́ъркейс] *n* стъ́лбище

stamp [ста-мп] *n* по́щенска ма́рка

stand [ста-нд] *v* стоя́, нами́рам, търпя́; *n* пози́ция, щанд

standard [ста́-ндърд] *n* станда́рт, но́рма; *adj* станда́ртен

star [стар] *n* звезда́

start [старт] *v* тръ́гвам, запо́чвам

starve [старв] *v* глад́увам

state [стейт] *n* състоя́ние, държа́ва, щат; *v* заявя́вам; *adj* държа́вен

statement [сте́йтмънт] *n* изявле́ние

statesman [стéйтсмън] *n* държáвник

station [стéйшън] *n* гáра, стáнция

statistics [стътúстикс] *n* статúстика

statue [стá-тю] *n* стáтуя

status [стéйтъс] *n* положéние

stay [стей] *v* остáвам, престоЯвам; *n* престóй

steak [стейк] *n* пържóла

steam [стийм] *n* пáра

steel [стийл] *n* стомáна

step [степ] *n* стъ́пка; *v* стъ́пвам

stick [стик] *n* пръ́чка, пáлка

stick [стик] *v* пъ́хам, лепЯ

still [стил] *adj* тих, неподвúжен

stillness [стúлнис] *n* тишинá

stitch [стич] *n* бод; *v* шúя

stockholder [стóкхóулдър] *n* акционéр

stomach [стъ́мък] *n* стомáх

stone [стóун] *n* кáмък, костúлка

stop [стоп] *v* спúрам, престáвам; *n* спúране, спúрка

storage [стóридж] *n* съхранéние, склад

store [стор] *n* запáс; *v* складúрам

storm [сторм] *n* бýря

story [стóри] *n* прúказка

straight [стрейт] *adj* прав, пряк, чéстен, úскрен; *adv* тóчно

strange [стрейндж] *adj* стрáнен, чужд

stranger [стрéйнджър] *n* непознáт

strategy [стрá-тиджи] *n* стратéгия

strawberry [стро́бъри] *n* я́года

stream [стрийм] *n* пото́к; *v* тека́, струя́

street [стрийт] *n* у́лица

strength [стрент] *n* си́ла

strengthen [стре́нтън] *v* заси́лвам, укре́пвам

stretch [стреч] *v* опъ́вам

strict [стрикт] *adj* строг

strictly [стри́ктли] *adv* стро́го, то́чно

strike [страйк] *v* у́дрям, стачку́вам; *n* ста́чка

string [стринг] *n* връв, стру́на

strip [стрип] *n* и́вица, ле́нта

stroll [строл] *v* разхо́ждам се; *n* разхо́дка

strong [стронг] *adj* си́лен, твърд, як

struggle [стръ́гъл] *v* бо́ря се, мъ́ча се; *n* борба́

student [стю́дънт] *n* студе́нт

studio [стю́диоу] *n* сту́дио, ателие́

study [стъ́ди] *v* у́ча, сле́двам; *n* кабине́т, сту́дия

stuff [стъф] *n* вещество́, мате́рия

stupid [стю́пид] *adj* глу́пав, тъп

style [стайл] *n* стил, на́чин, мо́да

subject [съ́бджикт] *n* по́даник, по́длог, те́ма, предме́т

submit [събми́т] *v* подчиня́вам се, представя́м

subscribe [събскра́йб] *v* абони́рам се

subscription [събскри́пшън] *n* абонаме́нт

substance [събстънс] *n* субстанция,
вещество
substitute [събститют] *v* заменям; *n*
заместник, заместител
substitution [събститюшън] *n* заместване
subway [събуей] *n* метро
succeed [съксийд] *v* успявам, наследявам
success [съксес] *n* успех
successful [съксесфул] *adj* успешен,
сполучлив
such [съч] *pron* такъв, такива
suck [сък] *v* суча, смуча
sudden [съдън] *adj* внезапен
sue [сю] *v* давам под съд
suffer [сфър] *v* страдам
sufficient [съфишънт] *adj* достатъчен
sugar [шугър] *n* захар
suggest [съджест] *v* подсказвам, внушавам,
предлагам
suicide [сюсайд] *n* самоубийство
suit [сют] *n* костюм, комплект, процес; *v*
подхождам, задоволявам
suitcase [сюткейс] *n* куфар
suite [суийт] *n* апартамент
sum [съм] *n* сума, сбор
summer [съмър] *n* лято
summit [съмит] *n* връх, връхна точка
sun [сън] *n* слънце
Sunday [сънди] *n* неделя
sunrise [сънрайз] *n* изгрев

sunset [сънсет] *n* залез
superficial [сýпърфишъл] *adj* повърхностен
superior [супúърър] *adj* по́-висш
superiority [супúприóрити] *n* превъзхо́дство
superstition [сýпърстúшън] *n* суеве́рие
supervise [сýпървайз] *v* надзира́вам
supervision [сýпървúжън] *n* надзо́р
supper [сѫпър] *n* вече́ря
supply [сѫплáй] *v* снабдя́вам, доставя́м; *n*
снабдя́ване, предла́гане
support [сѫпóрт] *v* поддъ́ржам, издъ́ржам;
n поддръ́жка, опо́ра
supporter [сѫпóртър] *n* поддръ́жник
suppose [сѫпóуз] *v* предпола́гам, мú́сля
sure [шýър] *adj* сúгурен, уве́рен; *adv*
разбú́ра се
surface [сѫрфис] *n* повъ́рхност
surgeon [сѫрджън] *n* хирýрг
surgery [сѫрджъри] *n* хирургúя
surname [сѫрнейм] *n* пре́зиме
surprise [сѫпрáйз] *n* изнена́да, учу́дване; *v*
изнена́двам
survival [сѫрвáйвъл] *n* оцеля́ване
survive [сѫрвáйв] *v* оцеля́вам
suspect [сѫспект] *n* заподозря́но лице́
suspect [сѫспе́кт] *v* подозúрам
suspicion [сѫспúшън] *n* подозре́ние
suspicious [сѫспúшъс] *adj* подозрúтелен
swallow [суóлоу] *v* гъ́лтам
swear [суе́ър] *v* кълна́ се, псу́вам

sweat [суéт] *n* пот; *v* потя́ се
sweater [суéтър] *n* пуло́вер
sweep [суи́йп] *v* метá
sweeper [суи́пър] *n* метáч
sweet [суи́йт] *adj* слáдък, мил; *n* бонбóн, сладки́ш
sweetness [суи́йтнис] *n* слáдост
swell [суéл] *v* подýвам се
swift [суи́фт] *adj* бърз
swiftness [суи́фтнис] *n* бързинá
swim [суи́м] *v* плýвам; *n* плýване
swimmer [суи́мър] *n* плувéц
sword [суóрд] *n* меч, сáбя
syllable [си́лъбл] *n* сри́чка
symbol [си́мбъл] *n* знак, си́мвол
symmetry [си́митри] *n* симéтрия
sympathize [си́мпътайз] *v* съчýвствувам
sympathy [си́мпъти] *n* съчýвствие
symphony [си́мфъни] *n* симфóния
synonym [си́нъним] *n* синони́м
syrup [сáйръп] *n* сирóп
system [си́стъм] *n* систéма

T

table [тéйбъл] *n* мáса, тáблица
tact [та-кт] *n* такт
tactics [тá-ктикс] *noun pl* тáктика

tag [та-г] *n* етикет

tail [тейл] *n* опашка, край, тура́

tailor [те́йлър] *n* шива́ч

take [тейк] *v* взе́мам, зана́сям, заве́ждам

talent [та́-лънт] *n* тала́нт

talk [ток] *n* ра́зговор, бесе́да; *v* разгова́рям, гово́ря

tall [тол] *adj* висо́к

tank [та-нк] *n* танк, резервоа́р

tap [та-п] *n* кран, чешма́, поту́ване; *v* то́ча питие́, поту́пвам

tape [тейп] *n* ле́нта; *v* завъ́рзвам

target [та́ргит] *n* цел, мише́на

tariff [та́-риф] *n* тари́фа

task [та-ск] *n* зада́ча

taste [тейст] *n* вкус; *v* опи́твам

tax [та-кс] *n* да́нък; *v* обла́гам с да́нък

taxation [та-ксе́йшън] *n* обла́гане, да́нъчна систе́ма

taxi [та́-кси] *n* такси́

taxpayer [та́-кспейър] *n* данъкопла́тец

tea [тий] *n* чай

teach [тийч] *v* обуча́вам, препода́вам

teacher [тийчър] *n* учи́тел, преподава́тел

team [тийм] *n* отбо́р, тим, кома́нда

tear [ти́ър] *n* сълза́

tear [те́ър] *v* къ́сам, дера́

teaspoon [ти́йспун] *n* ча́ена лъжи́чка

technical [те́кникъл] *adj* техни́чески

technology [текно́лъджи] *n* те́хника, техноло́гия

telephone [те́лифоун] *n* телефо́н; *v* телефони́рам

television [те́ливижън] *n* телеви́зия

tell [тел] *v* ка́звам, разка́звам, различа́вам

temperature [те́мпричър] *n* температу́ра

temporary [те́мпърəри] *adj* вре́менен

tempt [темпт] *v* изкуша́вам, съблазня́вам

temptation [темпте́йшън] *n* изкуше́ние, събла́зън

ten [тен] *num* де́сет

tenant [те́нънт] *n* наема́тел, квартира́нт

tender [те́ндър] *adj* не́жен, кре́хък

tenderness [те́ндърнис] *n* не́жност

tennis [те́нис] *n* те́нис

tension [те́ншън] *n* напреже́ние

tent [тент] *n* пала́тка

term [търм] *n* срок, те́рмин, усло́вия

terrible [те́ръбл] *adj* ужа́сен

terrify [те́рифай] *v* ужася́вам

territory [те́ритъри] *n* терито́рия

terror [те́рър] *n* у́жас, теро́р

test [тест] *n* прове́рка, изпита́ние; *v* изпи́твам, проверя́вам

testify [те́стифай] *v* свиде́телствувам, удостоверя́вам

text [текст] *n* текст

textbook [те́кстбук] *n* уче́бник

textile [те́кстайл] *n* тексти́л

than [да-н] *conj* отколкото
thank [та-нк] *v* благодаря́
that [да-т] *pron* то́зи, о́нзи, ко́йто; *conj* че, за да
theater [ти́ътър] *n* теа́тър
theatrical [тиа́-трикъл] *adj* театра́лен
theft [тефт] *n* кра́жба
their [де́ър] *pron* те́хен
them [дем] *pron* тях, ги
theme [тийм] *n* те́ма
themselves [демсе́лвз] *pron* себе́ си, се
then [ден] *adv* тога́ва, след това́
theory [ти́ъри] *n* тео́рия
there [де́ър] *adv* там
thermometer [търмо́митър] *n* термоме́тър
these [дийз] *pron* те́зи
they [дей] *pron* те, ня́кой
thick [тик] *adj* дебе́л, гъст
thickness [ти́книс] *n* гъстота́
thief [тийф] *n* краде́ц
thigh [тай] *n* бедро́
thin [тин] *adj* тъ́нък, слаб, ря́дък
thing [тинг] *n* не́що, ра́бота, предме́т
think [тинк] *v* ми́сля, смя́там
thirst [търст] *n* жа́жда
thirsty [тъ́рсти] *adj* жа́ден
thirteen [търти́йн] *num* трина́десет
thirty [тъ́рти] *num* триде́сет
this [дис] *pron* то́зи, та́зи, това́
thorn [торн] *n* трън

thorough [търо] *adj* пълен, съвършен

those [дòуз] *pron* онèзи

thought [тот] *n* мѝсъл

thousand [тàузънд] *num* хиляда

thread [тред] *n* конèц

threat [трет] *n* заплàха

three [три] *num* три

throat [трòут] *n* гъ̀рло

throw [трòу] *v* хвъ̀рлям; *n* хвъ̀рляне

thumb [тъм] *n* пàлец

thunder [тъ̀ндър] *n* гръм; *v* гърмя̀

thunderstorm [тъ̀ндърсторм] *n* бỳря с гръмотèвици

ticket [тѝкит] *n* билèт, етикèт

tide [тайд] *n* прѝлив и òтлив

tidy [тàйди] *adj* спрèтнат

tie [тай] *v* връ̀звам; *n* вратовръ̀зка

tiger [тàйгър] *n* тѝгър

tight [тайт] *adj* як, стèгнат, опъ̀нат

tile [тайл] *n* керемѝда

time [тайм] *n* врèме, епòха

timetable [тàймтейбл] *n* разписàние

tin [тин] *n* калàй, тенекѝя, консèрвна кутѝя; *v* консервѝрам

tiny [тàйни] *adj* мъ̀ничък

tip [тип] *n* край, връ̀хче, бакшѝш

tire [тàйър] *n* въ̀ншна гỳма на колелò; *v* уморя̀вам, омръ̀зва ми

tissue [тѝшю] *n* тъ̀кан

title [тàйтъл] *n* заглàвие, тѝтла

to [ту] *prep* към, за, в, според, до, по;
conj за да

tobacco [тъба́-коу] *n* тютю́н

today [тъде́й] *adv* днес

toe [то́у] *n* пръст

together [тъге́дър] *adv* за́едно

tolerance [то́лърънс] *n* търпи́мост,
толера́нтност

tolerate [то́лърейт] *v* търпя́, пона́сям

toll [тол] *n* та́кса

tomato [тъма́тоу] *n* дома́т

tomb [тум] *n* гроб

tomorrow [тъмо́роу] *adv* у́тре

ton [тан] *n* тон

tone [то́ун] *n* тон, нюа́нс

tongue [танг] *n* ези́к

tonight [тънайт] *adv* та́зи ве́чер, дове́чера

too [ту] *adv* съ́що, твъ́рде

tool [ту́ул] *n* инструме́нт

tooth [ту́ут] *n* зъб

toothache [ту́утейк] *n* зъбобо́л

top [топ] *n* връх; *adj* го́рен, най-голя́м

topic [то́пик] *n* предме́т, те́ма

torture [то́рчър] *n* мъче́ние; *v* измъ́чвам

total [то́утъл] *adj* пъ́лен, цял

touch [тъч] *v* пи́пам, доко́свам

tough [тъф] *adj* тру́ден, упори́т

tour [ту́ър] *n* обико́лка, пътеше́ствие; *v*
пъту́вам

tourist [ту́ърист] *n* тури́ст

towards [тъуо́рдз] *prep* към, по отноше́ние на, о́коло, приблизи́телно

towel [та́уъл] *n* къ́рпа за лице́

tower [та́уър] *v* изди́гам се; *n* ку́ла

town [та́ун] *n* град

toy [той] *n* игра́чка

trade [трейд] *n* търгови́я, заня́т; *v* търгу́вам

trade union [тре́йд ю́ниън] *n* професиона́лен съ́юз

tradition [тръди́шън] *n* тради́ция, преда́ние

traditional [тръди́шънъл] *adj* традицио́нен

traffic [тра́-фик] *n* движе́ние

tragedy [тра́-джиди] *n* траге́дия

tragic [тра́-джик] *adj* траги́чен

train [трейн] *n* влак; *v* обуча́вам, трени́рам

trainer [тре́йнър] *n* треньо́р

transform [трансфо́рм] *v* преобразя́вам, превръ́щам

transformation [тра́-нсформе́йшън] *n* преобразя́ване, преустро́йство

translate [тра-нсле́йт] *v* преве́ждам

translation [тра-нсле́йшън] *n* прево́д

translator [тра-нсле́йтър] *n* преводáч

transmission [тра-нсми́шън] *n* трансми́сия, преда́ване

transmit [тра-нсми́т] *v* преда́вам

transport [тра-нспо́рт] *v* прена́сям, прево́звам

transport [тра́-нспорт] *n* пре́воз, транспо́рт

travel [тра́-вълл] *v* пътувам; *n* пътуване
traveler [тра́-вълър] *n* пътник
tray [трей] *n* табла, поднос
treasure [тре́жър] *n* съкровище
treat [трийт] *v* отнасям се; *n* удоволствие
treatment [три́йтмънт] *n* отношение, лечение
treaty [три́йти] *n* договор
tree [трий] *n* дърво
tremble [тре́мбл] *v* треперя
trend [тренд] *n* тенденция, насока
trial [тра́йъл] *n* изпитание, дело
triangle [тра́йа-нгъл] *n* триъгълник
tribe [трайб] *n* племе, род
trick [трик] *n* хитрост, фокус
trip [трип] *v* спъвам; *n* пътуване
triumph [тра́йъмф] *n* сполука, триумф; *v* тържествувам
trouble [трабл] *n* неприятности; *v* безпокоя
trousers [тра́узърз] *noun pl* панталони
truck [трък] *n* камион
true [тру] *adj* верен, истински; *adv* точно
trunk [трънк] *n* стъбло, ствол
trust [тръст] *n* доверие, отговорност; *v* доверявам, вярвам
truth [трут] *n* истина
try [трай] *v* опитвам, изпитвам
tube [тюб] *n* туба
Tuesday [тю́зди] *n* вторник

tuition [тюи́шън] *n* обуче́ние, уче́бна та́кса
tunnel [тѣнъл] *n* туне́л
turn [тѫрн] *v* въртя́, превръ́щам; *n* обра́т
twelve [туе́лв] *num* двана́десет
twenty [туе́нти] *num* двадесе́т
twin [туи́н] *n* близна́к; *adj* една́къв
twist [туи́ст] *v* изви́вам, изкри́вявам; *n*
изкри́вяване, особеност
two [ту] *num* две
type [тайп] *n* вид, тип, шрифт; *v* пи́ша
на пи́шеща маши́на
typewriter [та́йпра́йтър] *n* пи́шеща маши́на
typical [ти́пикъл] *adj* типи́чен, характе́рен
typist [та́йпист] *n* машинопи́сец,
машинопи́ска

U

ugliness [ѣглинис] *n* грозота́
ugly [ѣгли] *adj* гро́зен
umbrella [ъмбре́ла] *n* чадъ́р
unable [ейбл] *adj* неспосо́бен
uncle [ѣнкъл] *n* чи́чо, ву́йчо
uncomfortable [ънкѣмфъта́бл] *adj* неудо́бен
under [а́ндър] *prep* под, на, по́-ма́лко от,
при, в
underclothes [а́ндърклоудэ] *noun pl* до́лни
дре́хи

understand [áндърстá-нд] *v* разбѝрам

underwear [áндъруеър] *n* дóлни дрéхи

unemployed [ънимплóйд] *adj* безрабóтен

unemployment [ънимплóймънт] *n* безрабóтица

unfair [ънфéър] *adj* несправедлѝв, непочтéн

uniform [юниформ] *adj* еднообрáзен; *n* унифóрма

union [юниън] *n* съюз, обединéние

unit [юнит] *n* единѝца

unity [юнити] *n* едѝнство

universal [юнивъ̀рсъл] *adj* собщ, универсáлен

universe [юнивърс] *n* вселéна

university [юнивъ̀рсити] *n* университéт

unknown [ъннóун] *adj* непознáт, неизвéстен

unlock [ънлóк] *v* отключвам

until [ънтѝл] *prep* до; *conj* докатó

unusual [ънню̀жуъл] *adj* необикновéн

up [ап] *adv* гóре, стáнал прав, надѝгнал се; *prep* нагóре

upper [апър] *adj* гóрен, висш

urgent [ѐрджънт] *adj* неотлóжен

us [ъс] *pron* нас

use [юс] *n* пóлза, употрéба

use [юз] *v* изпóлзувам, употребя́вам

useful [ю̀сфул] *adj* полéзен

useless [ю̀слис] *adj* безполéзен

usual [южуъл] *adj* обикновен, обичаен
usually [южуъли] *adv* обикновено

V

vacancy [вейкънси] *n* вакантно място
vacation [въкейшън] *n* освобождаване,
ваканция
vaccination [ва-ксинейшън] *n* ваксинация
valid [ва-лид] *adj* валиден, в сила
valley [ва-ли] *n* долина
valuable [ва-люъбл] *adj* ценен
value [ва-лю] *n* стойност, цена
vapor [вейпър] *n* пара
variety [върайъти] *n* разнообразие,
разновидност
various [вериъс] *adj* различен,
разнообразен
vary [ва-ри] *v* меня се, варирам
vase [ваз] *n* ваза
vast [васт] *adj* обширен, огромен
veal [вийл] *n* телешко месо
vegetable [веджитъбл] *n* растителен,
зеленчуков; *n* зеленчук
vegetation [веджитейшън] *n* растителност,
растене
vehicle [вийкъл] *n* превозно средство, кола
verb [върб] *n* глагол

verdict [въ́рдикт] *n* присъ́да
verse [върс] *n* стих, поéзия
version [въ́ржън] *n* вéрсия
vertical [въ́ртикъл] *adj* вертикáлен
very [вéри] *adv* мнóго
vessel [вéсъл] *n* съд
veteran [вéтърън] *n* ветерáн
via [вáйъ] *prep* през
vibration [вайбрéйшън] *n* трепéрене
vicinity [висúнити] *n* окóлност
victim [вúктим] *n* жéртва
victory [вúктъри] *n* побéда
view [вю] *n* úзглед, мнéние
village [вúлидж] *n* céло
vinegar [вúнигър] *n* оцéт
violate [вáйълейт] *v* нарушáвам
violation [вайълéйшън] *n* нарушáване
violence [вáйълънс] *n* насúлие
violent [вáйълнт] *adj* сúлен, бýен
violin [вáйълин] *n* цигýлка
visible [вúзъбл] *adj* очевúден
vision [вúжън] *n* зрéние
visit [вúзит] *n* посещéние, вúзита; *v* посещáвам
visitor [вúзитър] *n* посетúтел, гост
vocabulary [въкá-бюлъри] *n* рéчник, запáс от дýми
vocal [вóукъл] *adj* глáсен
voice [войс] *n* глас, залóг
volcano [волкéйноу] *n* вулкáн

volume [во́люм] *n* том, кни́га, объе́м

voluntary [во́лънтъри] *adj* доброво́лен

volunteer [во́лънти́ър] *n* доброво́лец; *v* предла́гам доброво́лно

vote [во́ут] *n* глас, гласу́ване; *v* гласу́вам

voter [во́утър] *n* избира́тел, гласоподава́тел

vowel [ва́уъл] *n* гла́сна

voyage [во́ядж] *n* пъту́ване

W

wage [уе́йдж] *n* на́дница

waist [уе́йст] *n* та́лия

wait [уе́йт] *v* ча́кам, прислу́жвам

waiter [уе́йтър] *n* сервитьо́р

wake [уе́йк] *v* събу́ждам се

walk [уо́к] *n* разхо́дка; *v* хо́дя

wall [уо́л] *n* стена́

wallet [уо́лит] *n* портфе́йл

want [уо́нт] *v* и́скам, нужда́я се

war [уо́р] *n* война́

wardrobe [уо́рдроуб] *n* гардеро́б

warehouse [уе́ърхаус] *n* склад

warm [уо́рм] *adj* то́пъл, сърде́чен

warning [уо́рнинг] *n* предупрежде́ние

wash [уо́ш] *v* ми́я, пера́; *n* пране́

washing [уо́шинг] *n* пране́

waste [уейст] *v* хабя́, прахо́свам; *n* отпа́дъци

watch [уо́ч] *v* наблюда́вам, внима́вам; *n* ръ́чен часо́вник

water [уо́тър] *n* вода́

waterfall [уо́търфол] *n* водопа́д

watermelon [уо́търмелън] *n* ди́ня

wave [уейв] *n* вълна́, ма́хане с ръка́; *v* разма́хвам, развя́вам

way [уей] *n* път, начи́н

weak [уийк] *adj* слаб

weakness [уи́книс] *n* сла́бост

wealth [уелт] *n* бога́тство, изоби́лие

wealthy [уе́лти] *adj* бога́т

weapon [уе́пън] *n* оръ́жие

wear [уе́ър] *v* но́ся

weather [уе́дър] *n* вре́ме

wed [уед] *v* венча́вам

wedding [уе́динг] венча́вка, сва́тба

Wednesday [уе́нзди] *n* сря́да

week [уийк] *n* се́дмица

weigh [уей] *v* те́гля, тежа́

weight [уейт] *n* тежина́, тегло́

welcome [уе́лкъм] *interj* добре́ дошъ́л; *v* приве́тствувам

well [уел] *n* кла́денец; *adv* добре́

west [уест] *n* за́пад

western [уе́стърн] *adj* за́паден

wet [ует] *adj* мо́кър; *v* мо́кря

what [уо́т] *pron* какво́, що, какъ́в, това́, кое́то

wheat [уи́йт] *n* пшени́ца, жи́то

wheel [уи́йл] *n* колело́

when [уе́н] *conj* кога́то

which [уи́ч] *pron* кой, ко́йто

while [уа́йл] *conj* дока́то

whisky [уи́ски] *n* уи́ски

whistle [уи́съл] *n* сви́рка; *v* сви́ря с уста́

white [уа́йт] *adj* бял, бле́ден

who [ху] *pron* кой, ко́йто

whole [хо́ул] *adj* цял

wholesale [хо́улсейл] *n* прода́жба на е́дро

whose [хуз] *pron* чий, чи́йто

why [уа́й] *adv* защо́

wide [уа́йд] *adj* широ́к, голя́м, обши́рен

widen [уа́йдън] *v* разширя́вам

widow [уи́доу] *n* вдови́ца

width [уи́дт] *n* широчина́

wife [уа́йф] *n* съпру́га

wild [уа́йлд] *adj* див, необузда́н

will [уил] *v* ще, и́скам, жела́я, завеща́вам; *n* во́ля, завеща́ние

win [уи́н] *v* пече́ля

wind [уи́нд] *n* вя́тър

window [уи́ндоу] *n* прозо́рец

wine [уа́йн] *n* ви́но

wing [уи́нг] *n* крило́, кули́си

winner [уи́нър] *n* победи́тел

winter [уи́нтър] *n* зи́ма; *v* зиму́вам